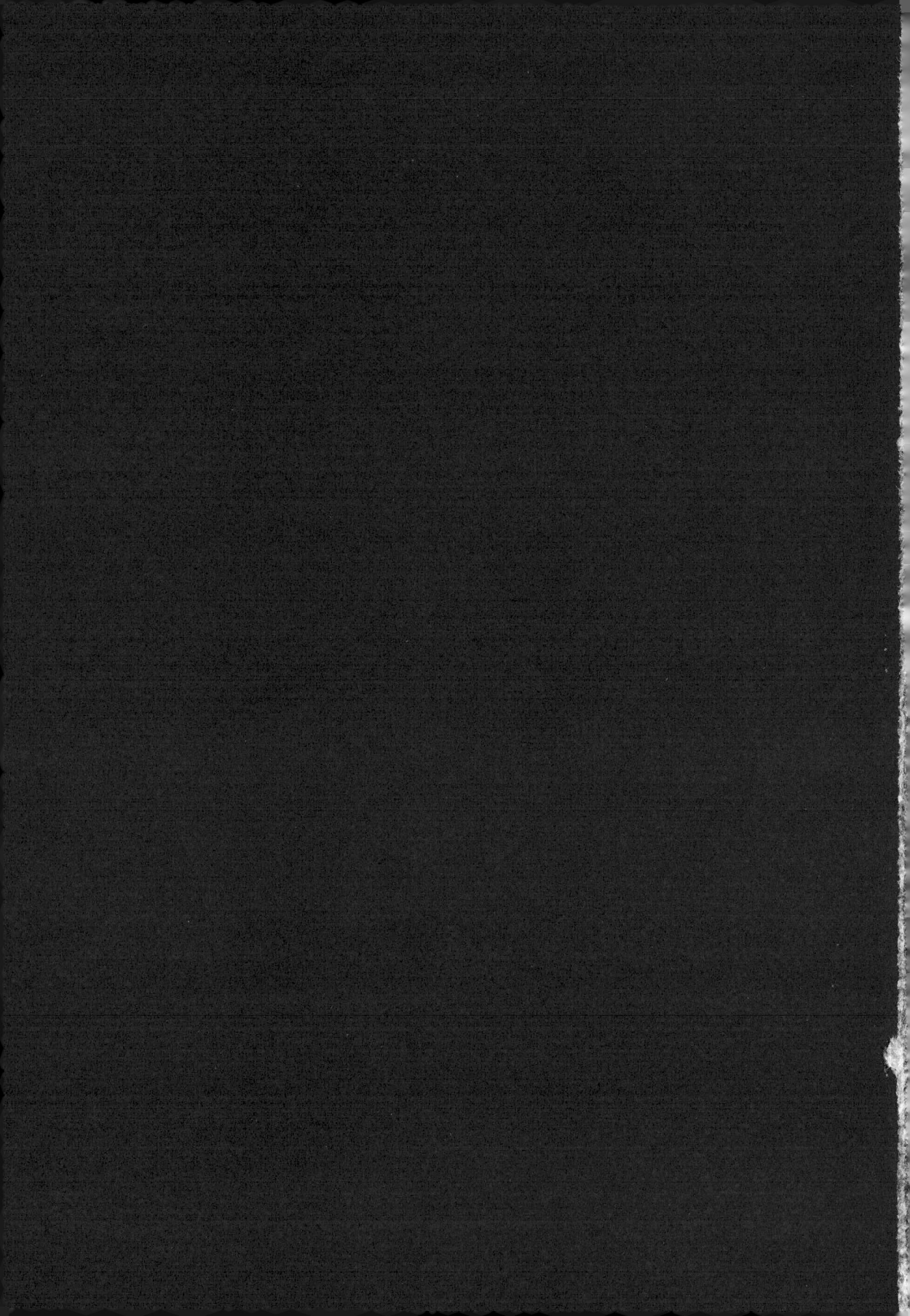

SANS IN USE

A COLLECTION OF
SANS-SERIF
TYPEFACES

FROM A TO Z

576 PAGES

PROJECTS

ISBN
978-988-76844-2-8
VICTIONARY.COM

Published and distributed by
viction:workshop ltd

viction:ary™

viction:workshop ltd
Unit C, 7/F, Seabright Plaza,
9-23 Shell Street,
North Point, Hong Kong
Url: www.victionary.com
Email: we@victionary.com

 @victionworkshop
 @victionworkshop
Bē @victionary
 @victionary

Edited and produced by viction workshop ltd
Creative direction: Victor Cheung
Art direction and design: Ben Lee@BD85BD85
Editorial: Ynes Filleul, YL Lim
Coordination: Katherine Wong, Jeanie Choy
Production: Bryan Leung
Typefaces: Fraktion Mono, Aeonik Pro

Second Edition

ISBN 978-988-76844-2-8
Printed and bound in China

BY DANIEL MCQUEEN
(FOUNDER OF TDF,
THE DESIGNERS FOUNDRY)

TO THE VAST MAJORITY OF HUMANS AROUND THE WORLD, THE ART OF TYPEFACE DESIGN GOES UNNOTICED. IT IS SIMPLY NOT SOMETHING THAT WILL ENTER THEIR THOUGHTS OFTEN, IF AT ALL. TYPEFACES TO MOST ARE JUST A BACKDROP TO THE MESSAGE BEING COMMUNICATED. THIS UNDERSTATED PRESENCE IS OFTEN A TESTAMENT TO A TYPE DESIGNER'S SUCCESS. WHEN WE CREATE TYPEFACES, OUR AIM IS TO DESIGN A SET OF GLYPHS THAT SEAMLESSLY FACILITATES COMMUNICATION REINFORCING THE INTENDED EMOTIONS, MESSAGE AND VOICE OF THE AUTHOR. WHEN A TYPEFACE HARMONISES WITH ITS CONTEXT, WE CAN DEEM THE MISSION ACCOMPLISHED. THIS IS NOT TO BE MISUNDERSTOOD THAT A TYPEFACE SHOULD BE PLAIN IN FORM; BUT IT SHOULD BE APPROPRIATE AND INTENTIONAL. THERE IS A SUITABLE PLACE FOR EVERYTHING FROM A NEO GROTESQUE SANS-SERIF TO A 3D BRUSH SCRIPT.

SUCCESSFUL INTEGRATIONS GIVE VERY LITTLE CONTEXT OR PRAISE TO THE NEVER-ENDING DEDICATION OF TYPE DESIGNERS WHO INVEST YEARS HONING THEIR CRAFT, SOLVING NEW PROBLEMS, AND CREATING TYPOGRAPHIC SOLUTIONS TO BE USED IN THE WORLD AROUND US WHILE PUSHING FONT TECHNOLOGIES SUCH AS VARIABLE FONTS INTO NEW TERRITORY. TYPE DESIGNERS MUST CONSTANTLY ADAPT TO NEW INDUSTRIES AND DEMANDS PUT ON TYPEFACES; MEANING THERE WILL ALWAYS BE A NEED FOR NEW TYPEFACES, WHETHER THE WORLD NOTICES THEM OR NOT.

WITH THAT SAID, IN THIS BOOK, WE WILL TAKE THE OPPORTUNITY TO SHINE A SPOTLIGHT ON THE ARTISTRY THAT IS TYPEFACE DESIGN. IMMERSE YOURSELF IN A COLLECTION OF TYPEFACES, MASTERFULLY DESIGNED BY TALENTED INDIVIDUALS AND TEAMS FROM ALL AROUND THE WORLD, EXPERTLY CURATED BY VICTIONARY. THROUGH MY OWN EXPERIENCES RUNNING THE DESIGNERS FOUNDRY FOR OVER A DECADE NOW, I LOOK TO ALL THE TYPEFACES GRACING THESE PAGES WITH EXCITEMENT FOR THE FUTURE TO SEE WHAT COMES NEXT AND WHERE WE WILL PUSH EACH OTHER TO GO. FOR US AT TDF, WE HAVE AN ALL NEW WEBSITE LAUNCHING IN A MATTER OF WEEKS AFTER OVER 18 MONTHS IN DEVELOPMENT AND ALSO MULTIPLE EXCITING VARIABLE TYPEFACES TO FOLLOW!

I WILL LEAVE YOU NOW TO ENJOY THESE ENSUING PAGES AND HOPE YOU COME AWAY WITH A GREATER APPRECIATION OF THE SKILL AND DEDICATION REQUIRED TO DESIGN TYPEFACES.

CONTENTS

		HAIRLINE	THIN	EXTRA LIGHT	LIGHT	BOOK	REGULAR	MEDIUM
A	FFF ACID GROTESK			•	•	•	•	•
	AEONIK		•		•		•	•
	AEONIK FONO		•		•		•	•
	AEONIK MONO		•		•		•	•
	AEONIK PRO		•		•		•	•
	AGRANDIR		•		•		•	•
	AIR		•	•	•		•	•
	NB AKADEMIE™ PRO				•	•	•	•
	AKTIV GROTESK	•	•		•		•	•
	ALDGATE SANS	•	•		•		•	•
	ALTFORM		•	•	•		•	•
	AMBIT		•	•	•		•	•
	ANALOG		•		•		•	•
	ANTARCTICA	•	•	•	•	•	•	•
	AQUAWAX FX		•	•	•		•	•
	FOUNDRY ARKIAS	•	•	•	•		•	•
	ATLANTIC		•		•		•	•
	AUGURE		•	•	•		•	•
B	BAGOSS		•		•		•	•
	BAIKAL	•	•	•	•	•	•	•
	BASE NEUE		•	•	•		•	•
	BETATRON						•	
	BRIK						•	
C	CATEGORY						•	•
	COANDA		•		•		•	
	TT COMMONS™ PRO		•	•	•		•	•
D	DAZZED		•		•		•	•
	ABC DIATYPE		•		•		•	•
	DIGITAL SANS		•	•	•		•	•
	DIVERSE				•		•	•
E	EXTENDA							
F	ABC FAVORIT				•	•	•	•
	FORMULA		•	•	•		•	•
G	GAMUTH SANS			•	•		•	•
	GIRONA				•		•	•
	ABC GRAVITY							
	GREED				•		•	•
	GRIDULAR						•	
H	HARBER		•		•		•	•
I	INSITU				•		•	
	NB INTERNATIONAL™ PRO				•	•	•	•
J	F37 JUDGE		•				•	•
K	F37 K9				•		•	•
	KOBE						•	
	F37 KOOKIE						•	•
M	MACAN & MACAN STENCIL		•	•	•	•	•	•
	MAGNET				•		•	•
	MANUAL GROTESK A							
	MAXEVILLE						•	
	MONOPOL		•				•	
	ABC MONUMENT GROTESK		•				•	•
	MORI			•	•	•	•	•
N	NEOGEO		•	•			•	•
	NEUE MACHINA		•				•	•
	NEUE POWER				•		•	•
	MD NICHROME		•		•		•	
	TT NORMS PRO		•	•	•		•	•

SEMIBOLD	BOLD	EXTRA BOLD	BLACK	EXTRA BLACK	ITALIC	OTHERS	CONDENSED	MONO	EXTENDED	PAGE
	●	●	●		●	●				012
	●		●		●	●				018
	●		●			●				022
	●		●			●		●		026
	●		●			●				030
	●		●		●	●	●		●	034
●	●	●	●		●	●		●		038
●	●	●	●		●	●		●		042
●	●	●	●		●	●	●		●	048
●	●	●	●		●	●	●		●	052
●	●		●		●	●				056
●	●		●			●				060
	●				●					064
●	●	●	●	●	●	●	●		●	068
	●									074
●	●	●	●		●	●				078
●	●					●				082
	●		●		●					086
●	●		●		●	●	●		●	090
●	●	●	●	●	●	●	●		●	096
●	●	●	●		●	●	●		●	100
					●	●				106
					●	●	●			110
	●		●		●					114
	●		●							118
	●	●	●	●	●	●	●	●	●	122
●	●				●	●				126
	●		●		●	●	●	●	●	130
	●		●		●	●				134
	●	●	●		●	●				140
						●			●	146
	●				●	●		●	●	150
●	●	●	●		●	●	●		●	154
	●		●		●					158
●	●									162
					●	●	●		●	168
●	●				●	●	●		●	172
										178
	●		●			●				182
	●		●		●					188
	●				●	●		●		192
	●				●	●	●		●	196
	●				●	●				200
	●		●		●					204
●	●		●		●	●				210
●	●	●			●					214
	●		●		●	●				218
						●				224
	●				●	●		●		228
						●				232
	●		●		●	●		●		238
●	●	●			●					242
●	●	●	●		●	●				246
●	●		●		●	●				250
					●	●				256
	●		●		●	●				262
	●	●	●	●	●	●	●	●	●	266

TYPE CHECK

		HAIRLINE	THIN	EXTRA LIGHT	LIGHT	BOOK	REGULAR	MEDIUM
N	NOUVEAU				•		•	•
	NUCKLE	•	•	•	•		•	•
O	OFELIA		•	•	•		•	•
	OFFBIT						•	
	ONSITE		•	•	•		•	•
	F37 ORACLE				•		•	•
P	FT PILAR	•	•		•		•	•
	FOUNDRY PLEK				•		•	•
	GT PRESSURA				•		•	•
	MD PRIMER				•		•	•
R	RÄDER	•	•	•	•		•	•
	RAINER	•	•		•		•	•
	REWORK		•	•	•		•	
	RM MONO				•		•	
	RM NEUE				•		•	
	ABC ROM				•	•	•	•
	RULES				•		•	•
S	SANS PLOMB							
	SCANDIUM		•	•			•	
	SHAPE	•	•		•		•	•
	OR SIMILAR				•		•	•
	SNEAK				•		•	•
	SOLARIS				•		•	
	F37 SONIC				•		•	•
	FAIRE SPRIG SANS	•	•		•		•	•
	SURT		•	•	•		•	•
T	NB TELEVISION™ PRO						•	
	TOMATO GROTESK		•	•	•		•	•
	TT TRAILERS		•	•	•		•	•
U	KOMETA UNIFORMA	•	•	•	•		•	•
V	VCTR MONO		•		•		•	•
Z	ZETKIN				•		•	•
	ZIN SANS				•		•	•
	ZNVIT15						•	
	ZOOM PRO	•	•		•		•	•

SEMIBOLD	BOLD	EXTRA BOLD	BLACK	EXTRA BLACK	ITALIC	OTHERS	CONDENSED	MONO	EXTENDED	PAGE
●	●		●		●	●				270
●	●									274
●	●	●			●					278
	●					●				282
	●	●			●		●		●	288
●	●				●					292
	●		●							296
	●									300
	●		●		●	●		●	●	304
●	●		●							308
●	●				●					312
	●				●					316
●	●				●	●				320
●	●		●		●			●		326
●	●		●		●	●				330
	●		●		●	●	●	●	●	334
	●	●			●	●				338
					●	●				342
●	●		●		●	●				346
●	●		●		●	●				350
●	●		●		●					354
	●		●		●			●		358
	●				●					362
	●	●	●		●	●				366
	●		●		●	●				370
●	●	●	●		●	●			●	376
						●		●		380
●	●	●	●		●	●				386
	●	●	●		●	●				390
●	●		●		●					394
	●		●		●			●		398
	●		●		●	●				402
	●		●		●		●		●	406
										410
	●					●	●		●	414

```
TYPEFACE    :    FFF ACID GROTESK
DESIGNER    :    (FFF) FONTS FROM FOLCH
LOCATION    :    BARCELONA, SPAIN

                 PUBLISHED BY      :    (FFF) FONTS FROM FOLCH
                 CHRONOLOGY        :    2019 - 2020
                 RELEASED IN       :    2020

LINK        :    HTTPS://FONTSFROMFOLCH.COM
STYLES      :    ULTRA LIGHT, EXTRA LIGHT, LIGHT, BOOK, REGULAR,
                 MEDIUM, BOLD, EXTRA BOLD, BLACK + ITALICS + SOFT
```

ACID GROTESK SHOWCASES A UNIQUE CHARACTER, HARMONIOUSLY BLENDING A ROBUST APPEARANCE WITH SMOOTH CURVES AND ROUNDED VERTICES TO ACHIEVE A FLUID AND DYNAMIC AESTHETIC. AN EXPANSIVE FONT FAMILY ENCOMPASSING 9 WEIGHTS RANGING FROM EXTRA LIGHT TO BLACK, ACCOMPANIED BY MATCHING ITALICS AND A SOFT COUNTERPART, THE TYPEFACE INCLUDES ALL ITS DISTINCTIVE STYLISTIC SETS AND A WIDE RANGE OF OPENTYPE FUNCTIONS. ITS ADAPTABLE NATURE LENDS ITSELF SEAMLESSLY TO HEADLINES, BODY TEXTS, AND DISPLAYS, ALLOWING FOR THE CREATION OF A DIVERSE VISUAL LANGUAGE. NOTABLY, IT SEAMLESSLY COMBINES THIN SYMBOLS WITH ALL WEIGHT OPTIONS TO ELEVATE DESIGNS WITH ITS EXQUISITE BLEND OF STRENGTH, ELEGANCE, AND VERSATILITY.

CAP HEIGHT   REGULAR — 290PT

X-HEIGHT

Aa

BASELINE

FFFAcid Grotesk

THE QUICK BROWN

IT WOULD BE THE C

IT'S A LOVELY DAY IN

AND THE PUNGENT

PROMISE OF A SUM

THINKING ABOUT TI

THE LAZY DOG REM

LONG BLACK FUR FI

THE MOUNTAINS AF

AND THE PUDDLES .

IT'S A DOG'S LIFE, A

ABCDEƐFFFGGHIJKLMNOP
QRSSSTUVWXYYYZ
abcdeefgggghijklmnopqrs
sstuvwxyyz
0123456789®e$&

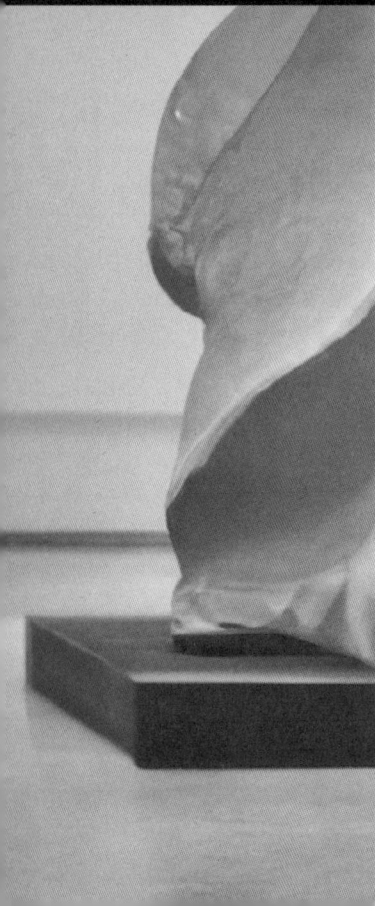

Life An
Death
Everyt

Mushy,
Squashy
&
Pappy.

Clubbing
Culture.

Enjoy the
Night.

BC

SSSSSSSSS

EL	UL	L	N	R	M	B	EB	BLK

SSSSSSSSS

ELI	ULI	LI	NI	RI	MI	BI	EBI	BLKI

Sans & Soft

Acid W
Tee.
Green
28€
XS S M

6

Yes,
No,
Maybe.

TYPEFACE	:	AEONIK
DESIGNER	:	MARK BLOOM, JOSEPH LEADBEATER
LOCATION	:	LONDON, UK

PUBLISHED BY	:	COTYPE FOUNDRY
CHRONOLOGY	:	2ND TYPEFACE RELEASE
RELEASED IN	:	2018

LINK	:	HTTPS://COTYPEFOUNDRY.COM/OUR-FONTS/AEONIK/
STYLES	:	14 STYLES, 7 WEIGHTS: AIR, THIN, LIGHT, REGULAR, MEDIUM, BOLD, BLACK + ITALICS

A STRUCTURAL WORKHORSE, AEONIK WAS CRAFTED WITH MECHANICAL DETAIL. CONCEIVED AS A "NEO-GROTESQUE WITH A GEOMETRIC SKELETON", IT HOLDS RIGIDITY AND COLDNESS THROUGH STRICT PERPENDICULAR TERMINALS: NOTICEABLY WITHIN THE "A", "T", "F" AND "J". THESE ARE OFFSET BY THE GEOMETRIC NATURE OF THE "C", "E", "O" AND "Y". SEVEN WEIGHTS AND ITALICS ENSURE ITS ECLECTIC USE AS A FAMILY. AEONIK'S CHARACTERS SPAN THE LATIN EXTENDED UNICODE RANGE, COVERING MOST LANGUAGES WRITTEN WITH THE LATIN SCRIPT. BOASTING ALMOST 700 CHARACTERS, ITS OPENTYPE FEATURES INCLUDE LIGATURES, OLD STYLE NUMERALS, FRACTIONS, CASE SENSITIVE PUNCTUATION, SYMBOLS, SHAPES, AND ARROWS.

CAP HEIGHT   REGULAR — 290PT

X-HEIGHT

Aa

BASELINE

Aeonik

THE QUICK BROWN FOX

IT WOULD BE THE CHEE

IT'S A LOVELY DAY IN TH

AND THE PUNGENT ARC

PROMISE OF A SUMPTU

THINKING ABOUT THE D

The quick brown fox jumps over a lazy dog. He didn't have to, it would be the cheeky thing to do. After all, he had a reputatic It's a lovely day in the neighbourhood, with the sun shining, the and the pungent aroma of fresh rubbish bins wafting through promise of a sumptuous meal. The sprightly fox rubs his paws thinking about the delicious treasures he's about to dig into. S the lazy dog remains unperturbed. With her long snout, droop long black fur fluttering in the breeze, she is in a dreamland fai the mountains are made of beefy treats, the valleys are filled v and the puddles are just the right temperature. Why be in the It's a dog's life, after all.

The quick brown fox jumps over a lazy dog. He didn't have to, but he thought it would be the cheeky thing to do. After all, he had a reputation to maintain. It's a lovely day in the neighbourhood, with the sun shining, the birds chirping, and the pungent aroma of fresh rubbish bins wafting through the air - the promise of a sumptuous meal. The sprightly fox rubs his paws together in glee, thinking about the delicious treasures he's about to dig into. Still in her spot, the lazy dog remains unperturbed. With her long snout, droopy jowls, and long black fur fluttering in the breeze, she is in a dreamland far away - where the mountains are made of beefy treats, the valleys are filled with tennis balls, and the puddles are just the right temperature. Why be in the rat race? It's a dog's life, after all.

747
747

LHR
LHR
LHR
ZRH
ZRH
ZRH

Zurich
Zurich
Zurich
Zurich
Zurich
Zurich

↑ ↑ ↑ ↑ ↑ ↑

London
London
London
London
London
London

Aeonik
Aeonik
Aeonik
Aeonik
Aeonik
Aeonik
Aeonik

↑ ↑ ↑ ↑ ↑
↑ ↑ ↑ ↑ ↑

AR7067494568901

LHR ZRH

LHR707 15 June BC1

ZRH

ZURICH

ZRH707 13 June BC1

LHR

HEATHROW

Aeonik

AR7067494568901

-1578
-1578
-1578
-1578
-1578
-1578
-1578
-1578
-1578

+ + + + + + + + +

HEATHROW
LHR
ZRH707 13 June BC1

ZURICH
ZRH
LHR707 15 June BC1

HEATHROW
LHR
ZRH707 13 June BC1

ZURICH
ZRH
LHR707 15 June BC1

ZRH707
ZRH707
ZRH707
ZRH707
ZRH707
LHR707
LHR707
LHR707
LHR707

-1547
-1547
-1547
-1547
-1547
-1547
-1547

Oslo Paris Berlin Zürich London Hong Kong Tokyo New York Stockholm Sydney

BUSINESS CLASS BUSINESS CLASS BUSINESS CLASS BUSINESS CLASS BUSINESS CLASS BUSINESS CLASS BUSINESS CLASS BUSINESS CLASS BUSINESS CLASS

BC1 BC1 BC1 BC1 BC1 BC1 BC1 BC1 BC1 BC1 BC1

13 → ← 13

AR70674945689U1

Aeonik

HEATHROW
LHR
ZRH707 13 June BC1

ZURICH
ZRH
LHR707 15 June BC1

LHR → ZRH

AR70674945689O1

```
TYPEFACE    :    AEONIK FONO
DESIGNER    :    COTYPE FOUNDRY
LOCATION    :    LONDON, UK

                 PUBLISHED BY    :    COTYPE FOUNDRY
                 CHRONOLOGY      :    11TH TYPEFACE RELEASE
                 RELEASED IN     :    2022

LINK        :    HTTPS://COTYPEFOUNDRY.COM/OUR-FONTS/AEONIK-FONO/
STYLES      :    7 WEIGHTS: AIR, THIN, LIGHT, REGULAR,
                 MEDIUM, BOLD, BLACK + A VARIABLE FONT
```

AEONIK FONO HAS BEEN DESIGNED TO LIVE IN THE SPACE BETWEEN THE CLASSICAL AEONIK AND AEONIK MONO. ITS LETTER SHAPES ARE SLIGHTLY LESS EXAGGERATED THAN A TRUE MONO FONT, MAKING IT EASIER TO READ. IT FEATURES PROPORTIONAL SPACING AND SOME KERNING, ALL OF WHICH MAKE TEXT SETTING A PLEASURE. IT IS AVAILABLE IN SEVEN WEIGHTS, RANGING FROM THIN TO BLACK. ITS EXTENSIVE LANGUAGE SUPPORT ALLOWS FOR TYPE SETTING IN MOST EUROPEAN LANGUAGES WRITTEN WITH THE LATIN SCRIPT. AEONIK FONO IS PARTICULARLY SUITABLE FOR EDITORIAL AND BRANDING PROJECTS, TAKING GROTESQUE TO ANOTHER DIMENSION WITH ITS MORE INTERESTING PROPORTIONS AND OVERSIZED SERIFS.

CAP HEIGHT   REGULAR — 290PT

X-HEIGHT

Aa

BASELINE

Aeonik Fono

THE QUICK BROWN FOX JU

IT WOULD BE THE CHEEKY

IT'S A LOVELY DAY IN THE

AND THE PUNGENT AROMA

PROMISE OF A SUMPTUOU

THINKING ABOUT THE DE

THE LAZY DOG REMAINS U

The quick brown fox jumps over a lazy dog. He d
it would be the cheeky thing to do. After all, he
It's a lovely day in the neighbourhood, with the
and the pungent aroma of fresh rubbish bins wa
promise of a sumptuous meal. The sprightly fox
thinking about the delicious treasures he's abo
the lazy dog remains unperturbed. With her long
long black fur fluttering in the breeze, she is i

The quick brown fox jumps over a lazy dog. He didn't have to, but he thought
it would be the cheeky thing to do. After all, he had a reputation to maintain.
It's a lovely day in the neighbourhood, with the sun shining, the birds chirping,
and the pungent aroma of fresh rubbish bins wafting through the air - the
promise of a sumptuous meal. The sprightly fox rubs his paws together in glee,
thinking about the delicious treasures he's about to dig into. Still in her spot,
the lazy dog remains unperturbed. With her long snout, droopy jowls, and
long black fur fluttering in the breeze, she is in a dreamland far away - where
the mountains are made of beefy treats, the valleys are filled with tennis balls,
and the puddles are just the right temperature. Why be in the rat race?
It's a dog's life, after all.

↓ Aeonik Mono Regular 134 pt

films

↓ Aeonik Fono Regular 134 pt

films

↓ Aeonik Mono Width

620
478

m

↓ Aeonik Fono Width

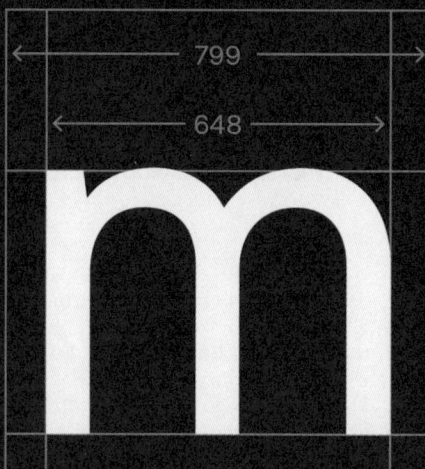

799
648

m

↓ Aeonik Mono Regular 54 pt

Biocompatible

↓ Aeonik Fono Regular 54 pt

Biocompatible

↓ Aeonik Mono Regular 18 pt

Typography is the art of arranging type to make written language legible, readable and appealing when displayed.

↓ Aeonik Fono Regular 18 pt

Typography is the art of arranging type to make written language legible, readable and appealing when displayed.

↓ Aeonik Mono Regular 10 pt
The arrangement of type involves selecting typefaces, point sizes, line lengths, line-spacing (leading), and letter-spacing (tracking).

↓ Aeonik Fono Regular 10 pt
The arrangement of type involves selecting typefaces, point sizes, line lengths, line-spacing (leading), and letter-spacing (tracking).

TYPEFACE	:	AEONIK MONO
DESIGNER	:	COTYPE FOUNDRY
LOCATION	:	LONDON, UK

		PUBLISHED BY	:	COTYPE FOUNDRY
		CHRONOLOGY	:	10TH TYPEFACE RELEASE
		RELEASED IN	:	2022

| LINK | : | HTTPS://COTYPEFOUNDRY.COM/OUR-FONTS/AEONIK-MONO/ |
| STYLES | : | 7 WEIGHTS: AIR, THIN, LIGHT, REGULAR, MEDIUM, BOLD, BLACK + A VARIABLE FONT |

AEONIK MONO WAS CREATED TO PICK UP ON THE FEATURES THAT MAKE THE ORIGINAL AEONIK A BELOVED CHOICE AMONGST DESIGNERS AND TRANSFORM IT INTO A TRUE MONOSPACED TYPE FAMILY FOR USE IN GRAPHIC DESIGN PROJECTS. AS IS CUSTOMARY FOR A FIXED-PITCH FONT, EACH CHARACTER IN AEONIK MONO FITS IN A BOX OF THE SAME WIDTH, WHICH IN THIS CASE IS 620 UNITS. AEONIK MONO IS AVAILABLE IN SEVEN WEIGHTS, RANGING FROM THIN TO BLACK. ITS EXTENSIVE LANGUAGE SUPPORT (LATIN EXTENDED A) ALLOWS FOR TYPE SETTING IN MOST EUROPEAN LANGUAGES WRITTEN WITH THE LATIN SCRIPT.

CAP HEIGHT   REGULAR – 290PT

X-HEIGHT

Aa

BASELINE

Aeonik Mono

THE QUICK BROWN FOX

IT WOULD BE THE CHE

IT'S A LOVELY DAY I

AND THE PUNGENT ARC

PROMISE OF A SUMPTU

THINKING ABOUT THE

THE LAZY DOG REMAIN

LONG BLACK FUR FLUT

THE MOUNTAINS ARE M

AND THE PUDDLES ARE

IT'S A DOG'S LIFE,

The quick brown fox jumps over a lazy dog. He didn't have to, but he thought it would be the cheeky thing to do. After all, he had a reputation to maintain. It's a lovely day in the neighbourhood, with the sun shining, the birds chirping, and the pungent aroma of fresh rubbish bins wafting through the air — the promise of a sumptuous meal. The sprightly fox rubs his paws together in glee, thinking about the delicious treasures he's about to dig into. Still in her spot, the lazy dog remains unperturbed. With her long snout, droopy jowls, and long black fur fluttering in the breeze, she is in a dreamland far away — where the mountains are made of beefy treats, the valleys are filled with tennis balls, and the puddles are just the right temperature. Why be in the rat race? It's a dog's life, after all.

Medium - 70pt
OAK

Medium - 53pt
BUZZ

Medium - 40pt
PIZZA

Medium - 33pt
QUARTZ

Medium - 28pt
BILLION

Medium - 25pt
CONCRETE

Medium - 22pt
FABRICATE

Medium - 20pt
STRAWBERRY

Medium - 16pt
OBJECTIFYING

Regular - 34pt
AFFORD
Combat
Demand

Regular - 22pt
MACAROONS
Dachshund
Radiators

Regular - 14pt
MULTIFREQUENCY
Contextualized
Subjectivising
Tranquillizers

Light - 22pt
BACKDRAFT
Gigapixel
Helpfully
Jellyfish

Light - 14pt
Apocalypse Now
Special Forces
Walter E.Kurtz
George Cantero

Light - 10pt
Apple Flagship Shop
@ 235 Regent Street
By appointment only
Saturday 10am - 7pm
Shopping and Pickup

ABCDEFGHIJJKLM
NOPQQRSTUVWXYZ
aɑabcdeffghijk
lmnopqrstuvwxy
yz/0123456789
£Ƀ$%&&?↯ßŧÄ⅛©¶

https://CoTypeFoundry.
com © 🅲🅸🅳🅴 x 7 weights
AeonikMono-Regular.otf
52 KB WOFF/WOFF2/OTF ¶
LDN,UK aalt/salt/frac/
◊ **aaaffyyJJQQ&&77** ↗£40
DPS: 240mm(H)x340mm(W)
CAPS + lwr INT ⑦ **Trial**
#Hashbrown Estd {②①①⑨}
¼lb ▶ 100% Beef @ 180°
ZQW / Zweibrücken €uro
Crypto ↔ **₿itcoin** / NFT
Like ✓ Chausseestraße?
Ωmega™ ⁑ Play ▶ STOP ■
¥en ↷ ₦aira ↗ ₺ira **U$D**
Peace ☮ Love & Unity ∞

```
TYPEFACE      :     AEONIK PRO
DESIGNER      :     COTYPE FOUNDRY
LOCATION      :     LONDON, UK

                    PUBLISHED BY        :     COTYPE FOUNDRY
                    CHRONOLOGY          :     5TH TYPEFACE RELEASE
                    RELEASED IN         :     2020

LINK          :     HTTPS://COTYPEFOUNDRY.COM/OUR-FONTS/AEONIK-PRO/
STYLES        :     14 STYLES, 7 WEIGHTS: AIR, THIN, LIGHT, REGULAR, MEDIUM,
                    BOLD, BLACK + ITALICS + A VARIABLE FONT INCLUDING LATIN,
                    GREEK AND CRYLLIC SUPPORT
CREDITS       :     SEMIOTIK DESIGN (SPECIMEN BOOK DESIGN)
```

IN CREATING AEONIK PRO, COTYPE FOUNDRY TOOK ITS BEST-SELLING AEONIK TYPE FAMILY AND REFINED IT FURTHER, WHILST ALSO ADDING SUPPORT FOR CYRILLIC AND GREEK. WITH MORE THAN 900 CHARACTERS AND PLENTY OF ALTERNATES TO CHOOSE FROM, THIS WORKHORSE TYPE FAMILY IS A MUST-HAVE IN ANY DESIGNER'S TOOLSET. WITH 17 STYLISTIC SETS, THE USER WILL FIND STYLISTIC ALTERNATES FOR PARTICULAR LOWERCASE OR CAPITAL LETTERS, ALTERNATE NUMERAL FORMS, WHITE AND BLACK CIRCLED NUMERALS, AS WELL AS ALTERNATE SHAPES FOR GREEK. TWO OF THE STYLISTIC SETS ALLOW FOR DIRECT ACCESS TO BULGARIAN AND SERBIAN CYRILLIC ALTERNATES.

CAP HEIGHT   REGULAR — 290PT

X-HEIGHT

Aa

BASELINE

Aeonik Pro

THE QUICK BROWN FOX J
IT WOULD BE THE CHEEK
IT'S A LOVELY DAY IN THE
AND THE PUNGENT AROM
PROMISE OF A SUMPTUO
THINKING ABOUT THE DE
THE LAZY DOG REMAINS
LONG BLACK FUR FLUTTE
THE MOUNTAINS ARE MA
AND THE PUDDLES ARE JU
IT'S A DOG'S LIFE, AFTER

The quick brown fox jumps over a lazy dog. He didn't have to, but he thought it would be the cheeky thing to do. After all, he had a reputation to maintain. It's a lovely day in the neighbourhood, with the sun shining, the birds chirping, and the pungent aroma of fresh rubbish bins wafting through the air - the promise of a sumptuous meal. The sprightly fox rubs his paws together in glee, thinking about the delicious treasures he's about to dig into. Still in her spot, the lazy dog remains unperturbed. With her long snout, droopy jowls, and long black fur fluttering in the breeze, she is in a dreamland far away - where the mountains are made of beefy treats, the valleys are filled with tennis balls, and the puddles are just the right temperature. Why be in the rat race? It's a dog's life, after all.

Cultural C.

Το ύφος της σχολής Μπαουχάους επέδρασε καταλυτικά στην εξέλιξη της σύγχρονης τέχνης, της αρχιτεκτονικής και του βιομηχανικού σχεδιασμού, ενώ, τα έργα που παράχθηκαν μέσα από τα εργαστήρια της σχολής έγιναν αντικείμενα εκτεταμένης αναπαραγωγής και συλλογής.

Λειτούργησε σε τρεις διαφορετικές πόλεις της Γερμανίας, στη Βαϊμάρη (1919–25), στο Ντεσάου (1925–32) και στο Βερολίνο (1932–33), υπό την διεύθυνση των Βάλτερ Γκρόπιους (1919–28), Χάνες Μέγιερ (1928–30) και Μις βαν ντερ Ρόε (1930–33), αντίστοιχα. Οι αλλαγές στην έδρα και την ηγεσία της συνδέονταν με αντίστοιχες διαφοροποιήσεις στην πολιτική της, καθώς και στα ιδιαίτερα χαρακτηριστικά του ύφους της. Ανάμεσα στις κεντρικές ιδέες που προώθησε η σχολή, ήταν η χρήση της τεχνολογίας για καλλιτεχνικούς σκοπούς, η απουσία διάκρισης μεταξύ καλών και εφαρμοσμένων τεχνών, καθώς, και η αναγκαιότητα της σφαιρικής διδασκαλίας όλων των μορφών τέχνης.[2] Επανέφερε τη διδασκαλία σε εργαστήρια, σε αντίθεση με τον τρόπο λειτουργίας των ακαδημιών, και στο μικρό χρονικό διάστημα που λειτούργησε, δίδαξαν σε αυτή επιφανείς καλλιτέχνες του 20ού αιώνα, όπως, ο Βασίλι Καντίνσκι, ο Γιοχάνες Ίτεν, ο Μαρσέλ Μπρόιερ και ο Πάουλ Κλέε.

Annual 5

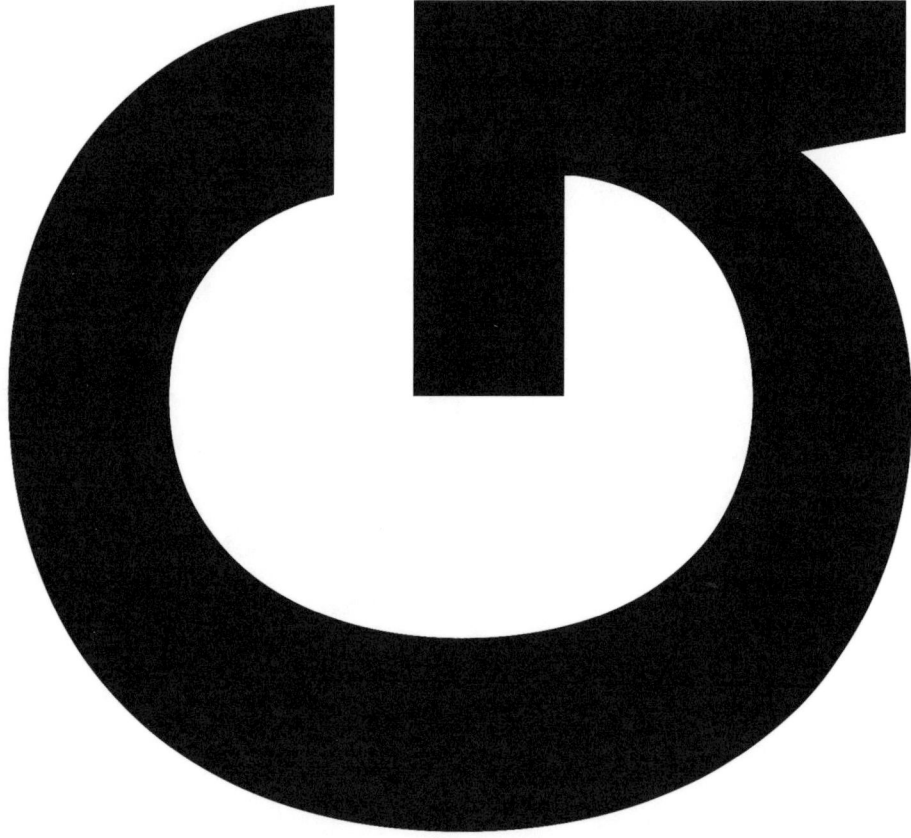

After closing and expulsion of the historical Bauhaus in Dessau on 30 September 1932 a long time of 44 years had to pass, before the Bauhaus Building could be used again in its original sense. In 1976, 50 years after its construction, the GDR government had reconstructed the historical monument and founded a "Scientific and cultural Centre". Assembly of a Bauhaus collection of its own began and the Bauhaus stage was once again used for concerts and plays. In 1986 the GDR celebrated the reopening of the Bauhaus as a "Centre for Design", tied in the eastern Germany's department of building.

After the German reunification it seemed to be completely unclear what the Bauhaus would evolve into during the following years. On 9 February 1994 the German Federal Government, the state of Saxony-Anhalt and the town Dessau finally founded[1] the Bauhaus Dessau Foundation.

From 1994 until 1998 Prof. Dr. Rolf Kuhn was the Executive Director of the Foundation. His successor Prof. Dr. Omar Akbar was in charge until 2009. Since 1 March 2009 the architect and publicist Prof. Philipp Oswalt is the head of the Foundation; his deputy is Dr. Regina Bittner, who is also responsible for the Foundation's Academy. Today, the Bauhaus Dessau Foundation is based in the

After closing and expulsion of the historical Bauhaus in Dessau on 30 September 1932 a long time of 44 years had to pass, before the Bauhaus Building could be used again in its original sense. In 1976, 50 years after its construction, the GDR government had reconstructed the historical monument and founded a "Scientific and cultural Centre". Assembly of a Bauhaus collection of its own began and the Bauhaus stage was once again used for concerts and plays. In 1986 the GDR celebrated the reopening of the Bauhaus as a "Centre for Design", tied in the eastern Germany's department of building.

After the German reunification it seemed to be completely unclear what the Bauhaus would evolve into during the following years. On 9 February 1994 the German Federal Government, the state of Saxony-Anhalt and the town Dessau finally founded[1] the Bauhaus Dessau Foundation.

From 1994 until 1998 Prof. Dr. Rolf Kuhn was the Executive Director of the Foundation. His successor Prof. Dr. Omar Akbar was in charge until 2009. Since 1 March 2009 the architect and publicist Prof. Philipp Oswalt is the head of the Foundation;

TYPEFACE	:	AGRANDIR
DESIGNER	:	ALEX SLOBZHENINOV
LOCATION	:	MONTREAL, CANADA

		PUBLISHED BY	:	PANGRAM PANGRAM® FOUNDRY
		CHRONOLOGY	:	N/A
		RELEASED IN	:	2018

| LINK | : | HTTPS://PANGRAMPANGRAM.COM/PRODUCTS/AGRANDIR |
| STYLES | : | 14 WEIGHTS X 5 WIDTHS + 4 TEXT WEIGHTS (TOTALLING 74 STYLES) WITH 443 GLYPHS EACH INCLUDING ITALIC SUPPORT |

AGRANDIR IS A CONTEMPORARY SERIFLESS TYPE FAMILY THAT CELEBRATES THE BEAUTY OF BEING IMPERFECT. IT WAS DESIGNED TO BE A BRAVE ANTIPODE TO NEUTRAL MODERNIST FONTS. AGRANDIR ACCEPTS ITS OWN SHAPES AS THEY ARE — UNALIGNED, QUIRKY AND FUNKY. IT CELEBRATES HUMANITY, NOT MACHINES. THE TYPE FAMILY FEATURES A FAIRLY GOOD NUMBER OF OPENTYPE STYLISTIC ALTERNATIVES, WHICH CAN BE TURNED ON FOR INDIVIDUAL LETTERS OR AS OVERALL PRESETS — DEFAULT, GROTESK AND GEOMETRIC. WITH ITS WIDE VARIETY OF FLAVOURS AND SUPER TIGHT SPACING, AGRANDIR WORKS WELL IN HEADLINES, WEBSITES, LOGOS, AND POSTERS, WHILE ITS NEW TEXT STYLES ARE GREAT FOR BODY COPY.

CAP HEIGHT

REGULAR — 290PT

X-HEIGHT

Aa

BASELINE

Agrandir

THE QUICK BROWN FOX J
IT WOULD BE THE CHEEKY
IT'S A LOVELY DAY IN THE N
AND THE PUNGENT AROM
PROMISE OF A SUMPTUO
THINKING ABOUT THE DEL
THE LAZY DOG REMAINS
LONG BLACK FUR FLUTTE
THE MOUNTAINS ARE MAD
AND THE PUDDLES ARE JL
IT'S A DOG'S LIFE, AFTER A

The quick brown fox jumps over a lazy dog. He didn't have to, but he thought it would be the cheeky thing to do. After all, he had a reputation to maintain. It's a lovely day in the neighbourhood, with the sun shining, the birds chirping, and the pungent aroma of fresh rubbish bins wafting through the air – the promise of a sumptuous meal. The sprightly fox rubs his paws together in glee, thinking about the delicious treasures he's about to dig into. Still in her spot, the lazy dog remains unperturbed. With her long snout, droopy jowls, and long black fur fluttering in the breeze, she is in a dreamland far away – where the mountains are made of beefy treats, the valleys are filled with tennis balls, and the puddles are just the right temperature. Why be in the rat race? It's a dog's life, after all.

AB

AGRANDIR

AGRANDIR

AGRANDIR

AGRANDIR

AGRANDIR

```
TYPEFACE    :    AIR
DESIGNER    :    MAT DESJARDINS, CAIO KONDO
LOCATION    :    MONTREAL, CANADA

                 PUBLISHED BY     :    PANGRAM PANGRAM® FOUNDRY
                 CHRONOLOGY       :    N/A
                 RELEASED IN      :    2023

LINK        :    HTTPS://PANGRAMPANGRAM.COM/PRODUCTS/AIR
STYLES      :    2 CUTS X 18 STYLES WITH 656 GLYPHS EACH + ITALICS
CREDITS     :    DEMANDE SPÉCIALE (VISUALS/COLLABORATION)
```

A HARMONIOUS COLLISION OF BRUTALISM, MINIMALISM, AND AEROSPACE, AIR IS A BREATH OF FRESH CREATIVITY. ORIGINALLY DESIGNED BY MAT DESJARDINS AND EXPANDED BY CAIO KONDO FROM INARI TYPE, IT EMBRACES THE DUALITY BETWEEN SIMPLICITY AND EXPERIMENTATION, OFFERING A VISUALLY APPEALING AND INTRIGUING AESTHETIC TO MAKE IT A TRUE PANGRAM PANGRAM FONT. ITS MASSIVE CHARACTER MAP INCLUDES A VARIETY OF ALTERNATE CHARACTERS, ALLOWING FOR GREATER CUSTOMISATION AND CREATIVE POSSIBILITIES. ADDITIONALLY, ABUNDANT PUNCTUATION AND A SET OF ARROWS ARE AVAILABLE, ADDING VERSATILITY AND FUNCTIONALITY TO ANY PROJECT. AIR COMES IN A HUGE RANGE OF WEIGHTS — FROM MONO TO ITALIC — AND EVEN HAS A VARIABLE VERSION THAT UNITES THESE AXES IN A SINGLE FILE.

CAP HEIGHT   REGULAR — 290PT

X-HEIGHT

Aa

BASELINE

Air

THE QUICK BROWN FOX JUMPS
IT WOULD BE THE CHEEKY THIN
IT'S A LOVELY DAY IN THE NEIGH
AND THE PUNGENT AROMA OF
PROMISE OF A SUMPTUOUS ME
THINKING ABOUT THE DELICIOU
THE LAZY DOG REMAINS UNPEF
LONG BLACK FUR FLUTTERING I
THE MOUNTAINS ARE MADE OF
AND THE PUDDLES ARE JUST T
IT'S A DOG'S LIFE, AFTER ALL.

The quick brown fox jumps over a lazy dog. He didn't have to, but he thought it would be the cheeky thing to do. After all, he had a reputation to maintain. It's a lovely day in the neighbourhood, with the sun shining, the birds chirping, and the pungent aroma of fresh rubbish bins wafting through the air - the promise of a sumptuous meal. The sprightly fox rubs his paws together in glee, thinking about the delicious treasures he's about to dig into. Still in her spot, the lazy dog remains unperturbed. With her long snout, droopy jowls, and long black fur fluttering in the breeze, she is in a dreamland far away - where the mountains are made of beefy treats, the valleys are filled with tennis balls, and the puddles are just the right temperature. Why be in the rat race? It's a dog's life, after all.

air

AIR

AA
IRR
IR

TYPEFACE	:	NB AKADEMIE™ PRO
DESIGNER	:	STEFAN GANDL
LOCATION	:	BERLIN, GERMANY

		PUBLISHED BY	:	NEUBAU
		CHRONOLOGY	:	2015 – 2016
		RELEASED IN	:	2016

| LINK | : | HTTPS://NEUBAULADEN.COM/PRODUCT/NB-AKADEMIE-EDITION/ |
| STYLES | : | 32 STYLES RANGING FROM LIGHT TO BLACK WITH ITALICS AND MONO |

NB AKADEMIE™ IS A CONTEMPORARY GROTESQUE TYPE SYSTEM COMPRISING 32 STYLES. ITS INFLUENCES AND NAMESAKE CAN BE ATTRIBUTED TO THE LEGENDARY GERMAN TYPE DESIGNER FERDINAND THEINHARDT AND HIS REVOLUTIONARY ROYAL GROTESK TYPESET (1880). AFTER HIS TYPE FOUNDRY (FERD. THEINHARDT SCHRIFTGIESSEREI BERLIN) WAS SOLD, THEINHARDT'S ROYAL GROTESK BECAME INTERNATIONALLY RENOWNED AS BERTHOLD'S AKZIDENZ GROTESK (1896) – THE GODMOTHER OF ALL MODERN GROTESQUE TYPEFACES.

CAP HEIGHT   REGULAR – 290PT

X-HEIGHT

Aa

BASELINE

^{NB}Akademie™ Pro

THE QUICK BROWN FO

IT WOULD BE THE CHI

ITS A LOVELY DAY IN T

AND THE PUNGENT A

PROMISE OF A SUMPT

THINKING ABOUT THE

THE LAZY DOG REMAI

LONG BLACK FUR FLU

THE MOUNTAINS ARE

The quick brown fox jumps over a lazy dog. He didn't have to, but he thought it would be the cheeky thing to do. After all, he had a reputation to maintain. Its a lovely day in the neighbourhood, with the sun shining, the birds chirping, and the pungent aroma of fresh rubbish bins wafting through the air - the promise of a sumptuous meal. The sprightly fox rubs his paws together in glee, thinking about the delicious treasures he's about to dig into. Still in her spot, the lazy dog remains unperturbed. With her long snout, droopy jowls, and long black fur fluttering in the breeze, she is in a dreamland far away - where the mountains are made of beefy treats, the valleys are filled with tennis balls, and the puddles are just the right temperature. Why be in the rat race? Its a dogs life, after all.

Printed in Germany, © XXXX 20XX

Königlich Preußische Nassau Akademie® Limited Edition (Flag) (—— 20) Draft

1	Light	04/05
2	*Light Italic*	06/07
3	Book	08/09
4	*Book Italic*	10/11
5	Regular	12/13
6	*Italic*	14/15
7	Medium	16/17
8	*Medium Italic*	18/19
9	SemiBold	20/21
10	*SemiBold Italic*	22/23
11	Bold	24/25
12	*Bold Italic*	26/27
13	ExtraBold	28/29
14	*ExtraBold Italic*	30/31
15	Black	32/33
16	*Black Italic*	34/35
17	Mono 200	36/37
18	*Mono 200 Italic*	38/39
19	Mono 300	40/41
20	*Mono 300 Italic*	42/43
21	Mono 400	44/45
22	*Mono 400 Italic*	46/47
23	Mono 500	48/49
24	*Mono 500 Italic*	50/51
25	Mono 600	52/53
26	*Mono 600 Italic*	54/55
27	Mono 700	56/57
28	*Mono 700 Italic*	58/59
29	Mono 800	60/61
30	*Mono 800 Italic*	62/63
31	Mono 900	64/65
32	*Mono 900 Italic*	66/67

Neubau
Akademie™

L L B B R R M M

[1] [2] [3] [4] [5] [6] [7] [8]

S S B B E E B B

[9] [10] [11] [12] [13] [14] [15] [16]

M M M M M M

[17] [18] [19] [20] [21] [22]

M M M M M M

[23] [24] [25] [26] [27] [28]

M M M M

[29] [30] [31] [32]

Neubau
Akademie™

[1] [2] [3] [4] [5] [6] [7] [8]

S P

[9] [10] [11] [14] [15] [16]

E C

[17] [18] [19] I [20] [21] [22]

[23] [24] [25] [26] [27]

[29] [30] [31] M E [32]

N

96/84 pt

Neubau
Akademie™

96/84 pt

Neubau
Akademie™

96/84 pt

Neubau
Akademie™

SP
C
E   I
ME
N

E   I
ME
N

SP
C

L L B B R/MM
SS BB EE BB
MM MM MM
MM MM MM MM

42/42 pt

B   D   L   L   I

M   R   S   S   E

B   M   S   E   M

B   B   E   M   B

Language Support

8/9   16/17   24/25   32/33
10/11   18/19   26/27   34/35
4/5   12/13   20/21   28/29   56/57
6/7   14/15   22/23   30/31

TYPEFACE	:	AKTIV GROTESK
DESIGNER	:	DALTON MAAG
LOCATION	:	LONDON, UK

	PUBLISHED BY	:	DALTON MAAG
	CHRONOLOGY	:	2010 - 2023
	RELEASED IN	:	2010 - 2023

LINK	:	HTTPS://WWW.DALTONMAAG.COM/PORTFOLIO/FONT-LIBRARY/
		AKTIV-GROTESK.HTML
STYLES	:	MULTI-AXIS VARIABLE FONTS + STATIC FONTS IN WEIGHTS &
		STYLES RANGING FROM CONDENSED HAIRLINE TO EXTENDED BLACK

AKTIV GROTESK WAS DESIGNED WITH A SINGLE GOAL IN MIND: TO CREATE A NEUTRAL BUT AUTHORITATIVE GROTESQUE TYPEFACE WELL-SUITED FOR THE 21ST CENTURY. WITHOUT THE TECHNICAL LIMITATIONS OF METAL TYPE AND BY AVOIDING THE APOLOGETIC APPROACH OF CLASSIC GROTESQUES FROM THE 1950'S, IT RESONATES AS CONTEMPORARY, FUNCTIONAL, AND APPROACHABLE. AKTIV GROTESK SUPPORTS OVER 220 LANGUAGES ACROSS 9 WRITING SYSTEMS, EACH WITH APPROPRIATE VARIABLE FONT AXIS SUPPORT. IT ALSO INCLUDES AN EXTENDED SET OF OVER 1,900 ICONS, MATHS SYMBOLS, TYPOGRAPHIC SYMBOLS, AND DINGBATS.

CAP HEIGHT   REGULAR — 290PT

X-HEIGHT

Aa

BASELINE

Aktiv Grotesk

THE QUICK BROWN
IT WOULD BE THE C
IT'S A LOVELY DAY II
AND THE PUNGENT
PROMISE OF A SUM
THINKING ABOUT TI

The quick brown fox jumps over a lazy dog. He didn't have to, but he thought it would be the cheeky thing to do. After all, he had a reputation to maintain. It's a lovely day in the neighbourhood, with the sun shining, the birds chirping, and the pungent aroma of fresh rubbish bins wafting through the air - the promise of a sumptuous meal. The sprightly fox rubs his paws together in glee, thinking about the delicious treasures he's about to dig into. Still in her spot, the lazy dog remains unperturbed. With her long snout, droopy jowls, and long black fur fluttering in the breeze, she is in a dreamland far away - where the mountains are made of beefy treats, the valleys are filled with tennis balls, and the puddles are just the right temperature. Why be in the rat race? It's a dog's life, after all.

The quick brown fox jumps over a lazy dog. He didn't have to, but he thought it would be the cheeky thing to do. After all, he had a reputation to maintain. It's a lovely day in the neighbourhood, with the sun shining, the birds chirping, and the pungent aroma of fresh rubbish bins wafting through the air - the promise of a sumptuous meal. The sprightly fox rubs his paws together in glee, thinking about the delicious treasures he's about to dig into. Still in her spot, the lazy dog remains unperturbed. With her long snout, droopy jowls, and long black fur fluttering in the breeze, she is in a dreamland far away - where the mountains are made of beefy treats, the valleys are filled with tennis balls, and the puddles are just the right temperature. Why be in the rat race? It's a dog's life, after all.

SHARPER

The Stardust Symphony

New Echoes of Euphoria

Sapphire Skyline **Moonlight** Vibe Vanguard

Radiant Rhapsody Midnight Mirage **Flow Frontiers**

Golden Groove **WILT** **Currents** *Velvet Vortex* **Prism Pulse** *Dreamer*

Eyes *Lost Lullabies* **Sapphire Skyline** Kid Khaos **Saliva** Infinite Inflections

Lil' Phoenix Golden Groove **Gritty G** DJ Dynamo *Siren Sizzle* Lullaby Luminescence

MC Matrix **Crystalizers** **Moonlit** Dreamscape **Horizon** Prince Prisma **Daddie** Bubblegum Ballads

Headcases **Toxic** Siren **Horizon** *Souls* **Queen Vibe** Prince Prisma **Grit & Gold** Neon Nocturnes **Daybreak Divas**

Electric Energy **Pop Prism** **Celestial Symphony** **Sugar Rush** Pop Paradise **Flashy Fever** Glitter Globe **Sonic Sultans** Beat Blitz **Mic Masters**

Aa *Aa* Aa *Aa* Aa *Aa*

Aa *Aa* Aa *Aa* Aa *Aa*

Aa *Aa* Aa *Aa* Aa *Aa*

Aa *Aa* Aa *Aa* Aa *Aa*

Aa *Aa* Aa *Aa* Aa *Aa*

Aa *Aa* Aa *Aa* Aa *Aa*

Aa *Aa* Aa *Aa* Aa *Aa*

Aa *Aa* Aa *Aa* Aa *Aa*

9 →
writing
systems

Arabic	عقل والوجدان وعليهم أن يعاملوا بعضهم بعضاً بروح الإخاء.
Armenian	Նկատի առնելով, որ մարդկային ընտանիքի բոլոր ս
Cyrillic	Все люди рождаются свободными и равными в св
Devanagari	चूंकि मानव परिवार के सभी सदस्यों के जन्मजात गौरव और समान त
Georgian	ყოველი ადამიანი იბადება თავისუფალი და ს
Greek	'Ολοι οι άνθρωποι γεννιούνται ελεύθεροι και ίσοι σ
Hebrew	ובמצפון, לפיכך חובה עליהם לנהוג איש ברעהו ברוח של אחוה.
Latin	All human beings are born free and equal in dignity a
Thai	มนุษย์ทั้งหลายเกิดมามีอิสระและเสมอภาคกันในเกียรติศักด

A ⟪ B ⟪ C ⟪ D
⇒ Dy − 1 + 4 = 0
A ⊐ B ⊐ C = ∅
a ✳ b ✳ c ✳ d
3x ≥ 0; x ∈ (∞)

JFK ✈ LAX
Ctrl + ⌥ + ⌫
⯒ captures ♛
✂ Cut Here ✂
☞ **Free trial** ⇒

TYPEFACE	:	ALDGATE SANS
DESIGNER	:	DALTON MAAG
LOCATION	:	LONDON, UK

PUBLISHED BY	:	DALTON MAAG
CHRONOLOGY	:	2023
RELEASED IN	:	2023

LINK	:	HTTPS://WWW.DALTONMAAG.COM/PORTFOLIO/FONT-LIBRARY/ ALDGATE-SANS.HTML
STYLES	:	MULTI-AXIS VARIABLE FONTS + STATIC FONTS IN WEIGHTS & STYLES RANGING FROM XCONDENSED HAIR TO XEXTENDED BLACK

ALDGATE SANS IS A MODERN HUMANIST SANS TYPEFACE INSPIRED BY THE DISTINCTLY BRITISH DESIGNS OF THE EARLY 1900'S. ITS GENEROUS PROPORTIONS ENSURE LEGIBILITY WITH AN APPROACHABLE TONE, WHILE ITS VARIABLE FONT OFFERS EXTENSIVE WEIGHT, WIDTH, AND ITALIC AXES FOR EXCEPTIONAL VERSATILITY.

CAP HEIGHT

REGULAR — 290PT

X-HEIGHT

Aa

BASELINE

Aldgate Sans

THE QUICK BROWN
IT WOULD BE THE
IT'S A LOVELY DAY
AND THE PUNGEN
PROMISE OF A SUN
THINKING ABOUT
THE LAZY DOG RE
LONG BLACK FUR
THE MOUNTAINS A

The quick brown fox jumps over a lazy dog. He didn't have to, but he thought it would be the cheeky thing to do. After all, he had a reputation to maintain. It's a lovely day in the neighbourhood, with the sun shining, the birds chirping, and the pungent aroma of fresh rubbish bins wafting through the air - the promise of a sumptuous meal. The sprightly fox rubs his paws together in glee, thinking about the delicious treasures he's about to dig into. Still in her spot, the lazy dog remains unperturbed. With her long snout, droopy jowls, and long black fur fluttering in the breeze, she is in a dreamland far away - where the mountains are made of beefy treats, the valleys are filled with tennis balls, and the puddles are just the right temperature. Why be in the rat race? It's a dog's life, after all.

Uprights

angle

angle

True italics

x19238

x19638

Tower Hamlets

Leadenhall Street

Æst Geat

The Minories Eagle

Handgloves

Handgloves

Handgloves

Handgloves

Handglov

Handglo

Handglo

Handgl

Hairline — Gateway

Thin — Lantern

Light — Archives

Regular — Taverns

Medium — Butcher

SemiBold — History

Bold — **Aldgate**

XBold — **Streets**

Black — **Culture**

G A T E

A

E

TYPEFACE	:	ALTFORM
DESIGNER	:	COTYPE FOUNDRY
LOCATION	:	LONDON, UK

		PUBLISHED BY	:	COTYPE FOUNDRY
		CHRONOLOGY	:	7TH TYPEFACE RELEASE
		RELEASED IN	:	2021

| LINK | : | HTTPS://COTYPEFOUNDRY.COM/OUR-FONTS/ALTFORM/ |
| STYLES | : | 14 STYLES, 7 WEIGHTS: THIN, EXTRALIGHT, LIGHT, REGULAR, SEMIBOLD, BOLD, BLACK + ITALICS + A VARIABLE FONT |

ALTFORM IS A SOLID AND DECEPTIVELY SIMPLE SANS SERIF FAMILY WITH AN ALTER-EGO. THE MARRIAGE BETWEEN A GEOMETRIC SANS AND A GROTESQUE, THIS TYPEFACE HAS A UNIVERSALLY NEUTRAL APPEAL. UPON CLOSER INSPECTION, THE READER WILL NOTICE TINY EXQUISITE CURVES IN SOME CHARACTERS WHICH GIVE ALTFORM A SUBTLE SOPHISTICATION AND RECOGNISABLE CHARACTER THAT REVEALS AN ALTERNATE SIDE THROUGH ITS OPENTYPE FEATURES. PERHAPS THE MOST INTERESTING SET OF STYLISTIC ALTERNATES ARE THE "WIND-BLOWN" "D", "I", "J", "L", "U", AND "Y", WHICH FEATURE A SLIGHT CURVATURE IN THE STEMS AND INFUSE THE TYPEFACE WITH A DYNAMIC QUALITY.

CAP HEIGHT

REGULAR — 290PT

X-HEIGHT

Aa

BASELINE

Altform

THE QUICK BROWN FOX J

IT WOULD BE THE CHEEKY

IT'S A LOVELY DAY IN THE

AND THE PUNGENT AROM

PROMISE OF A SUMPTUOU

THINKING ABOUT THE DEI

THE LAZY DOG REMAINS

LONG BLACK FUR FLUTTE

THE MOUNTAINS ARE MAD

AND THE PUDDLES ARE J

IT'S A DOG'S LIFE, AFTER A

The quick brown fox jumps over a lazy dog. He didn't have to, but he thought it would be the cheeky thing to do. After all, he had a reputation to maintain. It's a lovely day in the neighbourhood, with the sun shining, the birds chirping, and the pungent aroma of fresh rubbish bins wafting through the air - the promise of a sumptuous meal. The sprightly fox rubs his paws together in glee, thinking about the delicious treasures he's about to dig into. Still in her spot, the lazy dog remains unperturbed. With her long snout, droopy jowls, and long black fur fluttering in the breeze, she is in a dreamland far away - where the mountains are made of beefy treats, the valleys are filled with tennis balls, and the puddles are just the right temperature. Why be in the rat race? It's a dog's life, after all.

```
TYPEFACE     :     AMBIT
DESIGNER     :     COTYPE FOUNDRY
LOCATION     :     LONDON,  UK

                   PUBLISHED BY       :    COTYPE FOUNDRY
                   CHRONOLOGY         :    3RD TYPEFACE RELEASE
                   RELEASED IN        :    2019

LINK         :     HTTPS://COTYPEFOUNDRY.COM/OUR-FONTS/AMBIT/
                   CARDINAL_COLLECTION
STYLES       :     14 STYLES, 7 WEIGHTS: THIN, EXTRALIGHT, LIGHT,
                   REGULAR, SEMIBOLD, BOLD, BLACK + ITALICS
                   + A VARIABLE FONT
```

AMBIT IS AN ECCENTRIC AND UNIQUE SANS SERIF FONT INSPIRED BY EARLY GROTESQUES, BUT ADAPTED FOR THE 21ST CENTURY. ITS MOST STRIKING DETAILS ARE THE CURLY "F" AND "R" (THERE ARE ALSO SIMPLE ALTERNATE VERSIONS AVAILABLE VIA STYLISTIC SET 02). SHAPES LIKE "C/C" AND "S/S" SEEM TO CURL IN ONTO THEMSELVES, GIVING THIS TYPE FAMILY A VERY DISTINCTIVE LOOK. AMBIT FEATURES SEVEN WEIGHTS, EACH WITH OBLIQUE ITALICS. FEATURING A LATIN EXTENDED CHARACTER SET, IT COVERS MOST LANGUAGES WRITTEN WITH THE LATIN SCRIPT AND IS PERFECT FOR BRANDING, PACKAGING, AND EDITORIAL PROJECTS, BOTH PRINTED AND ONLINE.

CAP HEIGHT

REGULAR – 290PT

X-HEIGHT

BASELINE

Ambit

THE QUICK BROWN
IT WOULD BE THE C
IT'S A LOVELY DAY I
AND THE PUNGENT
PROMISE OF A SUM
THINKING ABOUT T
THE LAZY DOG REN

The quick brown fox jumps over a lazy dog. He didn't have to, it would be the cheeky thing to do. After all, he had a reputati It's a lovely day in the neighbourhood, with the sun shining, th and the pungent aroma of fresh rubbish bins wafting through promise of a sumptuous meal. The sprightly fox rubs his paws thinking about the delicious treasures he's about to dig into. S the lazy dog remains unperturbed. With her long snout, droo long black fur fluttering in the breeze, she is in a dreamland fa the mountains are made of beefy treats, the valleys are filled and the puddles are just the right temperature. Why be in the It's a dog's life, after all.

Apollo 11

July
20th
—
July
24th

1969

Apollo 11

The primary objective of Apollo 11 was to complete a national goal set by President John F. Kennedy on May 25, 1961: perform a crewed lunar landing and return to Earth.

Crew

Neil Armstrong
Commander

Edwin E. Aldrin Jr.
Lunar Module Pilot

Michael Collins
Command Module Pilot

Backup Crew

James A. Lovell
Commander

Fred W. Haise Jr.
Lunar Module Pilot

William A. Anders
Command Module Pilot

Payload

Columbia (CSM-107)
Eagle (LM-5)

Prelaunch Milestones

11/21/68
LM-5 Integrated
systems test

12/06/68
CSM-107 integrated
systems test

12/13/68
LM-5 acceptance test

01/08/69
LM-5 ascent stage
delivered to Kennedy

01/12/69
LM-5 descent stage
delivered to Kennedy

01/18/69
S-IVB ondock at Kennedy

01/23/69
CSM ondock at Kennedy

01/29/69
Command and service
module mated

02/06/69
S-II Ondock at Kennedy

02/20/69
S-IC Ondock at Kennedy

02/17/69
Combined CSM-107
systems tests

02/27/69
S-IU Ondock at Kennedy

03/24/69
CSM-107 Altitude testing

04/14/69
Rollover of CSM from the
operations and checkout
building to the vehicle
assembly building

04/22/69
Integrated systems test

05/05/69
CSM electrical mate to
Saturn V

05/20/69
Rollout to Launch Pad 39A

06/01/69
Flight readiness test

06/26/69
Countdown
Demonstration Test

Launch

July 16, 1969;
9:32 a.m. EDT

Launch Pad 39A

Saturn-V AS-506

High Bay 1

Mobile Launcher
Platform-1
Firing Room 1

Orbit

Altitude:
118.65 miles

Inclination

32.521 degrees

Orbits

30 revolutions

Duration

Eight days,
Three hours,
18 minutes,
35 seconds

Distance

953,054 miles

Lunar Location

Sea of Tranquility

Lunar Coordinates

.71 degrees North,
23.63 degrees East

Landing

July 24, 1969;
12:50 p.m. EDT
Pacific Ocean

Recovery Ship

USS Hornet

```
TYPEFACE     :    ANALOG
DESIGNER     :    TRAVIS KOCHEL
LOCATION     :    PORTLAND, US

                  PUBLISHED BY      :    VECTRO
                  CHRONOLOGY        :    2011 - 2013
                  RELEASED IN       :    2013

LINK         :    HTTPS://VECTROTYPE.COM
STYLES       :    THIN, THIN OBLIQUE, LIGHT, LIGHT OBLIQUE, REGULAR,
                  REGULAR OBLIQUE, MEDIUM, MEDIUM OBLIQUE, BOLD, BOLD OBLIQUE
```

ANALOG IS A NEW TAKE ON INDUSTRIAL SANS SERIFS THAT EMBODIES THE SPIRIT OF THE SOLID STATE ELECTRONICS REVOLUTION. ITS ENERGETIC, GENEROUSLY WIDE PROPORTIONS ARE BALANCED BY CONFIDENT, EFFICIENT STROKES WITH MINIMAL CONTRAST. IT EXPLORES THE USE OF PROPORTIONS AND OTHER SUBTLE FEATURES TO BRING PERSONALITY INTO ITS DESIGN TO MAKE IT LARGER THAN THE SUM OF ITS PARTS.

CAP HEIGHT   REGULAR - 290PT

X-HEIGHT

Aa

BASELINE

Analog

THE QUICK BROW

IT WOULD BE THE

ITS A LOVELY DAY

AND THE PUNGEN

PROMISE OF A SU

THINKING ABOUT

THE LAZY DOG RE

LONG BLACK FUR

THE MOUNTAINS A

AND THE PUDDLE

The quick brown fox jumps over a lazy dog. He didnt have to, but he thought it would be the cheeky thing to do. After all, he had a reputation to maintain. Its a lovely day in the neighbourhood, with the sun shining, the birds chirping, and the pungent aroma of fresh rubbish bins wafting through the air - the promise of a sumptuous meal. The sprightly fox rubs his paws together in glee, thinking about the delicious treasures hes about to dig into. Still in her spot, the lazy dog remains unperturbed. With her long snout, droopy jowls, and long black fur fluttering in the breeze, she is in a dreamland far away - where the mountains are made of beefy treats, the valleys are filled with tennis balls, and the puddles are just the right temperature. Why be in the rat race? Its a dogs life, after all.

A7 9 1
: . . .
? !
@
$ &
~

{[o%o#ffΩBex

TYPEFACE	:	ANTARCTICA		
DESIGNER	:	IAN PARTY		
LOCATION	:	LAUSANNE, SWITZERLAND		
		PUBLISHED BY	:	NEWGLYPH
		CHRONOLOGY	:	N/A
		RELEASED IN	:	2020
LINK	:	HTTPS://NEWGLYPH.COM/CLASSIC-COLLECTION/#FONT-ANTARCTICA		
STYLES	:	264 STYLES + A VARIABLE FONT		
CREDITS	:	IGINO MARINI (KERNING)		

THE ANTARCTICA TYPEFACE DERIVES ITS NAME AND INSPIRATION FROM EARTH'S SOUTHERNMOST CONTINENT. ECHOING THE ARCTIC'S ELEGANCE, THIS SANS SERIF FONT EXUDES SIMPLICITY, MINIMALISM, AND PURITY. ITS NEO-GROTESQUE STYLE TRANSCENDS TIME, AKIN TO THE ENDURING ANTARCTIC LANDSCAPE.

CAP HEIGHT

REGULAR — 290PT

X-HEIGHT

Aa

BASELINE

Antarctica

THE QUICK BROW

IT WOULD BE THE

IT'S A LOVELY DAY

AND THE PUNGEN

PROMISE OF A SUI

THINKING ABOUT

THE LAZY DOG RE

LONG BLACK FUR

THE MOUNTAINS A

AND THE PUDDLES

IT'S A DOG'S LIFE,

Antarctica
Antarctica
Antarctica
Antarctica
Antarctica
Antarctica

əuəu

əuəu

neue

əuəu

neue

əuəu

neue

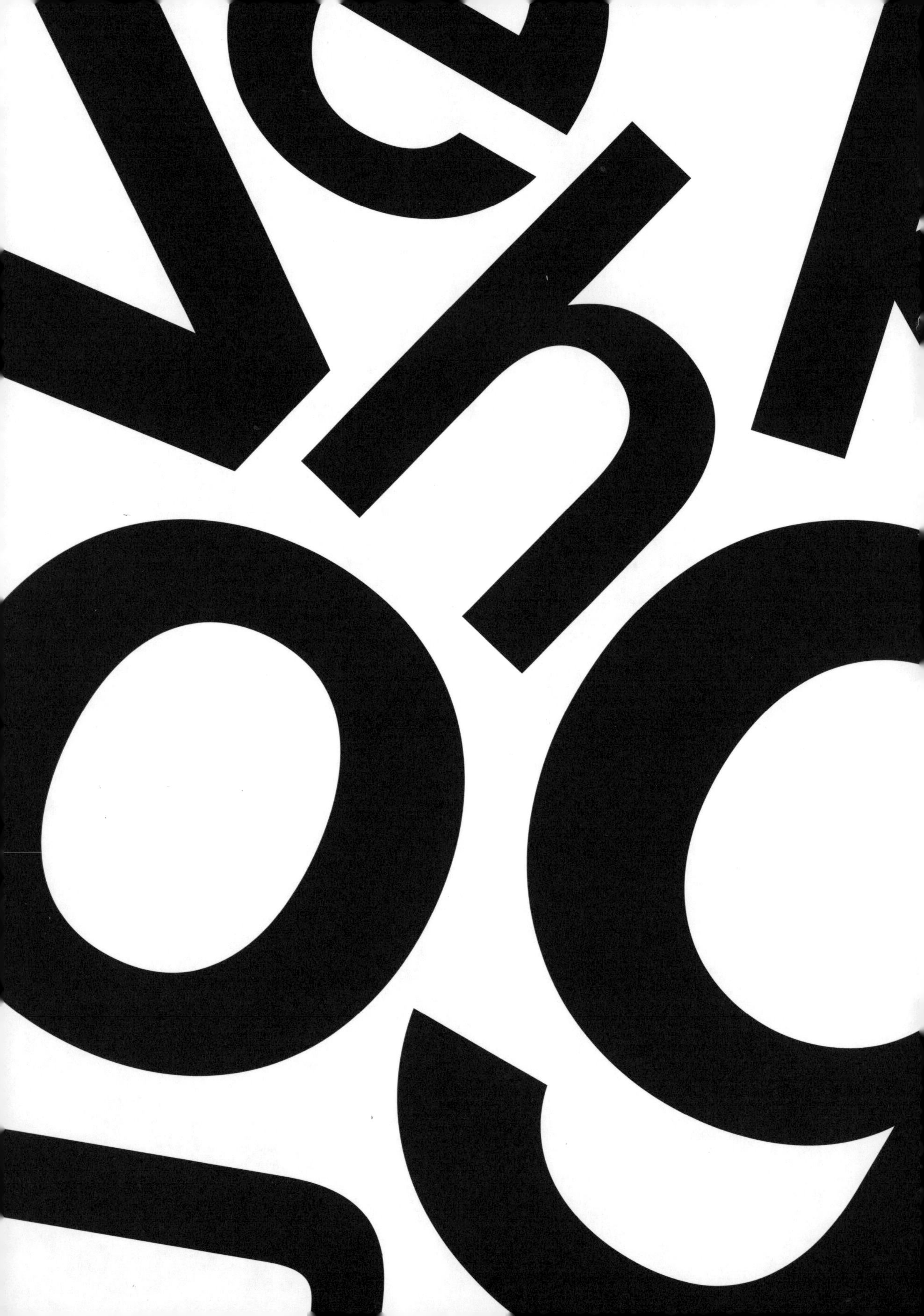

TYPEFACE   :   AQUAWAX FX
DESIGNER   :   FRANCESCO CANOVARO
LOCATION   :   FLORENCE, ITALY

               PUBLISHED BY   :   ZETAFONTS TYPE FOUNDRY
               CHRONOLOGY   :   2023
               RELEASED IN   :   2023

LINK   :   HTTPS://ZETAFONTS.COM/AQUAWAX-FX
STYLES   :   36 STYLES + 2 VARIABLE FONTS INCLUDING 9 WEIGHTS +
               ITALICS X 2 STYLES

AQUAWAX FX WAS DEVELOPED AS A VARIANT OF THE AQUAWAX TYPE FAMILY, ONE OF THE MOST BELOVED ZETAFONTS CLASSICS. THIS FONT FAMILY INCLUDES TWO VERSIONS (ROMAN AND SPACE), EACH WITH 9 WEIGHTS, RANGING FROM THIN TO HEAVY, AS WELL AS MATCHING ITALICS. WITH A TOTAL OF 36 VARIANTS PLUS ONE VARIABLE VERSION, AQUAWAX FX IS A VERSATILE TYPE FAMILY SUITABLE FOR A VARIETY OF DESIGN PROJECTS, FROM BRANDING AND PACKAGING TO EDITORIAL DESIGN AND ADVERTISING. IT OFFERS A FRESH RE-INTERPRETATION OF THE ORIGINAL AQUAWAX LETTERFORMS AND PROPORTIONS, WITH A DYNAMIC AND FLOWING LOOK THAT IS SURE TO MAKE ANY PROJECT STAND OUT.

CAP HEIGHT   REGULAR — 290PT

X-HEIGHT

Aa

BASELINE

Aquawax fx

THE QUICK BRO

IT WOULD BE T

IT'S A LOVELY D

AND THE PUNC

PROMISE OF A

THINKING ABO

THE LAZY DOG

LONG BLACK FI

THE MOUNTAIN

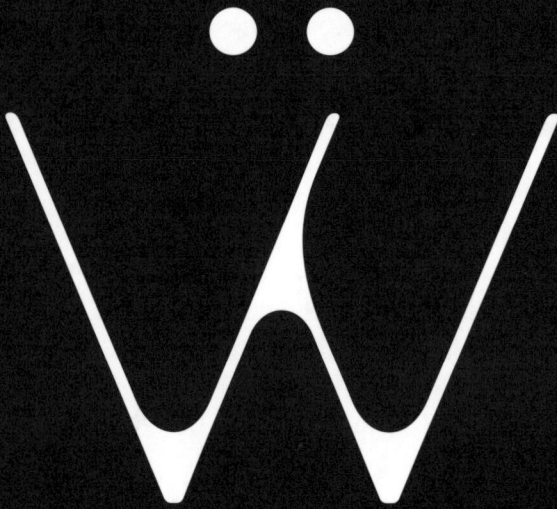
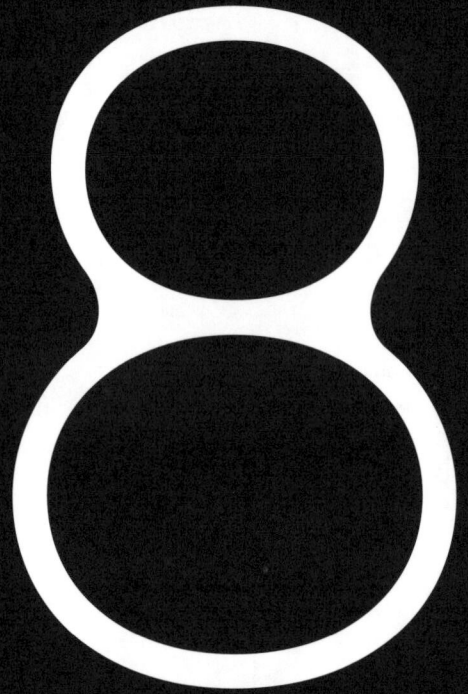

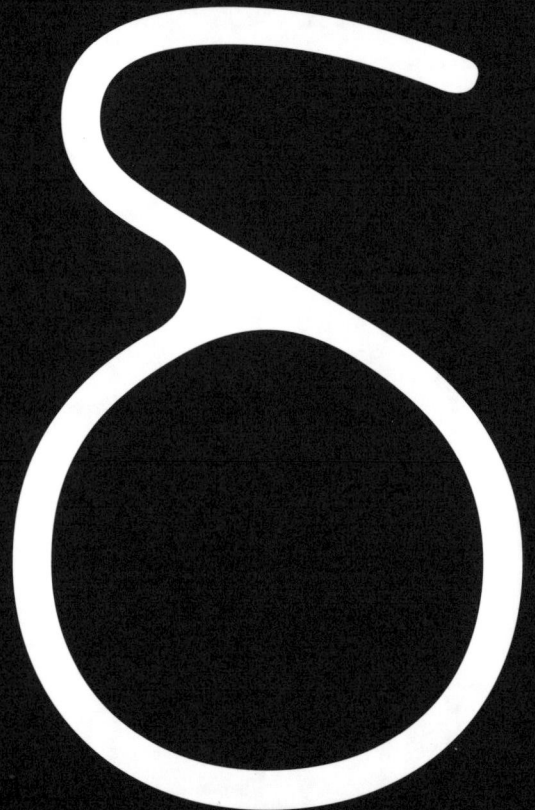
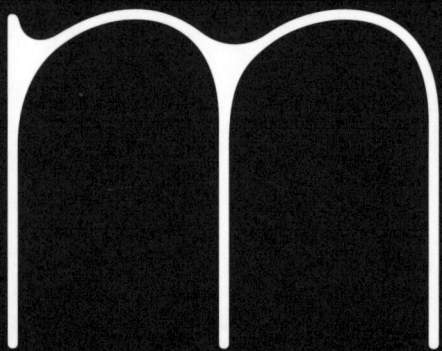

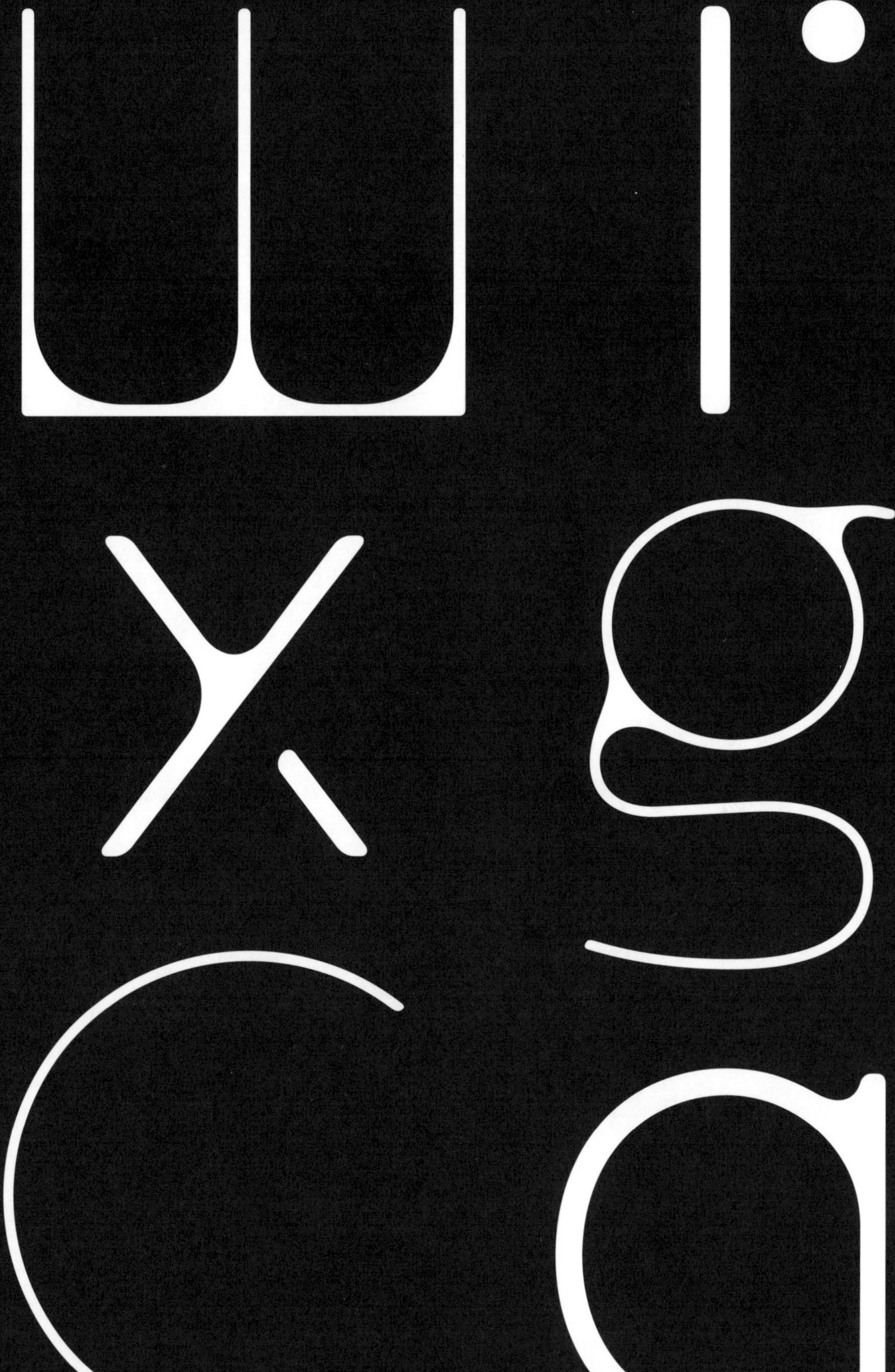
w i
x g
c a

TYPEFACE	:	FOUNDRY ARKIAS
DESIGNER	:	THE FOUNDRY TYPES
LOCATION	:	UK

PUBLISHED BY	:	THE FOUNDRY TYPES
CHRONOLOGY	:	2023
RELEASED IN	:	2023

LINK	:	HTTPS://WWW.THEFOUNDRYTYPES.COM
STYLES	:	39

INSPIRED BY THE CHARLES AND RAY EAMES LOUNGE CHAIR, THE CURVED LETTERFORMS AND TAPERING JUNCTIONS OF FOUNDRY ARKIAS PAY HOMAGE TO THOSE SOFT SHAPES. DISTINCTIVE, MODULAR, ROBUST, VIBRANT, CULTURED, AND CONTEMPORARY, IT IS A REFLECTION OF THE MODERNIST ARCHITECTURE AND GRAPHIC LANGUAGE OF THE 50-60'S. DESIGNED TO MAKE A POWERFUL STATEMENT, THE LIGHTER WEIGHTS MAKE A MORE SUBTLE APPEARANCE, WHILE THE VERTICAL AXIS, MODULAR FORMS, ALONG WITH THE NARROW PROPORTIONS BRING A ROBUST TONE OF VOICE. ITS STROKE WEIGHT CONTRAST IS EMPHASISED IN THE HEAVIER STYLES. THE MOST DISTINGUISHABLE FEATURE OF FOUNDRY ARKIAS IS ITS ARCHED FORMS, COINCIDING WITH THE PINCHED CONNECTING STROKES TO ERADICATE DARK SPOTS AT JUNCTIONS.

CAP HEIGHT

REGULAR — 290PT

X-HEIGHT

Aa

BASELINE

FOUNDRY Arkias

THE QUICK BROWN FOX JUMP

IT WOULD BE THE CHEEKY THIN

IT'S A LOVELY DAY IN THE NEIG

AND THE PUNGENT AROMA OF

PROMISE OF A SUMPTUOUS M

THINKING ABOUT THE DELICIOU

THE LAZY DOG REMAINS UNPE

LONG BLACK FUR FLUTTERING

The quick brown fox jumps over a lazy dog. He didn't have to, but he thought it would be the cheeky thing to do. After all, he had a reputation to maintain. It's a lovely day in the neighbourhood, with the sun shining, the birds chirping, and the pungent aroma of fresh rubbish bins wafting through the air - the promise of a sumptuous meal. The sprightly fox rubs his paws together in glee, thinking about the delicious treasures he's about to dig into. Still in her spot, the lazy dog remains unperturbed. With her long snout, droopy jowls, and long black fur fluttering in the breeze, she is in a dreamland far away - where the mountains are made of beefy treats, the valleys are filled with tennis balls, and the puddles are just the right temperature. Why be in the rat race? It's a dog's life, after all.

13

13 weights

39 styles

28,860 cultured glyphs

↕

Arki

Fou

39

ndry

as

pronounced aa-kee-uhs

DemiBold *Italic* Recline SemiBold *Italic* Recline Bold *Italic* Recline ExtraBold *Italic* Recline Bla

TYPEFACE	:	ATLANTIC
DESIGNER	:	HEAVYWEIGHT DIGITAL TYPE FOUNDRY
LOCATION	:	PRAGUE, CZECH REPUBLIC

		PUBLISHED BY	: HEAVYWEIGHT DIGITAL TYPE FOUNDRY
		CHRONOLOGY	: N/A
		RELEASED IN	: 2021

LINK	:	HTTPS://HEAVYWEIGHT-TYPE.COM/FONTS/ATLANTIC/DETAIL
STYLES	:	THIN, ULTRALIGHT, LIGHT, REGULAR, MEDIUM, SEMIBOLD, BOLD

ATLANTIC IS A DISPLAY TYPE WITH DISTINCTIVE FEATURES, DEVIATING FROM THE VERSATILE UNIVERSAL USE OF OTHER HEAVYWEIGHT ALPHABETS. DESPITE LACKING A CLEAR MODEL, IT COMBINES CALLIGRAPHIC ELEMENTS WITH GEOMETRIC INFLUENCES, REMINISCENT OF HERMANN ZAPF'S OPTIMA TYPE. THE FONT'S MOTIVATION EXTENDS BEYOND PORTFOLIO COMPLETION, EMPHASISING A UNIQUE STYLE AND A DESIRE TO ADVANCE CALLIGRAPHIC DRAWING.

CAP HEIGHT   REGULAR — 290PT

X-HEIGHT

BASELINE

Atlantic

THE QUICK BRO

IT WOULD BE TH

IT'S A LOVELY DA

AND THE PUNGE

PROMISE OF A S

THINKING ABOU

THE LAZY DOG

LONG BLACK FU

THE MOUNTAINS

m f e
a u t g e
l i d d , ,
K Z

TYPEFACE	:	AUGURE
DESIGNER	:	SIMON RENAUD
LOCATION	:	LYON, FRANCE

PUBLISHED BY	:	205TF
CHRONOLOGY	:	2023
RELEASED IN	:	2023

LINK : HTTPS://WWW.205.TF/AUGURE

STYLES : THIN, THIN SLANTED, EXTRALIGHT, EXTRALIGHT SLANTED, LIGHT, LIGHT SLANTED, REGULAR, SLANTED, MEDIUM, MEDIUM SLANTED, BOLD, BOLD SLANTED, BLACK, BLACK SLANTED

AUGURE IS BASED ON AN A PRIORI PARADOXICAL PRINCIPAL: HOW DO WE MOVE BEYOND TRADITIONAL LETTERFORMS WITHOUT UNDERMINING LEGIBILITY? TO THIS END, THIS TYPEFACE QUESTIONS THE CANONS INHERITED FROM ROMAN CAPITALS AND CAROLINGIAN MINUSCULES. AUGURE FREELY REFLECTS A RANGE OF DIVERSE INFLUENCES: SOMEWHERE BETWEEN THE HISTORICAL FORMS OF THE LATIN ALPHABET (INCLUDING UNCIALS), FORMS TAKEN FROM CRYPTOGRAPHY, AS WELL AS FORMS INSPIRED BY DIGITAL TECHNOLOGY AND ITS RATIONALITY. IT IS ALSO AVAILABLE IN A VARIABLE FONT FORMAT (WEIGHT AND SLANT), WHILE ALLOWING THE USER TO ACTIVATE ONE OF ITS THREE STYLISTIC SETS AVAILABLE — CLASSIC, ECLECTIC, OR CRYPTIC.

CAP HEIGHT

REGULAR — 290PT

X-HEIGHT

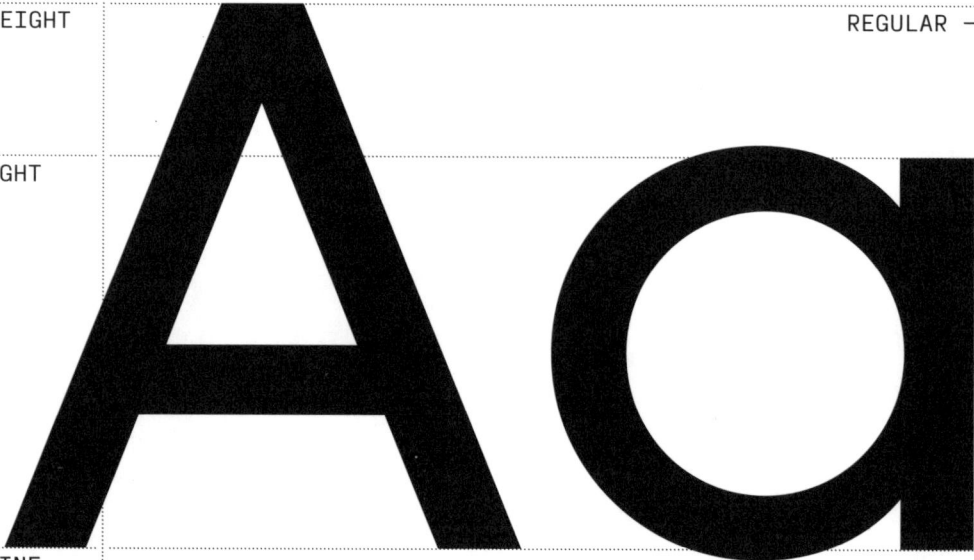

BASELINE

Augure

THE QUICK BROW
IT WOULD BE THE
IT'S A LOVELY DAY
AND THE PUNGEN
PROMISE OF A SU

The quick brown fox jumps over a lazy dog. He didn't have to, b
it would be the cheeky thing to do. After all, he had a reputation
It's a lovely day in the neighbourhood, with the sun shining, the
and the pungent aroma of fresh rubbish bins wafting through t
promise of a sumptuous meal. The sprightly fox rubs his paws to
thinking about the delicious treasures he's about to dig into. Stil
the lazy dog remains unperturbed. With her long snout, droopy
long black fur fluttering in the breeze, she is in a dreamland far
the mountains are made of beefy treats, the valleys are filled w
and the puddles are just the right temperature. Why be in the ra
It's a dog's life, after all.

The quick brown fox jumps over a lazy dog. He didn't have to, but he thought
it would be the cheeky thing to do. After all, he had a reputation to maintain.
It's a lovely day in the neighbourhood, with the sun shining, the birds chirping,
and the pungent aroma of fresh rubbish bins wafting through the air - the
promise of a sumptuous meal. The sprightly fox rubs his paws together in glee,
thinking about the delicious treasures he's about to dig into. Still in her spot,
the lazy dog remains unperturbed. With her long snout, droopy jowls, and
long black fur fluttering in the breeze, she is in a dreamland far away - where
the mountains are made of beefy treats, the valleys are filled with tennis balls,
and the puddles are just the right temperature. Why be in the rat race?
It's a dog's life, after all.

Standards

Control
Breakable
Memory
Safeguard
Network
Protection

Machines
Control
Protected
Backup
Decoding
Private
Variation

```
TYPEFACE    :    BAGOSS
DESIGNER    :    DISPLAAY TYPE FOUNDRY
LOCATION    :    PRAGUE, CZECH REPUBLIC

                 PUBLISHED BY       :    DISPLAAY TYPE FOUNDRY
                 CHRONOLOGY         :    2022 - 2023
                 RELEASED IN        :    2022

LINK        :    HTTPS://DISPLAAY.NET/TYPEFACE/BAGOSS-COLLECTION/
STYLES      :    THIN, LIGHT, REGULAR, MEDIUM, SEMIBOLD, BOLD, HEAVY
                 THIN ITALIC, LIGHT ITALIC, REGULAR ITALIC, MEDIUM ITALIC,
                 SEMIBOLD ITALIC, BOLD ITALIC, HEAVY ITALIC
```

THE ORIGINAL SKETCH OF THE BAGOSS TYPEFACE FEATURED A CRUDE CONDENSED SANS-SERIF CONSTRUCTION WITH A LARGE X-HEIGHT AND DIAGONAL TERMINALS. HOWEVER, AS THE TYPEFACE AGED, IT FOUND ITS DISTINCTIVENESS BY INCREASING THE CONTRAST OF THE STROKES AND DEVELOPING OTHER DETAILS SUCH AS A TINY SINGLE-EDGE SERIF. DURING THE MATURATION PHASE, THE FAMILY GREW INTO THREE SUB-FAMILIES, RANGING FROM CONDENSED TO EXPANDED WIDTHS. THE TYPEFACE REVEALS ITS CURSIVE FORMS WHEN ITS OPENTYPE FEATURES ARE TURNED ON, MAKING IT THE PERFECT TYPEFACE FOR ANY OCCASION WHERE A LITTLE CHARACTER IS NEEDED.

CAP HEIGHT   REGULAR — 290PT

X-HEIGHT

Bb

BASELINE

Bagoss

THE QUICK BROWN FOX JU

IT WOULD BE THE CHEEKY

IT'S A LOVELY DAY IN THE N

AND THE PUNGENT AROM

PROMISE OF A SUMPTUOU

THINKING ABOUT THE DEL

THE LAZY DOG REMAINS U

LONG BLACK FUR FLUTTEF

THE MOUNTAINS ARE MAD

AND THE PUDDLES ARE JU

IT'S A DOG'S LIFE, AFTER AL

The quick brown fox jumps over a lazy dog. He didn't have to, but he thought it would be the cheeky thing to do. After all, he had a reputation to maintain. It's a lovely day in the neighbourhood, with the sun shining, the birds chirping, and the pungent aroma of fresh rubbish bins wafting through the air - the promise of a sumptuous meal. The sprightly fox rubs his paws together in glee, thinking about the delicious treasures he's about to dig into. Still in her spot, the lazy dog remains unperturbed. With her long snout, droopy jowls, and long black fur fluttering in the breeze, she is in a dreamland far away - where the mountains are made of beefy treats, the valleys are filled with tennis balls, and the puddles are just the right temperature. Why be in the rat race? It's a dog's life, after all.

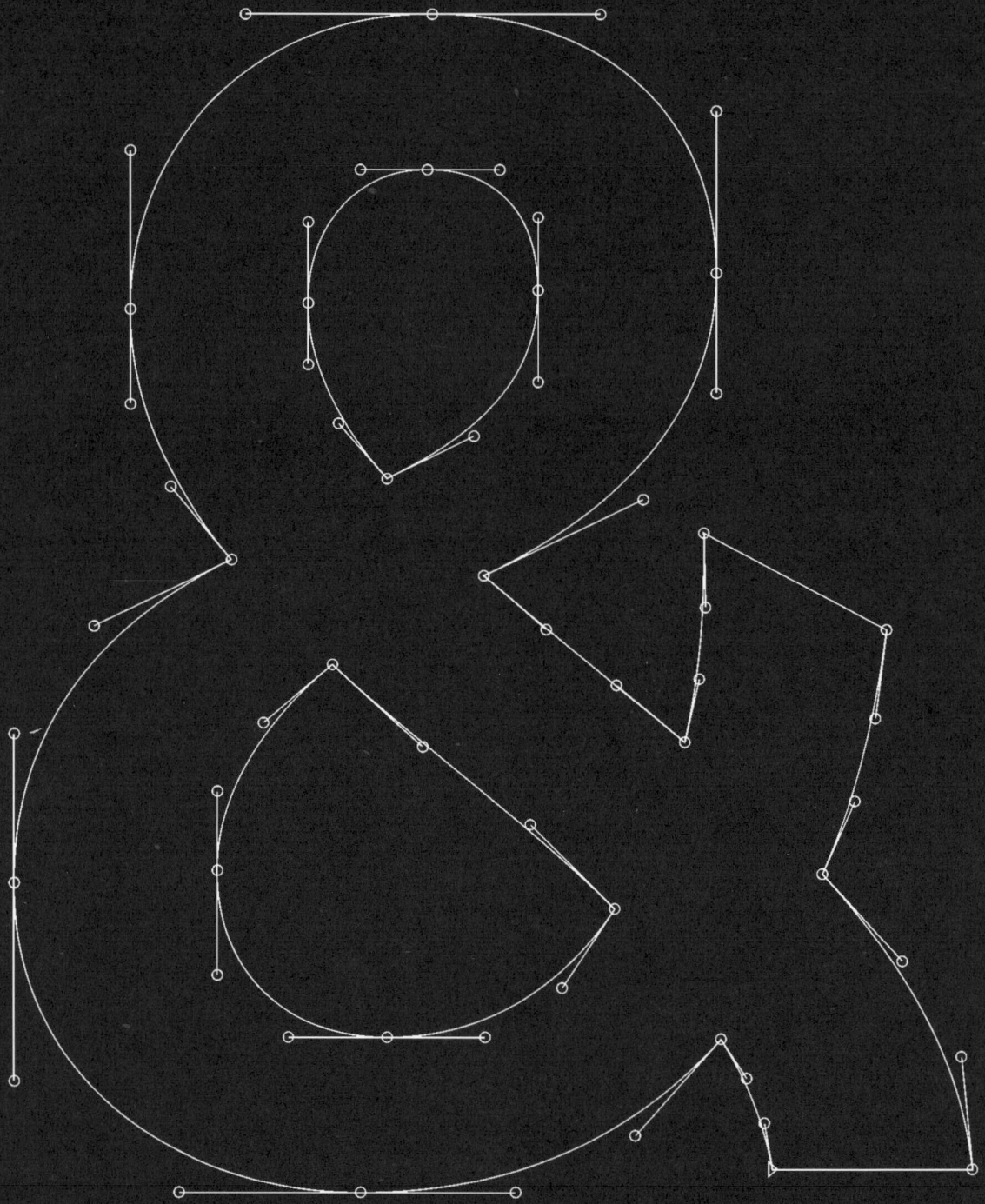

AäBbCcDdEeFfGgHh IiJjKk
RrŞsTtUuVvWwXxYyZz £123
<agf–a@, bgq? dpe G@&>

MmNnØoPpQq
4567890&@

Denominazi
di Origine Pr

Denominazi
di Origine Pr

Denominazi
di Origine Pr

one
otetta

one
otetta

one
otetta

```
TYPEFACE    :    BAIKAL
DESIGNER    :    IAN PARTY
LOCATION    :    LAUSANNE, SWITZERLAND

                 PUBLISHED BY      :    NEWGLYPH
                 CHRONOLOGY        :    2021
                 RELEASED IN       :    N/A

LINK        :    HTTPS://NEWGLYPH.COM/CLASSIC-COLLECTION/#FONT-BAIKAL
STYLES      :    132 STYLES + A VARIABLE FONT
CREDITS     :    IGINO MARINI (KERNING)
```

INSPIRED BY SWITZERLAND'S RICH TYPOGRAPHIC HISTORY AND TRADITION, BAIKAL IS A CONTEMPORARY SWISS VARIABLE FONT THAT SHOWCASES THE ESSENCE OF ITS HERITAGE.

CAP HEIGHT   REGULAR — 290PT

X-HEIGHT

Bb

BASELINE

Baikal

THE QUICK BROWN FOX J

IT WOULD BE THE CHEEKY

IT'S A LOVELY DAY IN THE

AND THE PUNGENT AROM

PROMISE OF A SUMPTUO

THINKING ABOUT THE DE

THE LAZY DOG REMAINS

LONG BLACK FUR FLUTTE

THE MOUNTAINS ARE MA

AND THE PUDDLES ARE J

IT'S A DOG'S LIFE, AFTER

The quick brown fox jumps over a lazy dog. He didn't have to, but he thought it would be the cheeky thing to do. After all, he had a reputation to maintain. It's a lovely day in the neighbourhood, with the sun shining, the birds chirping, and the pungent aroma of fresh rubbish bins wafting through the air - the promise of a sumptuous meal. The sprightly fox rubs his paws together in glee, thinking about the delicious treasures he's about to dig into. Still in her spot, the lazy dog remains unperturbed. With her long snout, droopy jowls, and long black fur fluttering in the breeze, she is in a dreamland far away - where the mountains are made of beefy treats, the valleys are filled with tennis balls, and the puddles are just the right temperature. Why be in the rat race? It's a dog's life, after all.

Bailey

kal
1e8

```
TYPEFACE     :    BASE NEUE
DESIGNER     :    POWER TYPE™ FOUNDRY
LOCATION     :    MAKASSAR, INDONESIA

                  PUBLISHED BY      :    POWER TYPE™ FOUNDRY
                  CHRONOLOGY        :    2023
                  RELEASED IN       :    2023

LINK         :    HTTPS://POWER-TYPE.COM/BASE-NEUE/
STYLES       :    THIN, EXTRA LIGHT, LIGHT, SUPER CONDENSED, MEDIUM,
                  SEMI BOLD, BOLD, EXTRA BOLD, BLACK
CREDITS      :    TEGUH ARIEF, AKOYA STUDIO
```

BASE NEUE IS THE REINCARNATION OF THE BASIC TYPOGRAPHY OF MODERN CIVILISATION. WITH INKTRAPS APPLIED, THIS TYPEFACE CAN BE USED FOR A RANGE OF APPLICATIONS, FROM VERY NARROW MEDIA TO EXTRA-LARGE PUBLICATIONS. ITS THIN TO BLACK WEIGHTS AND SUPER CONDENSED TO SUPER EXPANDED WIDTHS ALLOW IT TO BE USED IN ANYTHING FROM HEADINGS OR TITLES TO BODY TEXTS. BASE NEUE COMES IN A TOTAL OF 108 STYLES CONSISTING OF 782 GLYPHS PER STYLE. BESIDES SUPPORTING 95 DIFFERENT LANGUAGES, IT ALSO HAS ACCESS TO ALTERNATIVE LETTERS AND INTERESTING LIGATURES.

CAP HEIGHT

REGULAR — 290PT

X-HEIGHT

Bb

BASELINE

Base Neue

THE QUICK BROWN FOX JU

IT WOULD BE THE CHEEKY

IT'S A LOVELY DAY IN THE I

AND THE PUNGENT AROM

PROMISE OF A SUMPTUOL

THINKING ABOUT THE DEL

THE LAZY DOG REMAINS L

The quick brown fox jumps over a lazy dog. He didn't have to, but he thought it would be the cheeky thing to do. After all, he had a reputation to maintain. It's a lovely day in the neighbourhood, with the sun shining, the birds chirping, and the pungent aroma of fresh rubbish bins wafting through the air - the promise of a sumptuous meal. The sprightly fox rubs his paws together in glee, thinking about the delicious treasures he's about to dig into. Still in her spot, the lazy dog remains unperturbed. With her long snout, droopy jowls, and long black fur fluttering in the breeze, she is in a dreamland far away - where the mountains are made of beefy treats, the valleys are filled with tennis balls, and the puddles are just the right temperature. Why be in the rat race? It's a dog's life, after all.

The quick brown fox jumps over a lazy dog. He didn't have to, but he thought it would be the cheeky thing to do. After all, he had a reputation to maintain. It's a lovely day in the neighbourhood, with the sun shining, the birds chirping, and the pungent aroma of fresh rubbish bins wafting through the air - the promise of a sumptuous meal. The sprightly fox rubs his paws together in glee, thinking about the delicious treasures he's about to dig into. Still in her spot, the lazy dog remains unperturbed. With her long snout, droopy jowls, and long black fur fluttering in the breeze, she is in a dreamland far away - where the mountains are made of beefy treats, the valleys are filled with tennis balls, and the puddles are just the right temperature. Why be in the rat race? It's a dog's life, after all.

REMIX REMIX REMIX

WELL WELL WELL

BASE NEUE SUPER CONDENSED

BASE NEUE SUPER EXPANDED

Magenta magenta Magenta

Festival Festival Festival

today today today

(PT™F) (POWER TYPE) (BASE NEUE TYPEFACE)

14.50 PM

14.50 PM

14.50 PM

BASE NEUE
BASE NEUE

MR.BEATS FOLLOWING THE TONE WITH QUICK HEXAGONAL

MR.BEATS
FOLLOWING
THE TONE
WITH QUICK
HEXAGONAL

MR.BEATS
FOLLOWING
THE TONE
WITH QUICK
HEXAGONAL

INDEX INDEX

EDITORIAL
PREMIERE

Base Neue
Super Condensed
Black

Base Neue
Condensed
Semi Bold Oblique

Base Neue
Super Condensed
Extra Bold Oblique

Magenta

328pt

Vermilion

280pt

Scarlet

328pt

a (Alternate) .ss01

328pt

328pt

280pt

Base Neue
Super Condensed
Black

Base Neue
Super Condensed
Extra Bold Oblique

Base Neue
Condensed
Semi Bold Oblique

SUPREME

HYPER 🌐 📁

MEGAZONE

VOL.1 EDITION 1.00

EDITORIAL

GRAFIK + SIGN

PERFORMANCE

THE-BASIS©1996

SHOW TIME ROADMAP   CIRCA©1996

MILESTONE

TYPEFACE   :   BETATRON
DESIGNER   :   COTYPE FOUNDRY
LOCATION   :   LONDON, UK

             PUBLISHED BY   :   COTYPE FOUNDRY
             CHRONOLOGY   :   8TH TYPEFACE RELEASE
             RELEASED IN   :   2021

LINK   :   HTTPS://COTYPEFOUNDRY.COM/OUR-FONTS/BETATRON/
STYLES   :   1

INSPIRED BY SCI-FI MOVIES SET IN THE NOT TOO DISTANT FUTURE, BETATRON FEATURES SOLELY VERTICAL, HORIZONTAL, AND 45° DIAGONAL LINES AS IT TRIES TO CAPTURE EACH LETTERFORM IN AN ABSTRACT AND DYNAMIC WAY. ALTHOUGH IT IS A HAT TIP TO WIM CROUWEL'S PARAMETRIC NEW ALPHABET, BETATRON IS, HOWEVER, SHARPER AND MORE AUDACIOUS THAN COANDA, THE RETAIL TYPE FAMILY IT IS BASED ON.

CAP HEIGHT

REGULAR — 290PT

X-HEIGHT

BASELINE

Betatron

THE QUICK BROWN FOX

IT WOULD BE THE CHE

ITS A LOVELY DAY IN T

AND THE PUNGENT AR

PROMISE OF A SUMPT

THINKING ABOUT THE

THE LAZY DOG REMAIN

LONG BLACK FUR FLUT

THE MOUNTAINS ARE N

AND THE PUDDLES AR

The quick brown fox jumps over a lazy dog. He didnt have to, but he thought
it would be the cheeky thing to do. After all, he had a reputation to maintain.
Its a lovely day in the neighbourhood, with the sun shining, the birds chirping,
and the pungent aroma of fresh rubbish bins wafting through the air - the
promise of a sumptuous meal. The sprightly fox rubs his paws together in glee,
thinking about the delicious treasures hes about to dig into. Still in her spot,
the lazy dog remains unperturbed. With her long snout, droopy jowls, and
long black fur fluttering in the breeze, she is in a dreamland far away - where
the mountains are made of beefy treats, the valleys are filled with tennis balls,
and the puddles are just the right temperature. Why be in the rat race?
Its a dogs life, after all.

1082 — Blad
1085 — Back
1007 — The
1000 — The
2002 — Mino
2000 — Avat
2010 — Tron
2012 — Pron
2017 — Ghos

e Runner

to the Future

Fifth Element

Matrix

rity Report

ar

Legacy

netheus

t in the Shell

TYPEFACE   :   BRIK
DESIGNER   :   BURNTYPE
LOCATION   :   NEW ZEALAND

                 PUBLISHED BY   :   THE DESIGNERS FOUNDRY
                 CHRONOLOGY   :   N/A
                 RELEASED IN   :   2018

LINK   :   HTTPS://THEDESIGNERSFOUNDRY.COM/BRIK
STYLES   :   20

BRIK IS A BRUTALLY HONEST TYPE FAMILY AVAILABLE IN FIVE WEIGHTS ACROSS REGULAR, CONDENSED, AND OBLIQUE SUB-FAMILIES. ITS BLATANT BRICK-LIKE CONSTRUCTION IS HONEST, COARSE, AND UNAPOLOGETIC. THE FAMILY FEATURES CHARACTERISTIC HARD ANGLES, CHUNKY CORNERS, AND EXAGGERATED INKTRAPS THAT GIVE IT ITS DISTINCT EDGE. THESE HARDENED FEATURES ARE MET WITH SUBTLE CURVES AND STROKES THAT ADD CONTRAST AND FINESSE TO ITS PURPOSEFULLY RIGID FOUNDATION. REVISITED THROUGHOUT 2020, BRIK IS NOW WHIPPED INTO PRIME FIGHTING SHAPE, SPORTING EXPANDED GLYPH SUPPORT, COMPLETELY NEW KERNING, AND RECONSTRUCTED LETTERS. BRIK LOOKS GREAT WHEN DISPLAYED HUGE, BUT WORKS EVEN BETTER AT SCALE, ESPECIALLY WITH LARGER BODIES OF TEXT.

CAP HEIGHT   AR - 290PT

BASELINE

BRIK

THE QUICK BROWN FOX

IT WOULD BE THE CHEE

IT'S A LOVELY DAY IN T

AND THE PUNGENT AR

PROMISE OF A SUMPTU

THINKING ABOUT THE

THE LAZY DOG REMAIN

LONG BLACK FUR FLUT

THE MOUNTAINS ARE M

AND THE PUDDLES ARE

IT'S A DOG'S LIFE, AFT

EGO DEATH

LET'S GET OFF THIS WILD RIDE

GET DOWN MAKE LOVE!

TYPEFACE	:	CATEGORY
DESIGNER	:	VIOLAINE & JÉRÉMY
LOCATION	:	PARIS, FRANCE

PUBLISHED BY	:	VIOLAINE & JÉRÉMY
CHRONOLOGY	:	N/A
RELEASED IN	:	2023

| LINK | : | HTTPS://VJ-TYPE.COM/18-CATEGORY |
| STYLES | : | REGULAR, REGULAR ITALIC, MEDIUM, MEDIUM ITALIC, BOLD, BOLD ITALIC, BLACK, BLACK ITALIC |

CATEGORY IS A SANS SERIF FONT THAT BLENDS UTILITARIAN AND STYLISTIC FUNCTIONS. IT WAS DESIGNED TO ACHIEVE A SPECIFIC BALANCE SUITABLE FOR A VARIETY OF CONTENT, INCLUDING LONG TEXTS, BODY COPY, TITLES, AND LOGOTYPES. ORIGINATING FROM GEOMETRICAL SHAPES WITH LOW CONTRAST, ITS DESIGN INCORPORATES GRAPHIC SINGULARITIES, RENDERING IT BOTH PURE AND ELEGANT, WHILE MAINTAINING A REASONABLE CURVATURE AND A TOUCH OF HUMOUR. NOTABLY, THE LOWERCASE LETTERS "A", "G", "J", AND "Y" EXEMPLIFY THIS HARMONIOUS BALANCE. THE CBRP IMPARTS STYLE TO THE UPPERCASE SET WITH ITS ORIGINAL ANGLES, PROMPTING US TO ASSERT, PERHAPS AUDACIOUSLY, THAT CATEGORY EMBODIES A BLEND OF SQUARE YET ROUND CHARACTERISTICS.

CAP HEIGHT

REGULAR — 290PT

X-HEIGHT

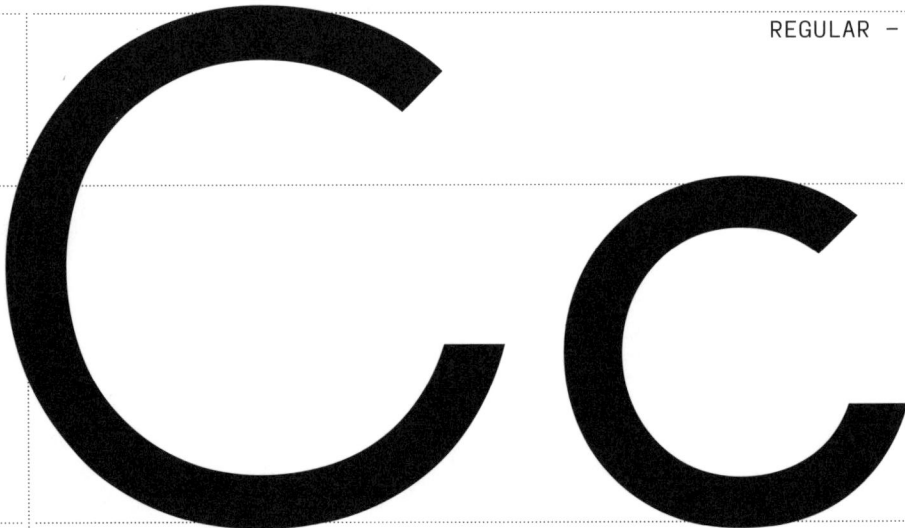

BASELINE

Category

THE QUICK BROWN

IT WOULD BE THE C

IT'S A LOVELY DAY

AND THE PUNGENT

PROMISE OF A SUM

THINKING ABOUT T

THE LAZY DOG REN

LONG BLACK FUR I

THE MOUNTAINS A

The quick brown fox jumps over a lazy dog. He didn't have to, but he thought it would be the cheeky thing to do. After all, he had a reputation to maintain. It's a lovely day in the neighbourhood, with the sun shining, the birds chirping, and the pungent aroma of fresh rubbish bins wafting through the air - the promise of a sumptuous meal. The sprightly fox rubs his paws together in glee, thinking about the delicious treasures he's about to dig into. Still in her spot, the lazy dog remains unperturbed. With her long snout, droopy jowls, and long black fur fluttering in the breeze, she is in a dreamland far away - where the mountains are made of beefy treats, the valleys are filled with tennis balls, and the puddles are just the right temperature. Why be in the rat race? It's a dog's life, after all.

OBJ

The
Cure

1979

N°08

ECT

Three
Imaginary
Boys

agenda

N°13

TYPEFACE	:	COANDA
DESIGNER	:	COTYPE FOUNDRY
LOCATION	:	LONDON, UK

		PUBLISHED BY	:	COTYPE FOUNDRY
		CHRONOLOGY	:	4TH TYPEFACE RELEASE
		RELEASED IN	:	2019

| LINK | : | HTTPS://COTYPEFOUNDRY.COM/OUR-FONTS/COANDA/ |
| STYLES | : | 1 |

COANDA IS AN IDEOLOGY OF THE FUTURE, CRAFTED FROM THE PAST. IT HONOURS THE AMBITIOUS OUTLOOK OF 20TH CENTURY DESIGNERS WIM CROUWEL AND MIMMO CASTELLANO, AND PAYS RESPECT TO THE METICULOUS DETAILS CRAFTED BY THE DESIGNERS REPUBLIC. ALTHOUGH MODULARITY AND STRICT MEASUREMENTS HAVE BEEN RETAINED THROUGHOUT LETTERFORMS AND CORNER COMPONENTS, COANDA OCCASIONALLY REPLACES STRICT RULES FOR LEGIBILITY AND OPTICAL ADJUSTMENTS — MAKING IT 95% TECHNOLOGICAL AND 5% HUMAN. COANDA CAN CREATE AN INCREDIBLY UNIQUE LOGOTYPE, BUT ALSO OFFERS FUNCTIONALITY WITHIN LARGER BODY COPY.

CAP HEIGHT

REGULAR — 290PT

X-HEIGHT

BASELINE

Coanda

THE QUICK

IT WOULD

IT'S A LOUS

AND THE P

PROMISE (

THINKING

THE LAZY

LONG BLAC

THE MOUN

MAX

VER

SILVERST

AREN

PRIX CIR

RACE LAP

Silverstone
Arena Grand Prix
Circuit (2020)

Race Lap Record
Max Verstappen
Red Bull, RB16, F1

Track Length:
5.901km / 3.667mi
Turns: 18

Coordinates:
52° 4'43" N 1° 1' 1"W
Time Zone: GMT

2020

STAPPEN

TONE

A GRAND

CUIT

RECORD

1:27.097

TYPEFACE	:	TT COMMONS™ PRO
DESIGNER	:	TYPETYPE.ORG
LOCATION	:	SAINT PETERSBURG, RUSSIA

	PUBLISHED BY	:	TYPETYPE.ORG
	CHRONOLOGY	:	2023
	RELEASED IN	:	2021

| LINK | : | HTTPS://TYPETYPE.ORG/FONTS/TT-COMMONS-PRO/ |
| STYLES | : | 102 STYLES + 2 VARIABLE FONTS |

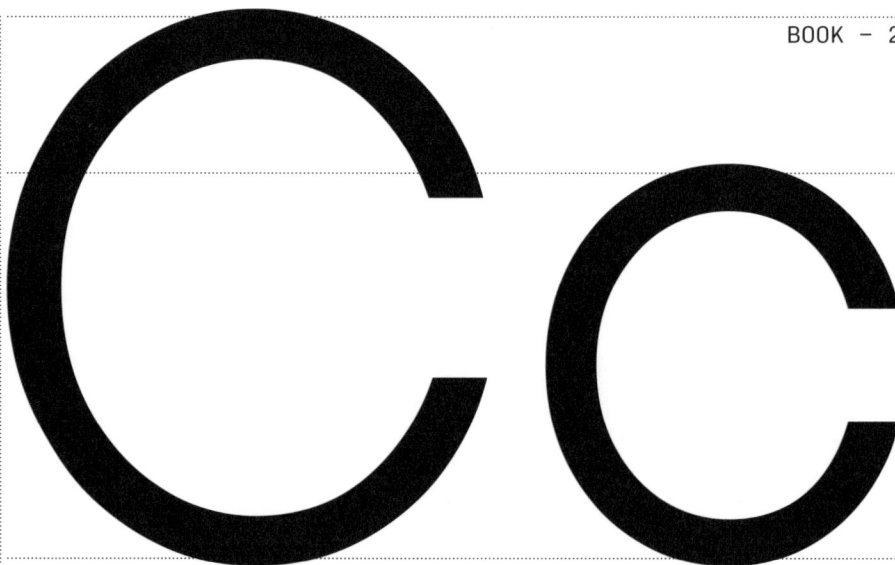

TT COMMONS™ PRO IS A VERSATILE GEOMETRIC SANS SERIF FONT HIGHLY FAVOURED FOR ITS MODERN AND TIMELESS DESIGN, READABILITY, AND ADAPTABILITY IN VARIOUS APPLICATIONS. IT OFFERS A COMPREHENSIVE RANGE OF STYLES, INCLUDING UPRIGHT AND ITALIC VARIATIONS IN NORMAL, CONDENSED, COMPACT, AND EXPANDED SUB-FAMILIES. THE FONT ALSO INCLUDES THE TT COMMONS PRO MONO SUB-FAMILY AND TWO VARIABLE FONTS: TT COMMONS PRO AND TT COMMONS PRO MONO. WITH A LARGE CHARACTER SET, SUPPORT FOR OVER 275 LANGUAGES, FUNCTIONAL OPENTYPE FEATURES, AND DIVERSE POSSIBILITIES, IT CATERS TO A WIDE ARRAY OF TYPOGRAPHIC NEEDS.

CAP HEIGHT

BOOK – 250PT

X-HEIGHT

Cc

BASELINE

^{TT}Commons™ Pro

THE QUICK BROWN FOX JU

IT WOULD BE THE CHEEKY

IT'S A LOVELY DAY IN THE N

AND THE PUNGENT AROM,

PROMISE OF A SUMPTUOU

THINKING ABOUT THE DEL

THE LAZY DOG REMAINS U

LONG BLACK FUR FLUTTEF

THE MOUNTAINS ARE MAD

AND THE PUDDLES ARE JU

The quick brown fox jumps over a lazy dog. He didn't have to, but he thoug
it would be the cheeky thing to do. After all, he had a reputation to maintair
It's a lovely day in the neighbourhood, with the sun shining, the birds chirp
and the pungent aroma of fresh rubbish bins wafting through the air - the
promise of a sumptuous meal. The sprightly fox rubs his paws together in g
thinking about the delicious treasures he's about to dig into. Still in her spc
the lazy dog remains unperturbed. With her long snout, droopy jowls, and
long black fur fluttering in the breeze, she is in a dreamland far away - wher
the mountains are made of beefy treats, the valleys are filled with tennis ba
and the puddles are just the right temperature. Why be in the rat race?
It's a dog's life, after all.

timeless
timeless
timeless

timeless
timeless

75%	90%	100%	125%
H	H	H	H	H

MONO   CONDENSED   COMPACT   NORMAL   EXPANDED

VARIABLE

VARIABLE

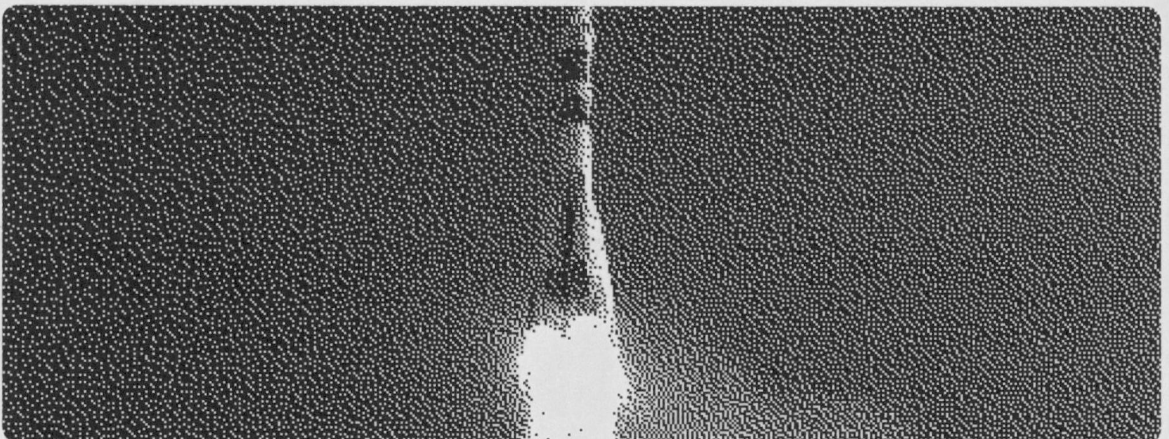

TT Commons™ Pro

TypeType

AaBbc
123&æ
DdEef

TT COMMONS™
PRO   COMPANY
CORPORATE   ↘
↖   TYPEFACE
WEB & PRINT

TYPEFACE	:	DAZZED
DESIGNER	:	MARTIN VÁCHA
LOCATION	:	PRAGUE, CZECH REPUBLIC

PUBLISHED BY	:	DISPLAAY TYPE FOUNDRY
CHRONOLOGY	:	2016 - 2023
RELEASED IN	:	2016

LINK	:	HTTPS://DISPLAAY.NET/TYPEFACE/DAZZED/
STYLES	:	THIN, LIGHT, REGULAR, MEDIUM, SEMIBOLD, BOLD,HEAVY
		THIN ITALIC, LIGHT ITALIC, REGULAR ITALIC, MEDIUM ITALIC,
		SEMIBOLD ITALIC, BOLD ITALIC, HEAVY ITALIC
CREDITS	:	ALEX SLOBZHENINOV (SPACING & KERNING)

DAZZED IS A SANS-SERIF TYPEFACE WITH NARROW PROPORTIONS WHICH STARTED AS A BESPOKE TYPEFACE FOR A CINEMATIC PROJECT PROPOSAL. IN THE SAME WAY THAT ALL KINDS OF MOVIES EXIST, DAZZED AIMS TO COMPRISE THEM IN ITS OVERALL LOOK. USERS WILL SEE COMIC, GROTESQUE, DRAMATIC AND QUIRKY MOMENTS IN "A", "E", "C", AND "G" MEETING TECHNICAL, STEEL-COLD, ACTION, CRIME AND SCI-FI SHAPES IN "T", "F", AND "R" WHERE THE TERMINALS ARE CUT OFF. THESE CONTRAST WITH THE CLASSICAL FORMS OF OTHER LETTERS. THE DOTS ARE ROUNDED FOR ACCENTS WHILE PUNCTUATION IS SQUARED FOR BETTER RECOGNITION. THE ITALICS ARE SET AT 18°, WITH CUSTOMISATION OPTIONS AVAILABLE UPON REQUEST.

CAP HEIGHT   REGULA   290PT

X-HEIGHT

Dd

BASELINE

Dazzed

THE QUICK BRO

IT WOULD BE T

IT'S A LOVELY D

AND THE PUNC

PROMISE OF A

THINKING ABO

THE LAZY DOG

LONG BLACK F

THE MOUNTAIN

the FOX Theather

The FOX THEATER

TYPEFACE	:	ABC DIATYPE
DESIGNER	:	DINAMO
LOCATION	:	BERLIN, GERMANY

PUBLISHED BY	:	DINAMO
CHRONOLOGY	:	N/A
RELEASED IN	:	2018

LINK	:	HTTPS://ABCDINAMO.COM/TYPEFACES/DIATYPE
STYLES	:	7 FAMILIES, 76 STYLES
CREDITS	:	JOHANNES BREYER, FABIAN HARB, ELIAS HANZER, ERKIN KARAMEMET & RENAN ROSSATI/DINAMO (DESIGN), IGINO MARINI (SPACING & KERNING), ROBERT JANES/DINAMO (PRODUCTION)

ABC DIATYPE IS A WARM YET SHARP GROTESQUE FONT, DESIGNED FOR OPTIMAL TEXT READABILITY ON SCREENS. ITS ORIGINS CAN BE TRACED BACK TO CO-FOUNDER FABIAN HARB'S STUDENT DAYS, WHERE IT EMERGED AS A KEEN EXPLORATION OF THE SWISS NEO-GROTESQUE GENRE. ITS NAME PAYS HOMAGE TO THE CLUNKY, PRE-DIGITAL TYPESETTING MACHINES THAT INFLUENCED ITS SHAPES. IN 2018, ELIAS HANZER, A LONGSTANDING MEMBER OF DINAMO, EXPANDED ABC DIATYPE FROM A SINGLE WEIGHT UPRIGHT AND ITALIC TO A COMPREHENSIVE FAMILY ENCOMPASSING THIN, LIGHT, REGULAR, MEDIUM, AND BOLD WEIGHTS, ALONG WITH CORRESPONDING MONOSPACE AND ITALICS.

CAP HEIGHT   REGULAR — 250PT

X-HEIGHT

Dd

BASELINE

ABCDiatype

THE QUICK BROWN

IT WOULD BE THE

IT'S A LOVELY DAY

AND THE PUNGEN

PROMISE OF A SUN

The quick brown fox jumps over a lazy dog. He didn't have to, but he tho
It would be the cheeky thing to do. After all, he had a reputation to maint
It's a lovely day in the neighbourhood, with the sun shining, the birds chi
And the pungent aroma of fresh rubbish bins wafting through the air - th
Promise of a sumptuous meal. The sprightly fox rubs his paws together i
Thinking about the delicious treasures he's about to dig into. Still in her s
The lazy dog remains unperturbed. With her long snout, droopy jowls, ar
Long black fur fluttering in the breeze, she is in a dreamland far away - w
The mountains are made of beefy treats, the valleys are filled with tennis
And the puddles are just the right temperature. Why be in the rat race?
It's a dog's life, after all.

The quick brown fox jumps over a lazy dog. He didn't have to, but he thought
it would be the cheeky thing to do. After all, he had a reputation to maintain.
It's a lovely day in the neighbourhood, with the sun shining, the birds chirping,
and the pungent aroma of fresh rubbish bins wafting through the air - the
promise of a sumptuous meal. The sprightly fox rubs his paws together in glee,
thinking about the delicious treasures he's about to dig into. Still in her spot,
the lazy dog remains unperturbed. With her long snout, droopy jowls, and
long black fur fluttering in the breeze, she is in a dreamland far away - where
the mountains are made of beefy treats, the valleys are filled with tennis balls,
and the puddles are just the right temperature. Why be in the rat race?
It's a dog's life, after all.

DIATYPE
DIATYP
DIATY
DIAT
DIA
DI
D

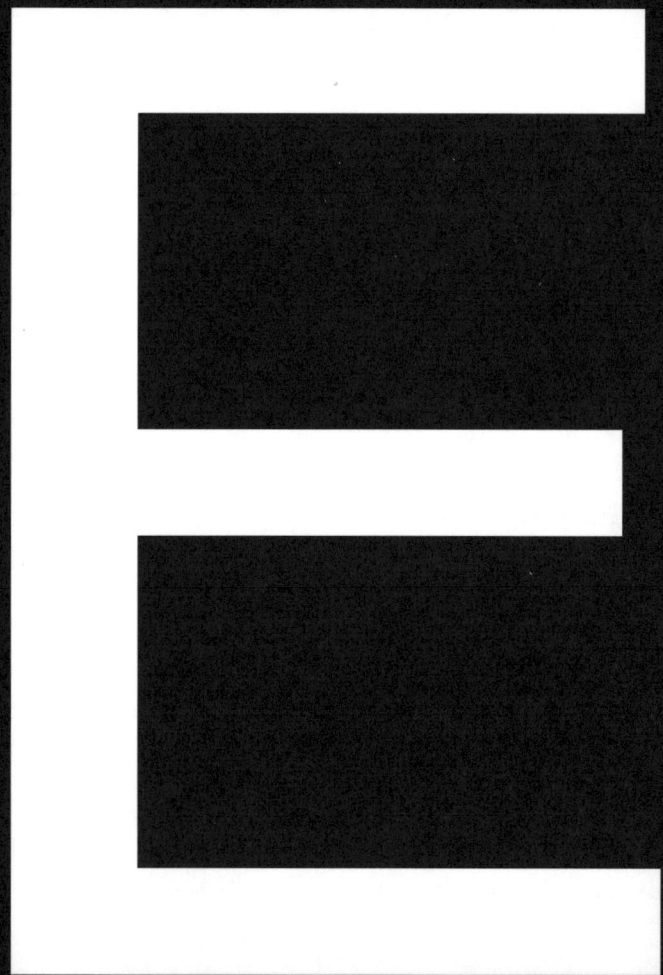

```
D   I       T
D   I   A   T
D   I   A   T
D   I   A   T  Y
DIIIATYP
DIATYPE
DIATPPE
DIAPEEE
```

TYPEFACE	:	DIGITAL SANS
DESIGNER	:	BLAZE TYPE
LOCATION	:	MARSEILLE, FRANCE

		PUBLISHED BY	:	BLAZE TYPE
		CHRONOLOGY	:	N/A
		RELEASED IN	:	2023

| LINK | : | HTTPS://BLAZETYPE.EU/TYPEFACES/DIGITAL-SANS |
| STYLES | : | SANS, UPRIGHT, ITALIC, GEOMETRIC, MODERN, CONTEMPORARY |

DIGITAL SANS IS A VERSATILE AND TIMELESS GEOMETRIC SANS FONT, DRAWING INSPIRATION FROM PAUL RENNER'S FUTURA. WITH SEVEN DIFFERENT WEIGHTS AND MATCHING ITALICS, IT CATERS TO A BROAD RANGE OF APPLICATIONS, FROM BODY TEXT TO HEADLINES AND LOGOTYPES. ACTING AS A BRIDGE BETWEEN THE 20'S AND CONTEMPORARY DESIGN, DIGITAL SANS GOES BEYOND A MERE INTERPRETATION, QUESTIONING GEOMETRIC SYSTEMS TO ESTABLISH ITS UNIQUE LANGUAGE. THE FONT FAMILY INCLUDES ALTERNATE GLYPHS, PROVIDING FLEXIBILITY FOR PLAYFUL DESIGN AND ALLOWING FOR TRANSITIONS BETWEEN DIFFERENT SETS WITH DIAGONAL OR VERTICAL CUTS AND SHARP ANGLES. IT OFFERS A DISTINCT LOOK WITH CONSTRUCTED ALTERNATES FOR CERTAIN LETTERS, MAKING IT HIGHLY FLEXIBLE FOR VARIOUS DESIGN MOODS AND SUITABLE FOR HEAVY TYPE USE IN BOTH SCREEN AND PRINT MEDIA.

CAP HEIGHT REGULAR 290PT

X-HEIGHT

BASELINE

Digital Sans

THE QUICK BROW
IT WOULD BE THE
IT'S A LOVELY DAY
AND THE PUNGEN
PROMISE OF A SUN
THINKING ABOUT

The quick brown fox jumps over a lazy dog. He didn't have to, but he thought it would be the cheeky thing to do. After all, he had a reputation to maintain. It's a lovely day in the neighbourhood, with the sun shining, the birds chirping, and the pungent aroma of fresh rubbish bins wafting through the air - the promise of a sumptuous meal. The sprightly fox rubs his paws together in glee, thinking about the delicious treasures he's about to dig into. Still in her spot, the lazy dog remains unperturbed. With her long snout, droopy jowls, and long black fur fluttering in the breeze, she is in a dreamland far away - where the mountains are made of beefy treats, the valleys are filled with tennis balls, and the puddles are just the right temperature. Why be in the rat race? It's a dog's life, after all.

The quick brown fox jumps over a lazy dog. He didn't have to, but he thought it would be the cheeky thing to do. After all, he had a reputation to maintain. It's a lovely day in the neighbourhood, with the sun shining, the birds chirping, and the pungent aroma of fresh rubbish bins wafting through the air - the promise of a sumptuous meal. The sprightly fox rubs his paws together in glee, thinking about the delicious treasures he's about to dig into. Still in her spot, the lazy dog remains unperturbed. With her long snout, droopy jowls, and long black fur fluttering in the breeze, she is in a dreamland far away - where the mountains are made of beefy treats, the valleys are filled with tennis balls, and the puddles are just the right temperature. Why be in the rat race? It's a dog's life, after all.

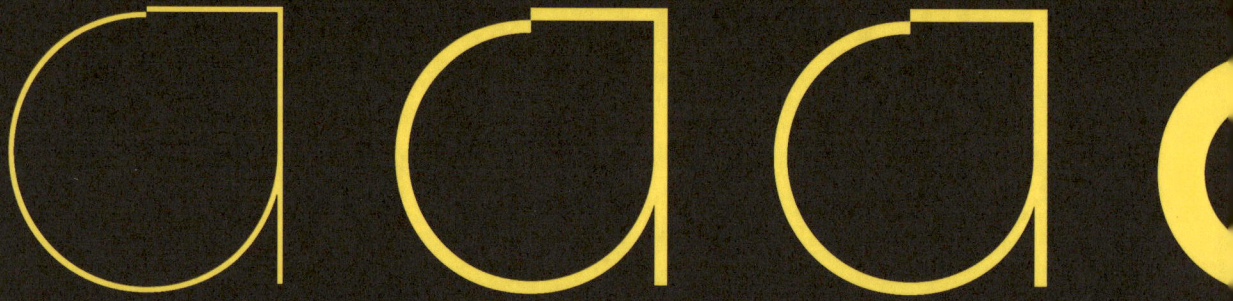

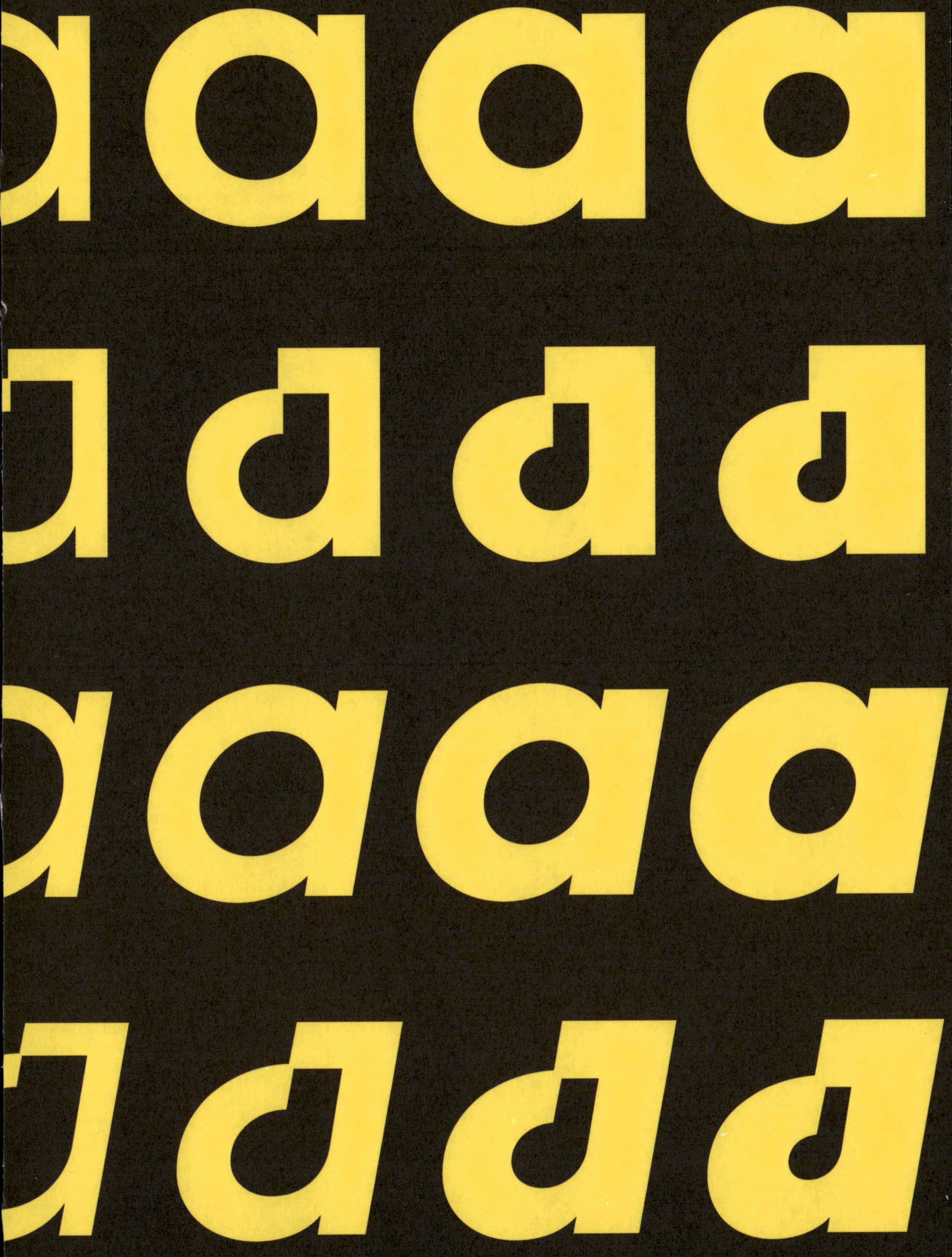

TYPEFACE   :   DIVERSE
DESIGNER   :   DDOTT
LOCATION   :   BARCELONA, SPAIN; COLOGNE, GERMANY

PUBLISHED BY   :   DDOTT
CHRONOLOGY   :   N/A
RELEASED IN   :   2022

LINK   :   HTTPS://DDOTT.NET/FONT/DIVERSE-C/
STYLES   :   36 STYLES, 3 FAMILIES
CREDITS   :   DOMINIK THIEME

DIVERSE, A HUMANIST SANS-SERIF TYPEFACE, OFFERS 36 FONTS DIVIDED INTO THREE FAMILIES (A, B, C) WITH VARIED STROKE CONTRASTS, INSPIRED BY NOORDZIJ'S CONTRAST MODEL. SIX YEARS OF DEVELOPMENT RESULTED IN DISTINCT STYLES, ALL SHARING THE EARLY HUMANIST SKELETON FROM JOHNSTON AND GILL SANS. EACH FAMILY REPRESENTS A DIFFERENT STROKE IMPRINT: MONOLINEAR (A), SUBTLE (B), AND HIGH CONTRAST (C). DIVERSE ALSO FEATURES EXTENSIVE OPENTYPE CAPABILITIES, ALLOWING FOR GEOMETRIC FORMS. THIS VERSATILE TYPEFACE IS SUITABLE FOR SMALL-SIZE READING WITH OPTICAL CORRECTIONS AND BOLD HEADLINES, EMBODYING A DEDICATED PROJECT THAT COMBINES TRADITION AND INNOVATION.

CAP HEIGHT   REG   — 290PT

X-HEIGHT

Dd

BASELINE

Diverse

THE QUICK BROW

IT WOULD BE THE

ITS A LOVELY DAY

AND THE PUNGEN

PROMISE OF A SU

THINKING ABOUT

THE LAZY DOG RE

LONG BLACK FUR

THE MOUNTAINS

The quick brown fox jumps over a lazy dog. He didnt have to, but he thought it would be the cheeky thing to do. After all, he had a reputation to maintain. Its a lovely day in the neighbourhood, with the sun shining, the birds chirping, and the pungent aroma of fresh rubbish bins wafting through the air - the promise of a sumptuous meal. The sprightly fox rubs his paws together in glee, thinking about the delicious treasures hes about to dig into. Still in her spot, the lazy dog remains unperturbed. With her long snout, droopy jowls, and long black fur fluttering in the breeze, she is in a dreamland far away - where the mountains are made of beefy treats, the valleys are filled with tennis balls, and the puddles are just the right temperature. Why be in the rat race Its a dogs life, after all.

M2ND

Regular

Brutal

Size: 80pt

↻ Est.

Leading: 70pt

15 12 97

M2ND

Regular

Brutal

Size: 129pt

↻ Est.

Leading: 114pt

15 12 97

M2ND

Regular

Size: 208pt

Leading: 174pt

Brutal

Est.

15 12

SQI

49s

B21

&

Gut

TYPEFACE	:	EXTENDA
DESIGNER	:	ZETAFONTS TYPE FOUNDRY
LOCATION	:	FLORENCE, ITALY

PUBLISHED BY	:	ZETAFONTS TYPE FOUNDRY
CHRONOLOGY	:	2018
RELEASED IN	:	2018

LINK	:	HTTPS://WWW.ZETAFONTS.COM/EXTENDA
STYLES	:	12 STYLES + 1 VARIABLE FONT: 10 PICA, 15 NANO, 20 MICRO, 30 DECA, 40 HECTO, 50 MEGA, 60 GIGA, 70 TERA, 80 PETA, 90 EXA, 100 YOTTA, EXTENDABLE

EXTENDA IS A VERSATILE VARIABLE WIDTH SANS-SERIF TYPE FAMILY DESIGNED FOR CREATING IMPACTFUL HEADLINES, LOGOS, AND DISPLAY TEXT WITH TIGHT SPACING AND MAXIMUM SPACE COVERAGE. INSTEAD OF OFFERING A RANGE OF WEIGHTS, IT PROVIDES A FINE-GRAINED SPECTRUM OF WIDTHS, ALLOWING FOR PRECISE CONTROL IN DISPLAY USES AND PROPORTIONAL SIZE VARIATION IN LOGOS. THE FONT INCLUDES A COMPREHENSIVE CHARACTER SET FOR LATIN, CYRILLIC, AND GREEK, COVERING OVER 200 LANGUAGES. EXTENDA ALSO FEATURES FULL OPENTYPE CAPABILITIES, INCLUDING SMALL CAPS, STYLISTIC ALTERNATES, POSITIONAL NUMBER FORMS, AND LIGATURES.

CAP HEIGHT

REGULAR — 290PT

X-HEIGHT

BASELINE

Extenda

THE QUICK BROWN

IT WOULD BE THE CH

IT'S A LOVELY DAY IN

AND THE PUNGENT A

THE QUICK BROWN FOX JUMPS OVER A LAZY DOG. HE

IT WOULD BE THE CHEEKY THING TO DO. AFTER ALL, HE

IT'S A LOVELY DAY IN THE NEIGHBOURHOOD, WITH THE

AND THE PUNGENT AROMA OF FRESH RUBBISH BINS W

PROMISE OF A SUMPTUOUS MEAL. THE SPRIGHTLY FO

THINKING ABOUT THE DELICIOUS TREASURES HE'S ABO

THE LAZY DOG REMAINS UNPERTURBED. WITH HER LO

LONG BLACK FUR FLUTTERING IN THE BREEZE, SHE IS IN

THE CREATIVE FASHIO

A CAUTIONARY TALE BY **OUR RESIDENT SNOI**

DO БРИЛЛИАНТЫ ЗАСТАВЛЯЕТ МИР ВРАЩАТЬСЯ ВОКРУГ

DO

WHAT MAKES YOU **FEEL** BEAUTIFUL

Forschung & Wißenschaft

ОЧЕНЬ ЛЮДНО

SMART THERMOSTAT

N WORLD

OGRAPHER

FOR ORIGINALITY
SEARCH DEEP INSIDE YOURSELF
DUDE

DREAMS

AT THE CATWALK'S HEART

The Quick Brown Fox Jumps Over

DESTINY OF WOMANKIND

HEAVEN CALLS UPON US QUIETLY, AS IN MURMURS

TYPEFACE	:	ABC FAVORIT
DESIGNER	:	DINAMO
LOCATION	:	BERLIN, GERMANY

PUBLISHED BY	:	DINAMO
CHRONOLOGY	:	N/A
RELEASED IN	:	2014

LINK	:	HTTPS://ABCDINAMO.COM/TYPEFACES/FAVORIT
STYLES	:	40 STYLES, 5 FAMILIES
CREDITS	:	JOHANNES BREYER, FABIAN HARB, ELIAS HANZER, ERKIN KARAMEMET & IMMO SCHNEIDER/DINAMO (DESIGN), IGINO MARINI (SPACING & KERNING), ROBERT JAMES/DINAMO (PRODUCTION)

ABC FAVORIT IS A STRAIGHTFORWARD, LOW-CONTRAST GROTESQUE FONT THAT COMBINES GEOMETRIC RIGIDITY WITH SUBTLE ODDITIES AND A TOUCH OF HUMOUR. IT COMES IN FIVE WEIGHTS WITH CORRESPONDING ITALICS, SPECIAL CUTS, AND AN UNDERLINED VERSION CALLED FAVORIT LINING. ADDITIONAL VARIATIONS INCLUDE ABC FAVORIT EXTENDED, ABC FAVORIT EXPANDED, AND THE MONOSPACED VERSION ABC FAVORIT MONO. ABC FAVORIT LINING, THE YOUNGER SIBLING OF ABC FAVORIT, FEATURES A "SMART UNDERLINE" BUILT DIRECTLY INTO THE FONT.

CAP HEIGHT ⋯⋯⋯⋯⋯⋯ ULAR — 290PT

Ff

X-HEIGHT

BASELINE

ABCFavorit

THE QUICK BROWN FO

IT WOULD BE THE CHE

IT'S A LOVELY DAY IN T

AND THE PUNGENT AF

PROMISE OF A SUMPT

THINKING ABOUT THE

THE LAZY DOG REMAI

LONG BLACK FUR FLU

THE MOUNTAINS ARE

AND THE PUDDLES AR

The quick brown fox jumps over a lazy dog. He didn't have to, but he thought it would be the cheeky thing to do. After all, he had a reputation to maintain. It's a lovely day in the neighbourhood, with the sun shining, the birds chirping, and the pungent aroma of fresh rubbish bins wafting through the air - the promise of a sumptuous meal. The sprightly fox rubs his paws together in glee, thinking about the delicious treasures he's about to dig into. Still in her spot, the lazy dog remains unperturbed. With her long snout, droopy jowls, and long black fur fluttering in the breeze, she is in a dreamland far away - where the mountains are made of beefy treats, the valleys are filled with tennis balls, and the puddles are just the right temperature. Why be in the rat race? It's a dog's life, after all.

ABC FAVORIT FAMILY

8

Fa?
@liR
%°
37W

TYPEFACE   :   FORMULA
DESIGNER   :   MAT DESJARDINS
LOCATION   :   MONTREAL, CANADA

                  PUBLISHED BY   :   PANGRAM PANGRAM® FOUNDRY
                  CHRONOLOGY   :   N/A
                  RELEASED IN   :   2019, 2022

LINK   :   HTTPS://PANGRAMPANGRAM.COM/PRODUCTS/FORMULA
STYLES   :   108
CREDITS   :   HUGO JOURDAN (COLLABORATION, 2022)

FORMULA IS A COMPREHENSIVE AND VERSATILE TYPEFACE, SEAMLESSLY BLENDING A BOLD, DYNAMIC APPEARANCE WITH THE ADAPTABILITY OF A GROTESQUE. WITH A VARIETY OF STYLES, RANGING FROM CONDENSED TO EXTENDED, AND AN EXTENSIVE SET OF WEIGHTS SPANNING FROM THIN TO BLACK, EACH COMPLEMENTED BY ITS ITALIC COUNTERPART, IT OFFERS A WIDE SPECTRUM OF DESIGN POSSIBILITIES. CRAFTED TO MAKE A POWERFUL IMPACT IN DESIGNS, FORMULA PROVES SUITABLE FOR DIVERSE APPLICATIONS. WHETHER OPTING FOR THE CONDENSED BLACK ITALIC STYLE IN A RACING-INSPIRED CAMPAIGN OR CHOOSING THE REGULAR WEIGHT FOR BODY TEXT, THIS TYPEFACE STANDS READY TO MEET A RANGE OF DESIGN NEEDS.

CAP HEIGHT

X-HEIGHT

REGULAR — 290PT

BASELINE

Ff

Formula

THE QUICK BROWN FOX JU
IT WOULD BE THE CHEEKY
IT'S A LOVELY DAY IN THE N
AND THE PUNGENT AROMA
PROMISE OF A SUMPTUOUS

The quick brown fox jumps over a lazy dog. He didn't have to, but he thought it would be the cheeky thing to do. After all, he had a reputation to maintain. It's a lovely day in the neighbourhood, with the sun shining, the birds chirping, and the pungent aroma of fresh rubbish bins wafting through the air – the promise of a sumptuous meal. The sprightly fox rubs his paws together in glee, thinking about the delicious treasures he's about to dig into. Still in her spot, the lazy dog remains unperturbed. With her long snout, droopy jowls, and long black fur fluttering in the breeze, she is in a dreamland far away – where the mountains are made of beefy treats, the valleys are filled with tennis balls, and the puddles are just the right temperature. Why be in the rat race? It's a dog's life, after all.

The quick brown fox jumps over a lazy dog. He didn't have to, but he thought it would be the cheeky thing to do. After all, he had a reputation to maintain. It's a lovely day in the neighbourhood, with the sun shining, the birds chirping, and the pungent aroma of fresh rubbish bins wafting through the air – the promise of a sumptuous meal. The sprightly fox rubs his paws together in glee, thinking about the delicious treasures he's about to dig into. Still in her spot, the lazy dog remains unperturbed. With her long snout, droopy jowls, and long black fur fluttering in the breeze, she is in a dreamland far away – where the mountains are made of beefy treats, the valleys are filled with tennis balls, and the puddles are just the right temperature. Why be in the rat race? It's a dog's life, after all.

TYPEFACE	:	GAMUTH SANS
DESIGNER	:	MAX ESNÉE
LOCATION	:	PARIS, FRANCE; SHANGHAI, CHINA

PUBLISHED BY	:	PRODUCTION TYPE
CHRONOLOGY	:	2021 - 2024
RELEASED IN	:	UNRELEASED - BETA

| LINK | : | HTTPS://WWW.PRODUCTIONTYPE.COM/COLLECTION/GAMUTH_COLLECTION |
| STYLES | : | 12 STYLES + ROMAN & ITALIC |

GAMUTH SANS, INTRODUCED AFTER GAMUTH TEXT AND DISPLAY, IS DESIGNED FOR LOW-KEY UI APPLICATIONS SUCH AS NAVIGATION ELEMENTS AND FORMS. WHILE IDEAL FOR PRESENTING COMPLEX DATA, IT MAINTAINS READABILITY AT SMALLER SIZES WITH CLEAR LETTER SHAPES AND GENEROUS SPACING. THIS MULTIPLEXED TYPEFACE ALLOWS FOR EASY INTERCHANGEABILITY OF STYLES AND WEIGHTS, SIMPLIFYING TYPESETTING FOR UI ELEMENTS AND DATA TABLES. ITS VERSATILITY MAKES IT CONVENIENT FOR INTERACTIVE WEB APPLICATIONS AND ENGAGING GRAPHIC DESIGN PROJECTS.

CAP HEIGHT

REGULAR — 290PT

X-HEIGHT

Gg

BASELINE

Gamuth Sans

THE QUICK BROWN

IT WOULD BE THE C

ITS A LOVELY DAY

AND THE PUNGENT

PROMISE OF A SUM

THINKING ABOUT T

THE LAZY DOG REM

LONG BLACK FUR F

THE MOUNTAINS A

The quick brown fox jumps over a lazy dog. He didn't have to, but he thought it would be the cheeky thing to do. After all, he had a reputation to maintain. Its a lovely day in the neighbourhood, with the sun shining, the birds chirping, and the pungent aroma of fresh rubbish bins wafting through the air - the promise of a sumptuous meal. The sprightly fox rubs his paws together in glee, thinking about the delicious treasures he's about to dig into. Still in her spot, the lazy dog remains unperturbed. With her long snout, droopy jowls, and long black fur fluttering in the breeze, she is in a dreamland far away - where the mountains are made of beefy treats, the valleys are filled with tennis balls, and the puddles are just the right temperature. Why be in the rat race? Its a dogs life, after all.

S

Invertebrater
Bracelets
Specification
Thermomerter
Understandable
Communications
Standardization
Conversation
German 600,000
Memorable
Electronmagnet
Conventionalize

PUBLISHED BY	:	NARROW TYPE
CHRONOLOGY	:	2022
RELEASED IN	:	2022

| LINK | : | HTTPS://WWW.NARROWTYPE.COM |
| STYLES | : | LIGHT, REGULAR, MEDIUM, SEMIBOLD, BOLD |

GIRONA IS AN ELEGANT, CONTRASTING SANS-SERIF TYPE FAMILY THAT IS AVAILABLE IN FIVE WEIGHTS RANGING FROM LIGHT TO BOLD. FEATURING LARGE INKTRAPS AND PLAYFUL DETAILS, IT EMBODIES A MODERN TYPEFACE WITH A DISTINCTIVE APPEARANCE. THE FONT OFFERS NUMEROUS DISCRETIONARY AND STANDARD LIGATURES, AND ITS DIFFERENT STYLISTIC SETS ALLOW DESIGNERS TO SHIFT THE FEEL OF THEIR DESIGNS FROM SUBTLE TO EXPRESSIVE. GIRONA PROVES TO BE AN IDEAL CHOICE FOR BRANDING, EDITORIAL DESIGN, LOGO CREATION, AND VARIOUS APPLICATIONS. IT IS MOST EFFECTIVE WHEN USED IN LARGER SIZES OR FOR HEADLINES.

CAP HEIGHT

REGULAR — 290PT

X-HEIGHT

BASELINE

Girona

THE QUICK BROWN FOX JU
IT WOULD BE THE CHEEKY
ITS A LOVELY DAY IN THE NI
AND THE PUNGENT AROMA
PROMISE OF A SUMPTUOU
THINKING ABOUT THE DELI

The quick brown fox jumps over a lazy dog. He didn't have to, b
it would be the cheeky thing to do. After all, he had a reputatio
Its a lovely day in the neighbourhood, with the sun shining, the
and the pungent aroma of fresh rubbish bins wafting through t
promise of a sumptuous meal. The sprightly fox rubs his paws
thinking about the delicious treasures he's about to dig into. St
the lazy dog remains unperturbed. With her long snout, droopy
long black fur fluttering in the breeze, she is in a dreamland far
the mountains are made of beefy treats, the valleys are filled v
and the puddles are just the right temperature. Why be in the r
Its a dogs life, after all.

The quick brown fox jumps over a lazy dog. He didn't have to, but he thought
it would be the cheeky thing to do. After all, he had a reputation to maintain.
Its a lovely day in the neighbourhood, with the sun shining, the birds chirping,
and the pungent aroma of fresh rubbish bins wafting through the air - the
promise of a sumptuous meal. The sprightly fox rubs his paws together in glee,
thinking about the delicious treasures he's about to dig into. Still in her spot,
the lazy dog remains unperturbed. With her long snout, droopy jowls, and
long black fur fluttering in the breeze, she is in a dreamland far away - where
the mountains are made of beefy treats, the valleys are filled with tennis balls,
and the puddles are just the right temperature. Why be in the rat race?
Its a dogs life, after all.

1835–
"Hels
FINLA
SWED

-2013
inki"
ND
DEN?!

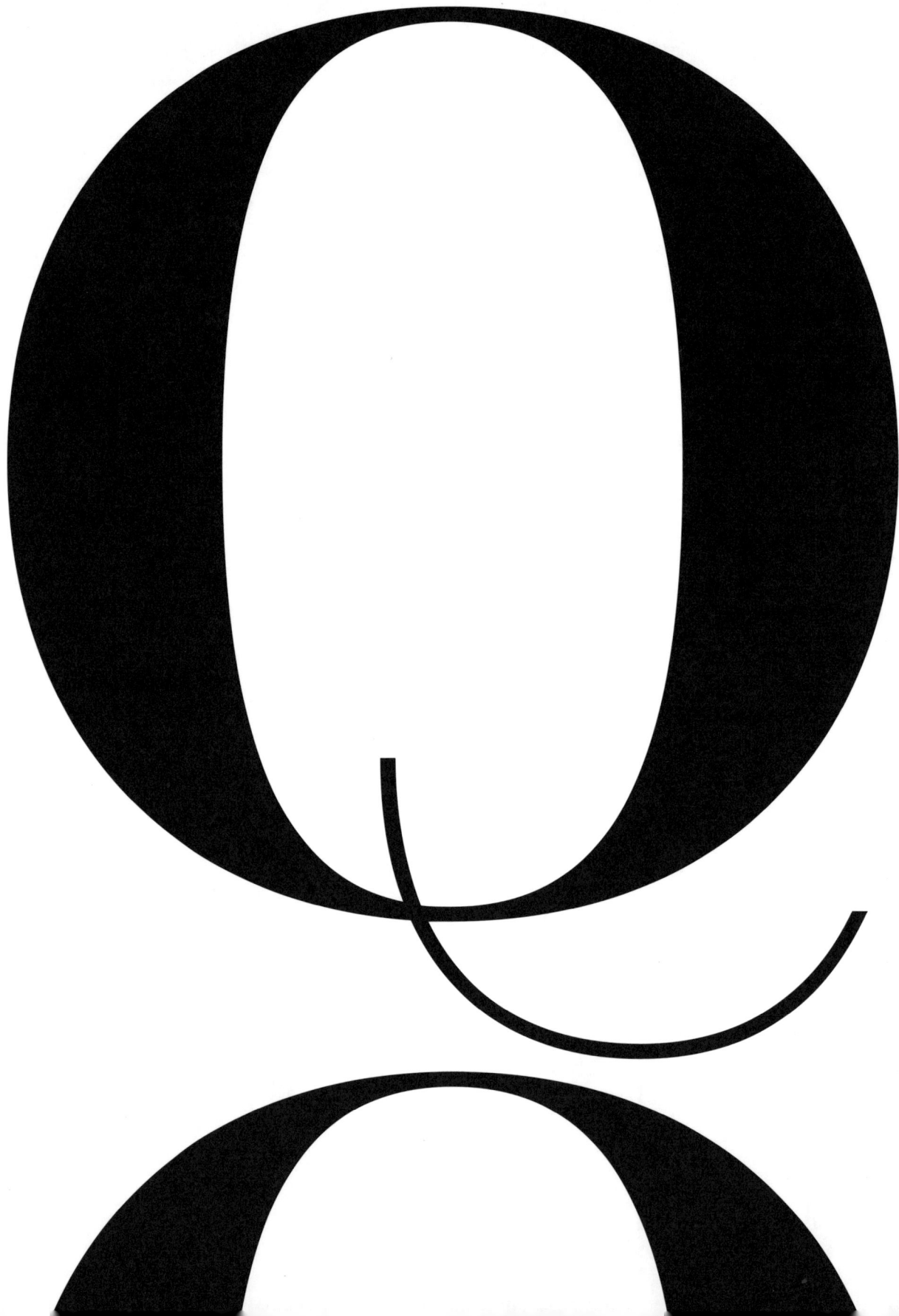

Q

CA

50%

e&

ffk

TYPEFACE   :   ABC GRAVITY
DESIGNER   :   DINAMO
LOCATION   :   BERLIN, GERMANY

             PUBLISHED BY   :   DINAMO
             CHRONOLOGY   :   N/A
             RELEASED IN   :   2021

LINK   :   HTTPS://ABCDINAMO.COM/TYPEFACES/GRAVITY
STYLES   :   24
CREDITS   :   JOHANNES BREYER, FABIAN HARB, ROBERT JANES, FABIOLA
                 MEJÍA & OLGA UMPELEVA/DINAMO (DESIGN), IGINO MARINI
                 (SPACING & KERNING), ROBERT JAMES/DINAMO (PRODUCTION)

ABC GRAVITY IS A HEADLINE TYPEFACE WITH A SINGLE WEIGHT AND 12 DIFFERENT WIDTHS. ITS NUMEROUS STYLISTIC ALTERNATES PROVIDE FLEXIBILITY FOR PLAYFUL SETTINGS AND SUPER COMPACT TITLE ARRANGEMENTS. THE FONT'S INITIAL SKELETON DRAWS INSPIRATION FROM THE HEAVY GROTESQUE TYPEFACES OF THE 60'S AND 70'S, WHICH WERE COMPRESSED AND STRETCHED TO EXTREME WIDTHS. AS A SPECIAL FEATURE, USERS CAN ARRANGE AND MODIFY THE POSITION OF CHARACTERS, ALLOWING THEM TO JUMP OVER THE BASELINE OR HANG FROM THE TOP. GRAVITY'S 12 STYLES CAN BE USED INDIVIDUALLY OR PACKAGED TOGETHER IN A SINGLE VARIABLE FONT FILE, ENABLING SEAMLESS MODULATION FROM XXXX COMPRESSED TO WIDE.

CAP HEIGHT   REGULAR — 290PT

X-HEI

Gg

BASELINE

ABCGravity

THE QUICK BRO

IT WOULD BE TH

IT'S A LOVELY D

AND THE PUNGI

PROMISE OF A S

THINKING ABOU

THE LAZY DOG

The quick brown fox jumps over a lazy dog. He didn't have to, but he th
it would be the cheeky thing to do. After all, he had a reputation to ma
It's a lovely day in the neighbourhood, with the sun shining, the birds c
and the pungent aroma of fresh rubbish bins wafting through the air -
promise of a sumptuous meal. The sprightly fox rubs his paws togethe
thinking about the delicious treasures he's about to dig into. Still in he
the lazy dog remains unperturbed. With her long snout, droopy jowls,
long black fur fluttering in the breeze, she is in a dreamland far away
the mountains are made of beefy treats, the valleys are filled with te
and the puddles are just the right temperature. Why be in the rat ra
It's a dog's life, after all.

ABC Gravity XXXX Compressed

ABC Gravity XXX Compressed

ABC Gravity XX Compressed

ABC Gravity X Compressed

ABC Gravity Compressed

ABC Gravity Extra Condensed

ABC Gravity SemiCondensed

ABC Gravity Normal

ABC Gravity Extended

ABC Gravity Expanded

ABC Gravity Wide

TYPEFACE	:	GREED
DESIGNER	:	MARTIN VÁCHA
LOCATION	:	PRAGUE, CZECH REPUBLIC

		PUBLISHED BY	:	DISPLAAY TYPE FOUNDRY
		CHRONOLOGY	:	2018 - 2023
		RELEASED IN	:	2019

LINK	:	HTTPS://DISPLAAY.NET/TYPEFACE/GREED/
STYLES	:	60 STYLES, 5 FAMILIES, 30 WEIGHTS
CREDITS	:	VIKTOR MIZERA (DESIGN ASSISTANCE),
		IGINO MARINI (SPACING & KERNING)

GREED, INITIALLY DESIGNED FOR THE POLANSKY GALLERY BY ANYMADE STUDIO, TAKES ITS NAME FROM A FICTIONAL FRAGRANCE COMMERCIAL DIRECTED BY ROMAN POLANSKI IN 2009. THIS SANS-SERIF FONT OFFERS VARIOUS WIDTHS, FROM CONDENSED TO EXTENDED, AND FEATURES ELEGANT CURVES AND STROKE CONTRAST FOR A DISTINCTIVE LOOK. THE ITALICS, ANGLED AT 14°, ADD FURTHER PERSONALITY TO THE TYPEFACE.

CAP HEIGHT

REGULAR — 180PT

X-HEIGHT

Gg

BASELINE

Greed

THE QUICK BROWN F
IT WOULD BE THE CH
IT'S A LOVELY DAY IN T
AND THE PUNGENT A
PROMISE OF A SUMPT
THINKING ABOUT THE
THE LAZY DOG REMA
LONG BLACK FUR FLU
THE MOUNTAINS ARE

The quick brown fox jumps over a lazy dog. He didn't have to, but he thought it would be the cheeky thing to do. After all, he had a reputation to maintain. It's a lovely day in the neighbourhood, with the sun shining, the birds chirping, and the pungent aroma of fresh rubbish bins wafting through the air - the promise of a sumptuous meal. The sprightly fox rubs his paws together in glee, thinking about the delicious treasures he's about to dig into. Still in her spot, the lazy dog remains unperturbed. With her long snout, droopy jowls, and long black fur fluttering in the breeze, she is in a dreamland far away - where the mountains are made of beefy treats, the valleys are filled with tennis balls, and the puddles are just the right temperature. Why be in the rat race? It's a dog's life, after all.

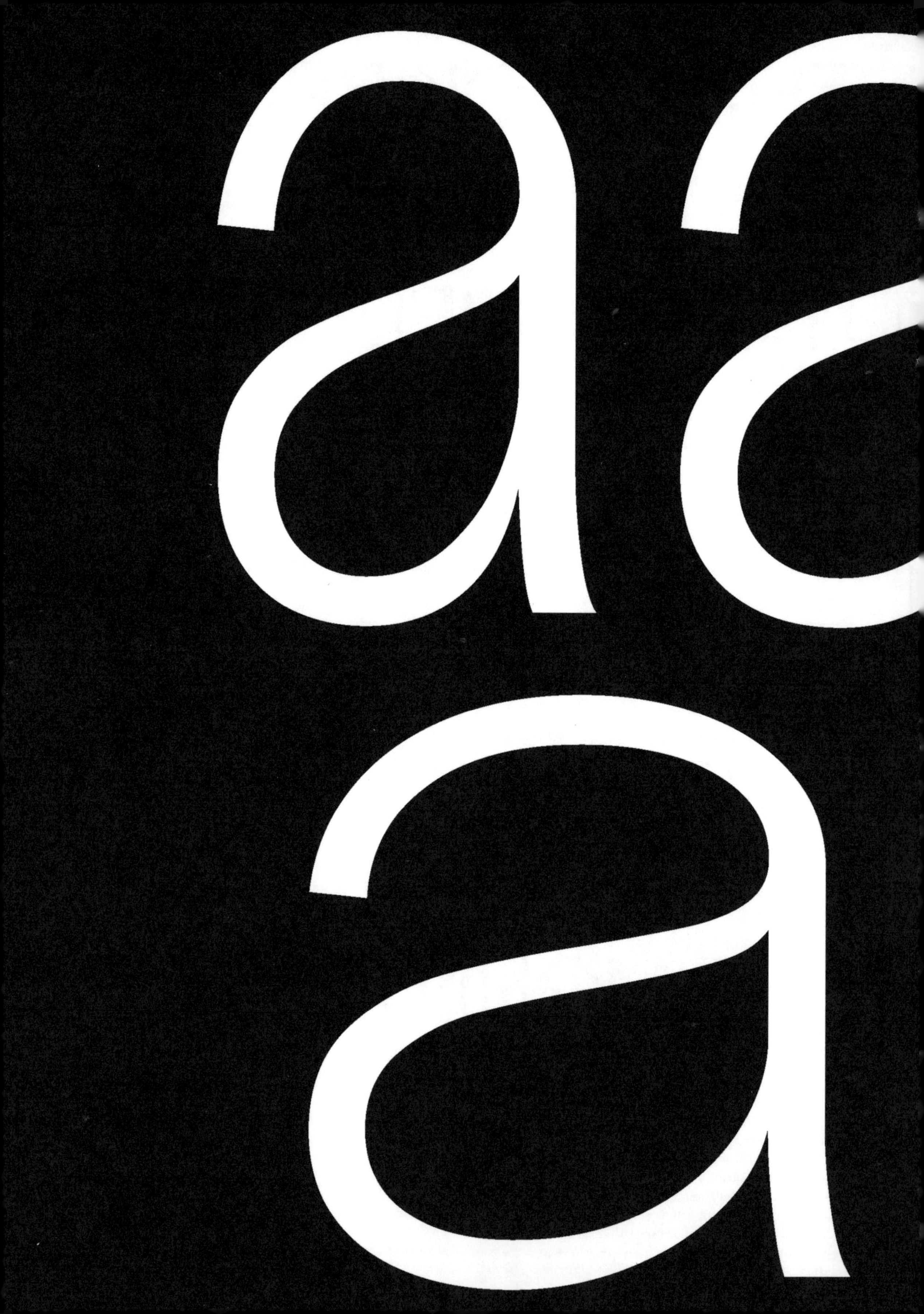

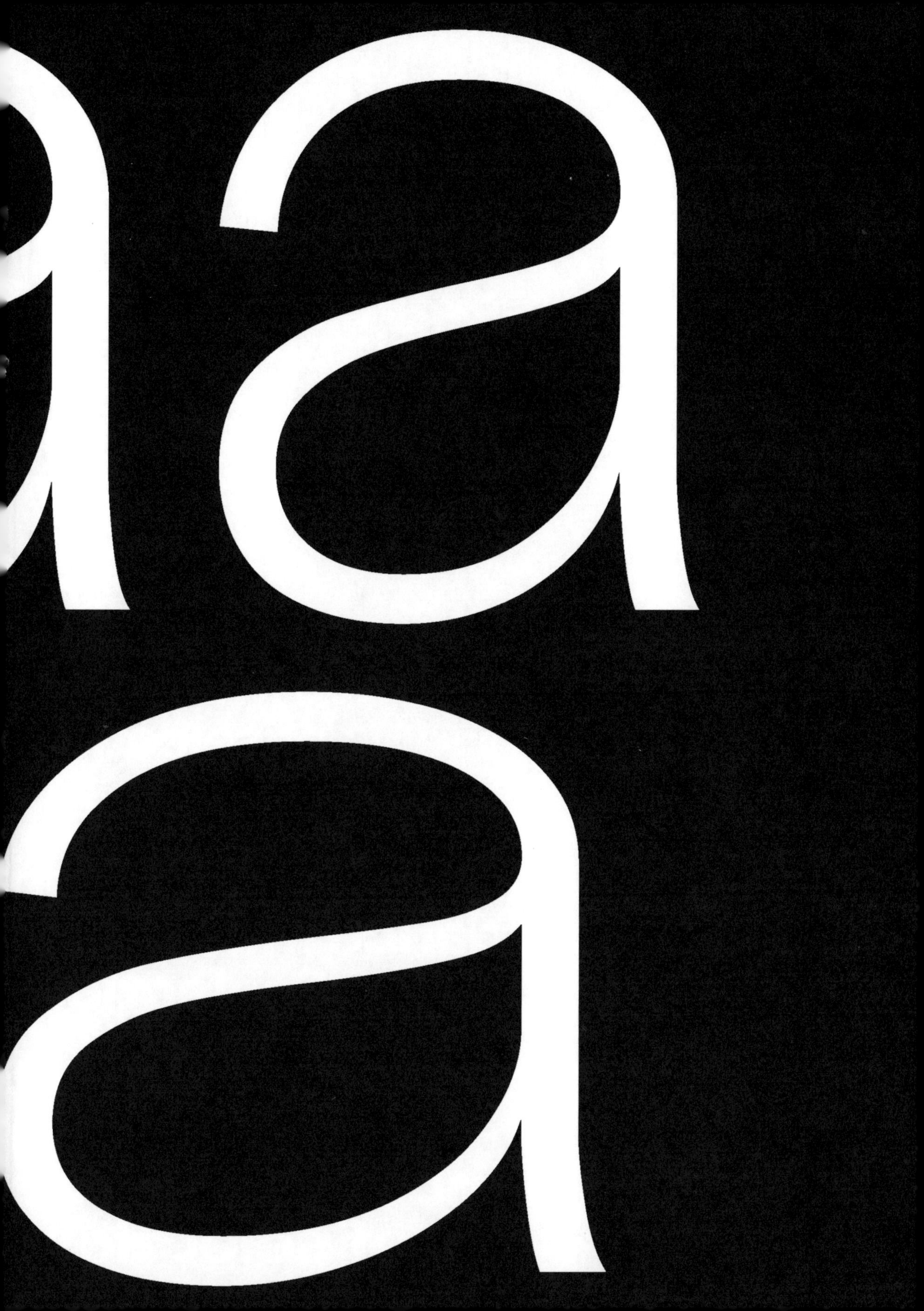

EROL
A 21st Cen
UK dance music grac
of selections

EROL
A 21st Cen
UK dance music grac
of selections

EROL
A 21st Cen
UK dance music grac
of selections

EROL
A 21st Cen
UK dance music grac
of selections

EROL
A 21st Cen
UK dance music grac
of selections

LKAN
ry titan of
NTS with two hours
very month.

LKAN
ry titan of
NTS with two hours
very month.

LKAN
ry titan of
NTS with two hours
every month.

LKAN
ry titan of
NTS with two hours
every month.

LKAN
ry titan of
NTS with two hours
every month.

TYPEFACE	:	GRIDULAR
DESIGNER	:	COTYPE FOUNDRY
LOCATION	:	LONDON, UK

		PUBLISHED BY	:	COTYPE FOUNDRY
		CHRONOLOGY	:	12TH TYPEFACE RELEASE
		RELEASED IN	:	2022

LINK	:	HTTPS://COTYPEFOUNDRY.COM/OUR-FONTS/GRIDULAR/
STYLES	:	1

GRIDULAR BEGAN AS AN EXPERIMENT BY MARK BLOOM, DRAWING INSPIRATION FROM WIM CROUWEL'S GRID-BASED TYPE DESIGNS, PARTICULARLY CROUWEL'S ARCHITYPE STEDELIJK TYPEFACE. ARCHITYPE STEDELIJK EMPLOYS A GRID OF INTERCONNECTED PIXELS WITH SLIGHTLY ROUNDED CORNERS AND CONNECTIONS. COTYPE'S GRIDULAR INTERPRETS THIS CONCEPT IN A MORE PLAYFUL MANNER, ACHIEVING A DYNAMIC BALANCE BETWEEN THE DECORATIVE AND THE FUNCTIONAL.

CAP HEIGHT

REGULAR — 290PT

X-HEIGHT

BASELINE

Gridular

THE QUICK BROWN

IT WOULD BE THE

ITS A LOVELY DAY

AND THE PUNGENT

PROMISE OF A SU

THINKING ABOUT

THE LAZY DOG RE

LONG BLACK FUR

THE MOUNTAINS A

AND THE PUDDLES

The quick brown fox jumps over a lazy dog. He didn't have to, but he thought
it would be the cheeky thing to do. After all, he had a reputation to maintain.
Its a lovely day in the neighbourhood, with the sun shining, the birds chirping,
and the pungent aroma of fresh rubbish bins wafting through the air - the
promise of a sumptuous meal. The sprightly fox rubs his paws together in glee,
thinking about the delicious treasures he's about to dig into. Still in her spot,
the lazy dog remains unperturbed. With her long snout, droopy jowls, and
long black fur fluttering in the breeze, she is in a dreamland far away - where
the mountains are made of beefy treats, the valleys are filled with tennis balls,
and the puddles are just the right temperature. Why be in the rat race?
Its a dogs life, after all.

Gridular —

RaBbCcDdEeF
KkLlMmMmNnO
UuVvWwWwXxY
0123456789

The International Typographic Style,
also known as the Swiss Style, is a
systemic approach to graphic design
that emerged in Switzerland during
the 1950s but continued to develop
internationally. It expanded on and
formalized the modernist typographic
innovations of the 20s that emerged
in part out of art movements such
as Suprematism and Constructivism
(Russia), De Stijl (The Netherlands)
and at the Bauhaus (Germany)

fF GgKHhIiJjj
oPpQqRrSsTtt
yZz.,;:!@¢£$%&()

stedelijk
museum
amsterdam
juni 87

tot 11/8
shinkichi tajiri
edelsmeden
frieda hunziker

tot 18/8
frieda hunziker
kitaj

tot 25/6
fotoprijs amersterdam 1976

tot 18/7
de wereld op papier

25/6 - 3/9
geld en glorie

TYPEFACE	:	HARBER
DESIGNER	:	BENOÎT BODHUIN
LOCATION	:	NANTES, FRANCE

PUBLISHED BY	:	BB-BUREAU
CHRONOLOGY	:	2023
RELEASED IN	:	2023

LINK	:	HTTPS://WWW.BB-BUREAU.FR
STYLES	:	THIN, LIGHT, REGULAR, MEDIUM, BOLD,
		BLACK + CUSTOM + A VARIABLE FONT

HARBER IS DESIGNED OF DOTS ON A GRID. ITS LETTERS ARE INVARIABLE, WHERE ONLY THE DOTS CHANGE, PARAMETERISED BY FIVE AXES: WEIGHT, SLANT, VOLUME, NOISE AND OPTICAL SIZE. THE NAME "HARBER" COMES FROM THE FIRST LETTERS DRAWN.

CAP HEIGHT

X-HEIGHT

REGULAR — 200PT

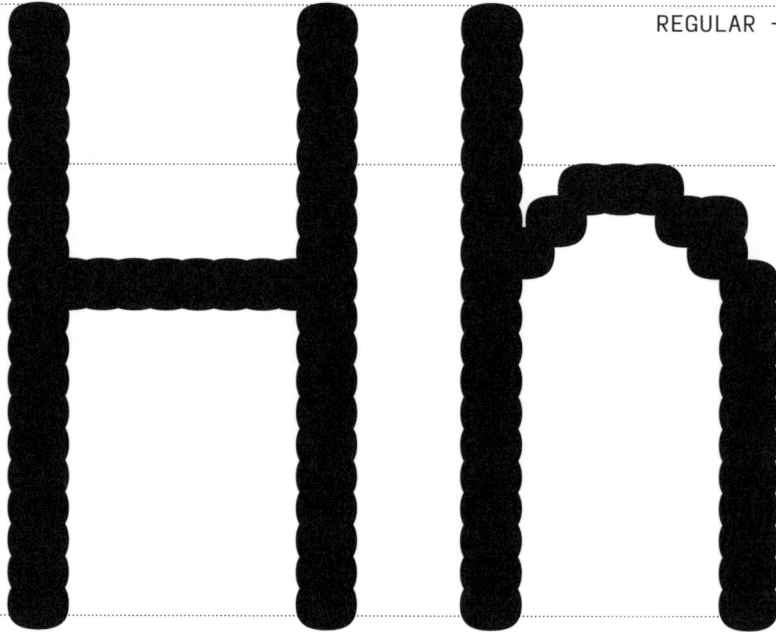

BASELINE

Harber

THE QUICK BR
IT WOULD BE
IT'S A LOVELY
AND THE PUN
PROMISE OF A
THINKING ABO
THE LAZY DOG
LONG BLACK F
THE MOUNTAIN
AND THE PUD
IT'S A DOG'S

@ § R s t

a. 132

17

TYPEFACE   :   INSITU
DESIGNER   :   EMMANUEL BESSE, LUCAS LE BIHAN
LOCATION   :   MARSEILLE, FRANCE

                 PUBLISHED BY   :   FORMAGARI
                 CHRONOLOGY   :   2017 - 2022
                 RELEASED IN   :   2022

LINK   :   HTTPS://FORMAGARI.COM/TYPEFACES/INSITU
STYLES   :   8 STYLES, 4 WEIGHTS: LIGHT, LIGHT ITALIC, REGULAR,
                 ITALIC, BOLD, BOLD ITALIC, BLACK, BLACK ITALIC

188

ORIGINALLY CREATED FOR THE ISELP ART INSTITUTE IN BRUSSELS AND FURTHER DEVELOPED FOR WEFRAC'S FRENCH REGIONAL CONTEMPORARY ART FUNDS OPEN DAYS EVENT, INSITU IS A NEO-GROTESQUE TYPEFACE CHARACTERISED BY TIGHT SPACING AND CONTRAST. DRAWING INSPIRATION FROM EARLY 20TH-CENTURY GOTHICS AND CLASSICS LIKE FOLIO, IT SERVES AS FORMAGARI'S INTERPRETATION OF A FRIENDLY AND ROBUST SANS-SERIF. INSITU IS TAILORED FOR THE SUCCINCT EXPRESSIONS OF CONCEPTUAL ART AND THE BOLD TITLES OF HEAVY MAGAZINES. WHILE IT EXCELS IN LARGE TYPE SETTINGS, IT MAINTAINS READABILITY AT SMALLER FONT SIZES AND INCLUDES ITALICS, ENSURING VERSATILITY ACROSS VARIOUS DESIGN SCENARIOS.

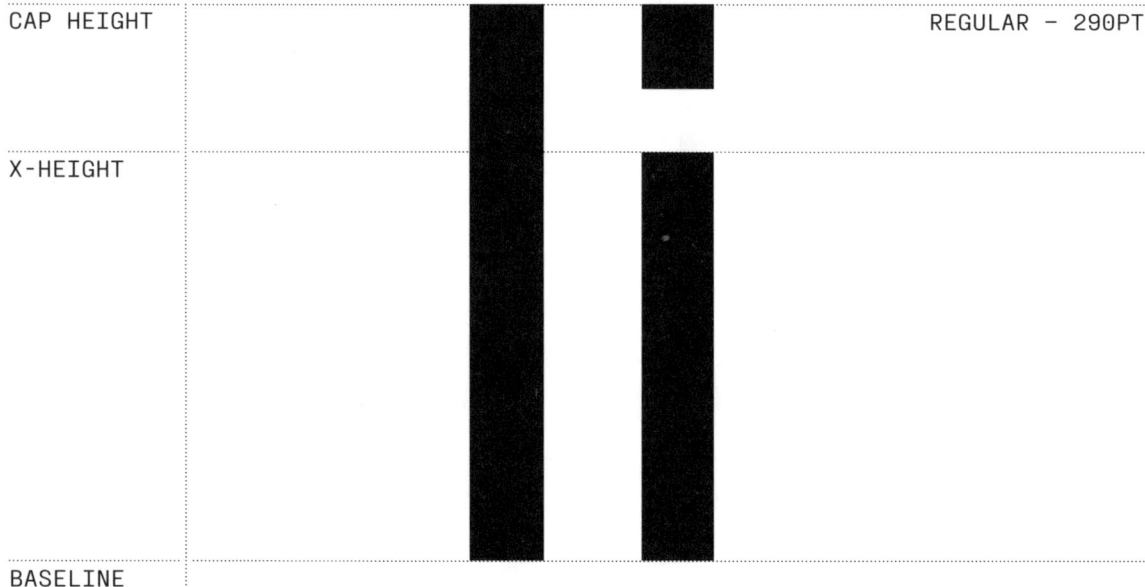

CAP HEIGHT   REGULAR — 290PT

X-HEIGHT

BASELINE

Insitu

THE QUICK BROWN FO

IT WOULD BE THE CHE

IT'S A LOVELY DAY IN

AND THE PUNGENT AF

PROMISE OF A SUMPT

THINKING ABOUT THE

THE LAZY DOG REMAI

LONG BLACK FUR FLU

The quick brown fox jumps over a lazy dog. He didn't have to, but he thought it would be the cheeky thing to do. After all, he had a reputation to maintain. It's a lovely day in the neighbourhood, with the sun shining, the birds chirping, and the pungent aroma of fresh rubbish bins wafting through the air - the promise of a sumptuous meal. The sprightly fox rubs his paws together in glee, thinking about the delicious treasures he's about to dig into. Still in her spot, the lazy dog remains unperturbed. With her long snout, droopy jowls, and long black fur fluttering in the breeze, she is in a dreamland far away - where the mountains are made of beefy treats, the valleys are filled with tennis balls, and the puddles are just the right temperature. Why be in the rat race? It's a dog's life, after all.

Catal
Raiso
Inven
1956-

ogue

onné:

taire

-1984

TYPEFACE	:	NB INTERNATIONAL™ PRO
DESIGNER	:	STEFAN GANDL
LOCATION	:	BERLIN, GERMANY

PUBLISHED BY	:	NEUBAU
CHRONOLOGY	:	2012 - 2014
RELEASED IN	:	2014

| LINK | : | HTTPS://NEUBAULADEN.COM/PRODUCT/NB-INTERNATIONAL-PRO/ |
| STYLES | : | 6 STYLES, 5 WEIGHTS: BOLD, BOLD ITALIC, MEDIUM, MEDIUM ITALIC, REGULAR, ITALIC, BOOK, BOOK ITALIC, LIGHT, LIGHT ITALIC, MONO |

NB INTERNATIONAL™ PAYS TRIBUTE TO THE POPULAR GROTESQUE TYPEFACES OF THE "INTERNATIONAL STYLE" ERA. IN REFERENCE TO TRADITIONAL LETTERPRESS PRINTING TECHNIQUES WITH A FOCUS ON DETAIL, EACH GLYPH FEATURES PRECISE FIVE-UNIT RADIUS CORNERS. THE RESULT IS A SOFT-EDGED, WARM CHARACTERISTIC THAT TRANSLATES BEAUTIFULLY BOTH IN PRINT AND ON SCREEN.

CAP HEIGHT   REGULAR — 290PT

X-HEIGHT

BASELINE

NBInternational™ Pro

THE QUICK BROWN

IT WOULD BE THE CH

IT'S A LOVELY DAY IN

AND THE PUNGENT

PROMISE OF A SUM

THINKING ABOUT TH

The quick brown fox jumps over a lazy dog. He didn't have to, but he thought it would be the cheeky thing to do. After all, he had a reputation to maintain. It's a lovely day in the neighbourhood, with the sun shining, the birds chirping, and the pungent aroma of fresh rubbish bins wafting through the air - the promise of a sumptuous meal. The sprightly fox rubs his paws together in glee, thinking about the delicious treasures he's about to dig into. Still in her spot, the lazy dog remains unperturbed. With her long snout, droopy jowls, and long black fur fluttering in the breeze, she is in a dreamland far away - where the mountains are made of beefy treats, the valleys are filled with tennis balls, and the puddles are just the right temperature. Why be in the rat race? It's a dog's life, after all.

The quick brown fox jumps over a lazy dog. He didn't have to, but he thought it would be the cheeky thing to do. After all, he had a reputation to maintain. It's a lovely day in the neighbourhood, with the sun shining, the birds chirping, and the pungent aroma of fresh rubbish bins wafting through the air - the promise of a sumptuous meal. The sprightly fox rubs his paws together in glee, thinking about the delicious treasures he's about to dig into. Still in her spot, the lazy dog remains unperturbed. With her long snout, droopy jowls, and long black fur fluttering in the breeze, she is in a dreamland far away - where the mountains are made of beefy treats, the valleys are filled with tennis balls, and the puddles are just the right temperature. Why be in the rat race? It's a dog's life, after all.

Neubau
Internation
Pro CG B¹ M

B^6 M^7 I^8 B^9

MMXXIV^E

Международа

Διεθνές^G

1	Bold	6	Bold Italic	11	Mono
2	Medium	7	Medium Italic	E	Edition
3	Regular	8	Italic	C	Cyrillic
4	Book	9	Book Italic	G	Greek
5	Light	10	Light Italic		

nal™

/I² R³ B⁴ L⁵

/_ 10 M¹¹

NB International® Pro CG Bold — NB International® Pro Bold

60
A view in to the f uture.

Σε μια από τις συνεντεύξεις με τον Neubau βρήκα την ομολογία ότι όλα ξεκίνησαν με τον Letraset. Όπως ίσως γνωρίζετε, το Letraset είναι ένα σύστημα μεταφοράς που περιέχει χαρακτήρες, σύμβολα ή εικόνες.

200

NB International® Pro Bold Italic — NB International® Pro Bold

60
For me Le traset has

flavour of the sixties, and brings back a lot of memories from this period, this enlightened decade with so much promises for a new society and better human understanding. The Paris student revolt,

200

NB International® Pro Regular — NB International® Pro Bold

30   The tragedy I faced while putting the publication together was that I had to compile columns of text in this typeface without having anything like a typesetter available. So, as an anachronism, I went to the Letraset company and had my typeface produced on a pile of transfer sheets that I could rub off on paper. Compared to the digital machinery it was a pre-historic way of doing.

24   In principle, it may elaborate on this theme, the Neubau work is pertinent for the 21st century. But why was it that, after my confrontation with their voluminous publications 'Neubau Modul' and 'Neubau Welt', my first reaction was: these are fundctin, they must be crazy! Catalogues of every thing, the whole tangible world on paper? I hardly understood this stupid task in compiling heavy volumes of systematically arranged patterns, illustrations and type. That can't be just modern Letraset.

200
'New Alpha bet'

NB International® Pro Italic — NB International® Pro Bold

30   While leafing through their books 'The whole earth catalogue' came to my mind. It was published for the first time in 1968, and became an immediate hit. Its purpose was to provide education and 'access to tools'; so a reader could 'find his own inspiration, shape his own environment, and share his adventure with whoever is interested.'

24   This publication used a broad definition of 'tools'. There were informative tools, such as books, maps, professional journals, courses, and classes. It also contained well-designed special-purpose utensils, including garden tools, carpenter's and masons' tools, welding equipment, chainsaws, fiberglass materials, tents, hiking shoes and potter's wheels. There were early synthesizers and personal computers.

59   Thus of a very well comparable with such chairs, constructions, and clean and smooth structures.

200
Hist oric re ferenc es.

NB International® Pro

48   Woodstock, and the first man on the moon. Our imagination was sky high! The Neubau boys were not yet born.

200
the Beatle s, hipp ies,

36
48   appeared in the printing industry. I remember well the first digital typesetting machines at the beginning of that decade.

200
Also the ear ly com puters

родный с

NB International® Pro

'CIA M', 'ISO TYPE'

48
The Neuba u idea.

These heavy orange books are first of all vertical columns of type, patterns and images, functioning as they say, like flash-backs.

200
typo graphi c syste m;

No. I lecture at the Yale University of Arts and therehas always a delight and fascination as they are referring to every kind of thing during several years.

W im Crouw el,

104 +

```
TYPEFACE     :    F37 JUDGE
DESIGNER     :    F37®
LOCATION     :    MANCHESTER, UK

                  PUBLISHED BY     :    F37®
                  CHRONOLOGY       :    2019 - 2023
                  RELEASED IN      :    2019

LINK         :    HTTPS://F37FOUNDRY.COM/FONTS/F37-JUDGE
STYLES       :    4 WEIGHTS, 4 WIDTHS WITH MATCHING OBLIQUES,
                  TOTALLING 32 STYLES
```

F37 JUDGE PAYS HOMAGE TO THE DEPENDABLE, UTILITARIAN FONT DIN AND DRAWS INSPIRATION FROM OLD WOOD-TYPE SPECIMEN BOOKS. THIS VERSATILE AND IMPACTFUL GEOMETRIC SANS-SERIF IS PARTICULARLY WELL-SUITED FOR XL SIZES, MAKING IT AN EXCELLENT CHOICE FOR HEADLINES THAT REQUIRE A STRONG VISUAL IMPACT, WHETHER FOR POSTERS OR EDITORIAL LAYOUTS.

CAP HEIGHT   REGULAR — 290PT

X-HEIGHT

Jj

BASELINE

F37 Judge

THE QUICK BROWN FOX JUMPS

IT WOULD BE THE CHEEKY THIN

IT'S A LOVELY DAY IN THE NEIGH

AND THE PUNGENT AROMA OF I

PROMISE OF A SUMPTUOUS ME

THINKING ABOUT THE DELICIOU

The quick brown fox jumps over a lazy dog. He didn't have to, but he thought it would be the cheeky thing to do. After all, he had a reputation to maintain. It's a lovely day in the neighbourhood, with the sun shining, the birds chirping, and the pungent aroma of fresh rubbish bins wafting through the air - the promise of a sumptuous meal. The sprightly fox rubs his paws together in glee, thinking about the delicious treasures he's about to dig into. Still in her spot, the lazy dog remains unperturbed. With her long snout, droopy jowls, and long black fur fluttering in the breeze, she is in a dreamland far away - where the mountains are made of beefy treats, the valleys are filled with tennis balls, and the puddles are just the right temperature. Why be in the rat race? It's a dog's life, after all.

The quick brown fox jumps over a lazy dog. He didn't have to, but he thought it would be the cheeky thing to do. After all, he had a reputation to maintain. It's a lovely day in the neighbourhood, with the sun shining, the birds chirping, and the pungent aroma of fresh rubbish bins wafting through the air - the promise of a sumptuous meal. The sprightly fox rubs his paws together in glee, thinking about the delicious treasures he's about to dig into. Still in her spot, the lazy dog remains unperturbed. With her long snout, droopy jowls, and long black fur fluttering in the breeze, she is in a dreamland far away - where the mountains are made of beefy treats, the valleys are filled with tennis balls, and the puddles are just the right temperature. Why be in the rat race? It's a dog's life, after all.

JUD

COMPRESSED

JUDGE *JU*

CONDENSED

JUDGE *JUDGE* **JUD**

REGULAR

JUDGE *JUDGE* **JUDGE** *JUD*

EXTENDED

DGE

JUDGE *JUDGE* JUDGE *JUDGE* **JUDGE** *JUDGE* **JUDGE** *JUDGE*

GE JUDGE *JUDGE* **JUDGE** *JUDGE* **JUDGE** *JUDGE*

E JUDGE JUDGE *JUDGE* JUDGE *JUDGE*

GE **JUDGE** *JUDGE* **JUDGE** *JUDGE*

TYPEFACE	:	F37 K9
DESIGNER	:	F37®
LOCATION	:	MANCHESTER, UK

PUBLISHED BY	:	F37®
CHRONOLOGY	:	2023
RELEASED IN	:	2023

| LINK | : | HTTPS://F37FOUNDRY.COM/FONTS/F37-K9 |
| STYLES | : | 4 WEIGHTS WITH A MATCHING UPRIGHT ITALIC, TOTALLING 8 STYLES |

F37 K9 SANS IS PART OF THE BROADER K9 COLLECTION. THE FAMILY'S FOUNDATIONAL CONSTRUCTION DRAWS INSPIRATION FROM CLARENDON-STYLE BRACKETED SLAB SERIFS COMMONLY FOUND IN WOOD-TYPE AND BILL POSTERS FROM THE LATE 19TH CENTURY. RATHER THAN A SPECIFIC REVIVAL, F37 K9 IS A BROAD HOMAGE TO THE GENRE. THE FONT FAMILY PACK INCLUDES SIX SUB-FAMILIES, EACH CHARACTERISED BY ITS DISTINCT PERSONALITY, FEATURING FOUR WEIGHTS AND A LIVELY UPRIGHT ITALIC STYLE TO COMPLEMENT THE COLLECTION.

CAP HEIGHT

X-HEIGHT

REGULAR — 290PT

BASELINE

F37 K9

THE QUICK BROWN FOX JUMPS OV

IT WOULD BE THE CHEEKY THING T

ITS A LOVELY DAY IN THE NEIGHBO

AND THE PUNGENT AROMA OF FRE

PROMISE OF A SUMPTUOUS MEAL.

THINKING ABOUT THE DELICIOUS T

THE LAZY DOG REMAINS UNPERTU

LONG BLACK FUR FLUTTERING IN T

THE MOUNTAINS ARE MADE OF BEE

The quick brown fox jumps over a lazy dog. He didnt have to, but he thought it would be the cheeky thing to do. After all, he had a reputation to maintain. Its a lovely day in the neighbourhood, with the sun shining, the birds chirping, and the pungent aroma of fresh rubbish bins wafting through the air the promise of a sumptuous meal. The sprightly fox rubs his paws together in glee, thinking about the delicious treasures hes about to dig into. Still in her spot, the lazy dog remains unperturbed. With her long snout, droopy jowls, and long black fur fluttering in the breeze, she is in a dreamland far away where the mountains are made of beefy treats, the valleys are filled with tennis balls, and the puddles are just the right temperature. Why be in the rat race Its a dogs life, after all.

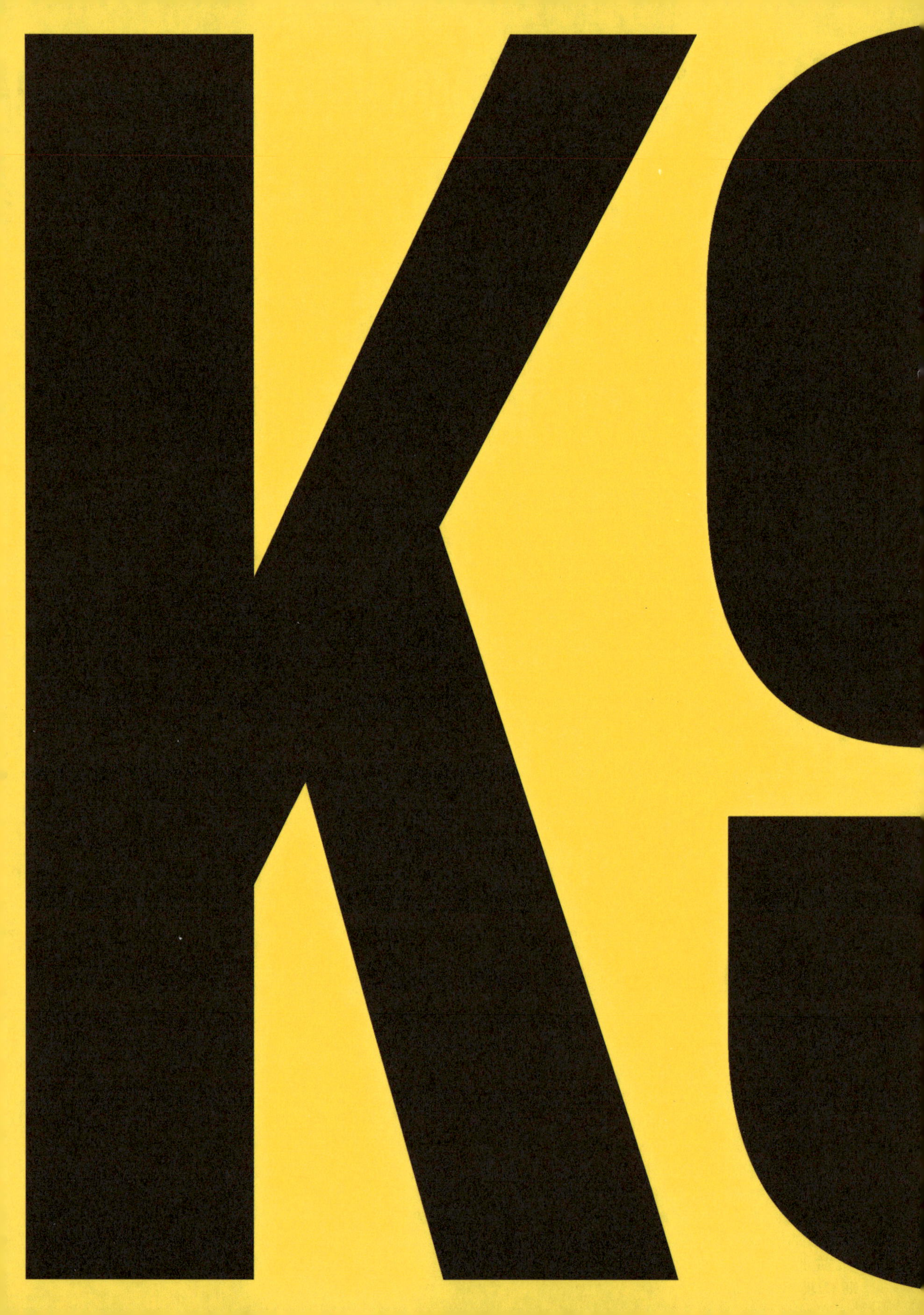
K

9 SANS

Light	**Walkies**
Light Italic	*Treats*
Regular	**Bones**
Regular Italic	*Tickles*
Medium	**Lead**
Medium Italic	*Paws*
Bold	**Zoom**
Bold Italic	***Cuddles***

TYPEFACE	:	KOBE
DESIGNER	:	VIOLAINE & JÉRÉMY
LOCATION	:	PARIS, FRANCE

		PUBLISHED BY	:	VIOLAINE & JÉRÉMY
		CHRONOLOGY	:	N/A
		RELEASED IN	:	2018, 2021

| LINK | : | HTTPS://VJ-TYPE.COM/9-KOBE |
| STYLES | : | BLACK, BOLD, REGULAR, BLACK OBLIQUE, BOLD OBLIQUE, REGULAR OBLIQUE |

KOBE, INITIALLY RELEASED IN 2018 AS A ONE-WEIGHT FONT, QUICKLY BECAME A STUDIO FAVOURITE DUE TO ITS VERSATILE AND WELL-PROPORTIONED MODULAR STRUCTURE. IT SEAMLESSLY BLENDS INTO BOTH TEXT AND DISPLAY APPLICATIONS WITH PLAYFUL TERMINALS AND ALTERNATES. THE FONT, DEFINED BY ITS TIMELESS APPEAL, HAS UNDERGONE A SUBTLE MAKEOVER, INTRODUCING FIVE ADDITIONAL WEIGHTS SUITABLE FOR TEXT. INSPIRED BY JAPANESE WRITING SHAPES, KOBE'S NUMEROUS LIGATURES AND STYLISTIC SETS CONTRIBUTE TO ITS DISTINCT CHARACTER. THE DARING SLANT OF ITS OBLIQUE SHOWCASES THE STUDIO'S UNCONVENTIONAL APPROACH TO FONT DESIGN.

CAP HEIGHT   REGULAR — 290PT

X-HEIGHT

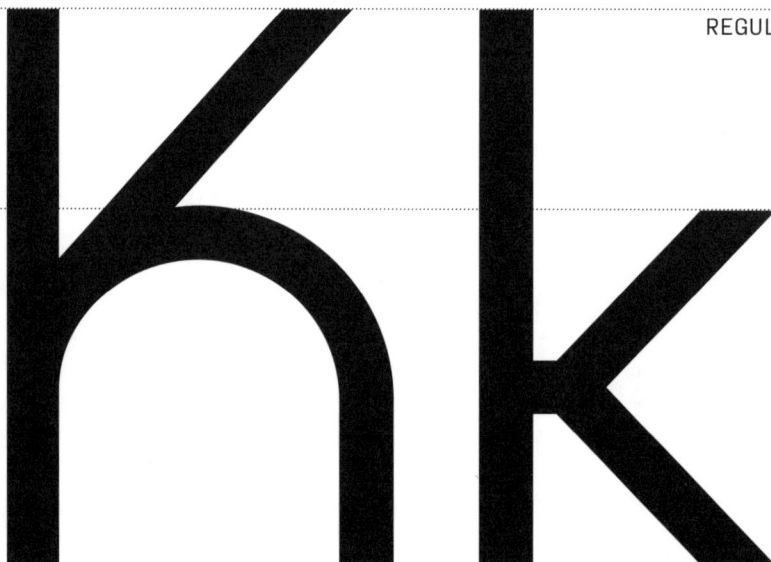

BASELINE

Kobe

THE QUICK BROW

IT WOULD BE THE

IT'S A LOVELY DAY

AND THE PUNGENT

PROMISE OF A SU

THINKING ABOUT

THE LAZY DOG RE

LONG BLACK FUR

THE MOUNTAINS A

Shibuya   Tokyo

k
style 2

Y
style 2

Kobe

Shintaro
Sakamoto

The
feeling of
love

You can
be a Ro

Let's
Dance Raw

Volta
e Meia

Herman

Melvi

TYPEFACE   :   F37 KOOKIE
DESIGNER   :   F37®
LOCATION   :   MANCHESTER, UK

             PUBLISHED BY   :   F37®
             CHRONOLOGY   :   2022
             RELEASED IN   :   2022

LINK   :   HTTPS://F37FOUNDRY.COM/FONTS/F37-KOOKIE
STYLES   :   6 WEIGHTS WITH MATCHING OBLIQUES, TOTALLING 12 STYLES

F37 KOOKIE BOASTS A NOTABLY TALL X-HEIGHT AND SHOWCASES UNIQUE VARIATIONS IN CHARACTERS SUCH AS "A", "G", "K", AND "Y". THE DIAGONAL LETTERS, INCLUDING VV, WW, AND XX, FEATURE A SUBTLE CURVATURE, ENHANCING ITS SOFT AND BOUNCY AURA. INSPIRED BY ORIGINAL LETTERING FROM LOGO EXPERT ROB CLARKE, F37 KOOKIE IS ENVISIONED FOR APPLICATIONS LIKE PICK-ME-UP PACKAGING AND IS PARTICULARLY SUITED FOR SPONGY CAKES AND CRUMBLY TREATS.

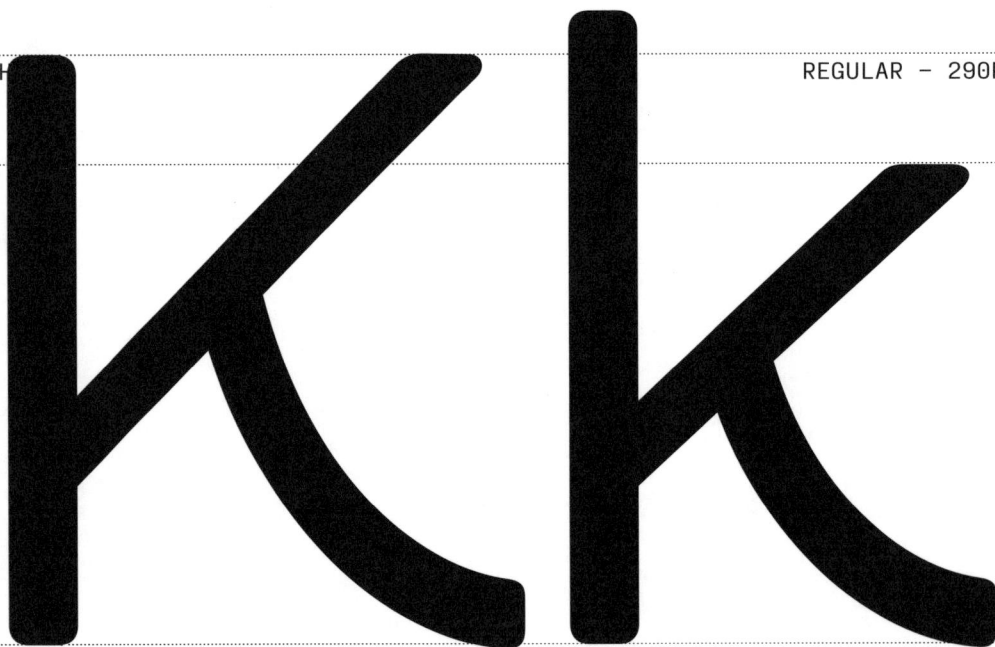

CAP HEIGHT

REGULAR — 290PT

X-HEIGHT

BASELINE

F37 Kookie

THE QUICK BR

IT WOULD BE

ITS A LOVELY

AND THE PUN

PROMISE OF A

THINKING ABC

THE LAZY DO

LONG BLACK

THE MOUNTA

Regular

Gomez,

Medium

Wednesda

SemiBold

Fester, Gr

Bold

Lurch, A

UltraBold

Cousin It

Black

The Adar

Morticia,

y, Pugsley,

ndmama,

ristotle,

, & Thing.

ns Family

```
TYPEFACE      :   MACAN & MACAN STENCIL
DESIGNER      :   TIGHTYPE
LOCATION      :   GERMANY

                  PUBLISHED BY    :    TIGHTYPE
                  CHRONOLOGY      :    N/A
                  RELEASED IN     :    2023

LINK          :   HTTPS://TIGHTYPE.COM/TYPEFACES/MACAN
STYLES        :   THIN, EXTRALIGHT, LIGHT, REGULAR, BOOK, MEDIUM,
                  SEMIBOLD, BOLD, EXTRABOLD + ITALICS
CREDITS       :   LÉON HUGUES, VASSILIS GEORGIOU (GREEK), JOVANA JOCIC
                  (CYRILIC), DONNY TRUONG (VIETNAMESE)
```

MACAN DRAWS INSPIRATION FROM THE GROTESQUE GENRE OF THE LAST CENTURY, THE INDUSTRIAL AESTHETICS OF STENCIL TYPEFACES, AND THE CAPTIVATING QUALITIES OF 90'S RAVE FLYERS, REMIXING THEM INTO A VERSATILE NEO-GROTESQUE TYPE FAMILY. IN ADDITION TO MACAN'S STANDARD VERSION, ITS STENCIL COMPANION IS A FUSION OF FUNCTIONALITY AND ORNAMENTATION. IT CREATIVELY TRANSLATES THE FUNCTIONAL ASPECTS OF STENCILS, SUCH AS CONNECTORS OR "BRIDGES", INTO AESTHETIC FEATURES THAT ARE BOTH ROUNDED AND STRAIGHT, FUNCTIONAL AND ORNAMENTAL, SEVERE AND QUIRKY. MACAN AND MACAN STENCIL WERE DEVELOPED IN HARMONY, INFLUENCING EACH OTHER'S CHARACTER SHAPES, RHYTHM, AND PROPORTIONS.

CAP HE   REGULAR — 270PT

X-HEIG

Mm

BASELINE

Macan & Macan Stencil

THE QUICK BR

IT WOULD BE

IT'S A LOVELY

AND THE PUN

PROMISE OF A

THINKING ABC

THE LAZY DOC

The quick brown fox jumps over a lazy dog. He didn't have to, but he thought it would be the cheeky thing to do. After all, he had a reputation to maintain. It's a lovely day in the neighbourhood, with the sun shining, the birds chirping, and the pungent aroma of fresh rubbish bins wafting through the air - the promise of a sumptuous meal. The sprightly fox rubs his paws together in glee, thinking about the delicious treasures he's about to dig into. Still in her spot, the lazy dog remains unperturbed. With her long snout, droopy jowls, and long black fur fluttering in the breeze, she is in a dreamland far away - where the mountains are made of beefy treats, the valleys are filled with tennis balls, and the puddles are just the right temperature. Why be in the rat race? It's a dog's life, after all.

XTAL
Original
Mix

Aphex
Twin
R&S
Records

7:53
114
BPM

TYPEFACE	:	MAGNET
DESIGNER	:	INGA PLÖNNIGS
LOCATION	:	BERLIN, GERMANY

218

PUBLISHED BY	:	FRERE-JONES TYPE
CHRONOLOGY	:	2021
RELEASED IN	:	2021

LINK	:	HTTPS://FREREJONES.COM/FAMILIES/MAGNET
STYLES	:	STANDARD: LIGHT, LIGHT ITALIC, REGULAR, REGULAR ITALIC,
		MEDIUM, MEDUM ITALIC, BOLD, BOLD ITALIC, BLACK,
		BLACK ITALIC
		HEADLINE: UPRIGHT, SLANTED, BACKSLANTED

MAGNET, A DYNAMIC SANS-SERIF FAMILY DESIGNED BY INGA PLÖNNIGS, FEATURES AN UNCONVENTIONAL FAMILY STRUCTURE, COMBINING AN EXTRA-COMPRESSED HEADLINE AND A VERSATILE STANDARD VARIANT WITHIN THE SAME NAME. MAGNET HEADLINE PRODUCES A DAZZLING PATTERN WITH TIGHTLY PACKED SHAPES, INTENSIFIED IN THE SLANTED AND BACKSLANTED STYLES. ON THE OTHER HAND, MAGNET STANDARD SERVES AS THE QUIETER SIBLING, BOASTING DEEPLY CUT NOTCHES AND UNIQUE WEIGHT TRANSITIONS. ITS BOXY CURVES EXCEL IN DENSE SETTINGS AND TIGHT LINE SPACING. PLÖNNIGS' YEARS OF EXPERIMENTATION WITH RIGID PATTERNS AND ORGANIC DETAILS RESULT IN A FAMILY THAT IS BOTH SURPRISING AND RELIABLE.

CAP

REGULAR — 250PT

X-

Mm

BASELINE

Magnet

THE QUICK BROWN FOX J
IT WOULD BE THE CHEEK
IT'S A LOVELY DAY IN THE
AND THE PUNGENT AROM
PROMISE OF A SUMPTUO
THINKING ABOUT THE DE
THE LAZY DOG REMAINS
LONG BLACK FUR FLUTTE
THE MOUNTAINS ARE MA
AND THE PUDDLES ARE J

The quick brown fox jumps over a lazy dog. He didn't have to, but he tho
it would be the cheeky thing to do. After all, he had a reputation to main
It's a lovely day in the neighbourhood, with the sun shining, the birds ch
and the pungent aroma of fresh rubbish bins wafting through the air - th
promise of a sumptuous meal. The sprightly fox rubs his paws together
thinking about the delicious treasures he's about to dig into. Still in her s
the lazy dog remains unperturbed. With her long snout, droopy jowls, an
long black fur fluttering in the breeze, she is in a dreamland far away - w
the mountains are made of beefy treats, the valleys are filled with tenni
and the puddles are just the right temperature. Why be in the rat race?
It's a dog's life, after all.

Magnets don't need power
Magnets don't need power
Magnets don't need power
Magnets don't need power
Magnets don't need power
Magnets don't need power
Magnets don't need power
Magnets don't need power
Magnets don't need power
Magnets don't need power
MAGNETS DON'T NEED POWER
MAGNETS DON'T NEED POWER
MAGNETS DON'T NEED POWER
MAGNETS DON'T NEED POWER
MAGNETS DON'T NEED POWER
MAGNETS DON'T NEED POWER
MAGNETS DON'T NEED POWER
MAGNETS DON'T NEED POWER
MAGNETS DON'T NEED POWER
MAGNETS DON'T NEED POWER

MAGNETS DON
MAGNETS DON
MAGNETS DON
T NEED POWER
T NEED POWER
T NEED POWER

T NEED POWER

T NEED POWER

T NEED POWER

MAGNETS DON

MAGNETS DON

MAGNETS DON

TYPEFACE	:	MANUAL GROTESK A
DESIGNER	:	SETUP TYPE
LOCATION	:	BRATISLAVA, SLOVAKIA

PUBLISHED BY	:	SETUP TYPE
CHRONOLOGY	:	2018
RELEASED IN	:	2018

LINK	:	HTTPS://WWW.SETUPTYPE.COM/FONTS/MANUAL-GROTESK-A
STYLES	:	1, 2, 3, 4, 5, 6

MANUAL GROTESK A IS A DIGITISED VERSION OF THE CLASSIC STREET PLATE TYPEFACE OF SLOVAKIA. IT FAITHFULLY REPRODUCES RICHARD PÍPAL'S ORIGINAL MODEL FOR A MANUALLY CONSTRUCTED TYPEFACE FROM THE MID-20TH CENTURY, WITH MINIMAL DIVERGENCES. THIS ICONIC TYPEFACE, PREVALENT DURING THE SOCIALIST ERA, IS NOW GRADUALLY DECLINING IN USAGE. THE DIGITISATION OF MANUAL GROTESK A SERVES THE PURPOSE OF PRESERVING AND REINTRODUCING THIS TYPEFACE FOR NEW CONTEXTS.

CAP HEIGHT

4 — 290PT

X-HEIGHT

Mm

BASELINE

Manual Grotesk A

THE QUICK BROWN FOX JU

IT WOULD BE THE CHEEKY

IT'S A LOVELY DAY IN THE M

AND THE PUNGENT AROMA

PROMISE OF A SUMPTUOUS

THINKING ABOUT THE DELIC

THE LAZY DOG REMAINS UN

LONG BLACK FUR FLUTTERI

THE MOUNTAINS ARE MADE

AND THE PUDDLES ARE JU

HVIEZDOSLAVOVO NÁMESTIE I

KRÁĽOVSKÁ CESTA

NÁBREŽIE ĽUBOMÍRA KADNÁRA

MÄSIARSKA
ULICA

NÁMESTIE
SLOVENSKÉHO NÁRODNÉHO POVSTANIA
IV

ČIPKÁRSKA
ULICA
II

```
TYPEFACE    :    MAXEVILLE
DESIGNER    :    SM FOUNDRY
LOCATION    :    APELDOORN, THE NETHERLANDS

                 PUBLISHED BY      :    SM FOUNDRY
                 CHRONOLOGY        :    N/A
                 RELEASED IN       :    2017

LINK        :    HTTPS://S-M.NU/TYPEFACES/MAXEVILLE
STYLES      :    MAXEVILLE TEKST: REGULAR, BOLD, CONSTRUCT, BOLD
                 CONSTRUCT + ITALICS
                 MAXEVILLE MONO: REGULAR, CONSTRUCT, BOLD, BOLD
                 CONSTRUCT
```

MAXEVILLE IS A NEO-GROTESQUE TYPEFACE WITH GEOMETRIC PROPERTIES, DRAWING INSPIRATION FROM THE VISUAL LANGUAGE ASSOCIATED WITH ART AND DESIGN MOVEMENTS FROM THE EARLY 20TH CENTURY, INCLUDING DE STIJL IN THE NETHERLANDS AND UNION DES ARTISTES MODERNES IN FRANCE. IT FOCUSES ON THE WORKS OF GERRIT RIETVELD AND JEAN PROUVÉ.

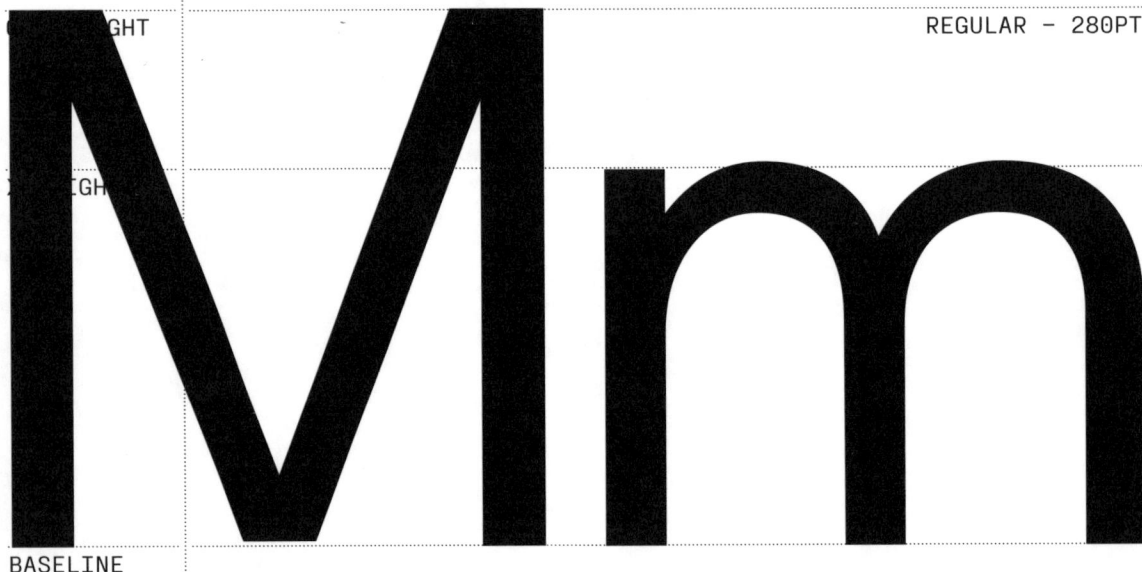

GHT

REGULAR — 280PT

GH

Mm

BASELINE

Maxeville

THE QUICK BROWN FOX JU

IT WOULD BE THE CHEEKY

IT'S A LOVELY DAY IN THE N

AND THE PUNGENT AROM

PROMISE OF A SUMPTUOL

THINKING ABOUT THE DEL

THE LAZY DOG REMAINS L

LONG BLACK FUR FLUTTEI

THE MOUNTAINS ARE MAD

AND THE PUDDLES ARE JL

The quick brown fox jumps over a lazy dog. He didn't h
it would be the cheeky thing to do. After all, he had a re
It's a lovely day in the neighbourhood, with the sun shin
and the pungent aroma of fresh rubbish bins wafting th
promise of a sumptuous meal. The sprightly fox rubs hi
thinking about the delicious treasures he's about to dig
the lazy dog remains unperturbed. With her long snout,
long black fur fluttering in the breeze, she is in a dream

14 pt	International Monument Foundatic
24 pt	Olympic Metabolism
34 pt	Rational Thought
44 pt	Offices For TI
54 pt	Wealth Refle
64 pt	Futurist Ins
74 pt	Artificial M
84 pt	Globalize
94 pt	Villager A

Structuralist Bureau Retrospective

xpression After Jazz

s Utilize Formats

e Generation

cts Phrases

titute Tasks

Manifesting

Objective

ssociates

TYPEFACE	:	MONOPOL
DESIGNER	:	NGUYEN GOBBER
LOCATION	:	VIENNA, AUSTRIA

PUBLISHED BY	:	NGUYEN GOBBER
CHRONOLOGY	:	2019
RELEASED IN	:	2020

LINK	:	HTTPS://NGUYENGOBBER.COM/TYPEFACES/MONOPOL
STYLES	:	REGULAR, THIN, KOMPAKT

MONOPOL IS A ROBUST DISPLAY TYPEFACE DESIGNED FOR IMPACTFUL HEADLINES, WORDMARKS, AND POSTER DESIGNS. WITH ITS UPPERCASE-ONLY STYLE, IT CONVEYS A BOLD AND ASSERTIVE TONE, IDEAL FOR DELIVERING STRONG MESSAGES. THE TYPEFACE FEATURES TWO RENDITIONS OF CHARACTERS WITH SHARP ANGLES LIKE "A", "M", "N", "V", AND "W" — ONE WITH EXPLICIT ANGULAR ELEMENTS FOR A MODULAR LOOK AND ANOTHER WITH A MORE SUBDUED APPEARANCE. THE "S" AND VARIOUS NUMERALS EVOKE A NOSTALGIC FEEL REMINISCENT OF 1980'S WORDMARKS.

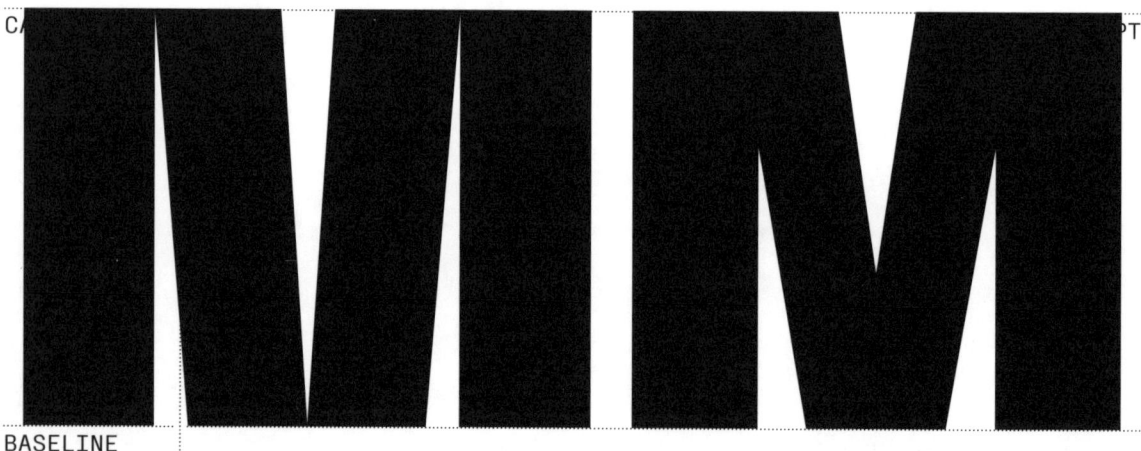

CA ... PT

MM

BASELINE

MONOPOL

THE QUICK BR

IT WOULD BE

IT'S A LOVELY

AND THE PUM

PROMISE OF

THINKING ABC

THE LAZY DOC

LONG BLACK

THE MOUNTA

€ 230,5

NEON' C

CASES

{ZOO} N

»ASTE

REDUC

50 Q&A Λ

COLORS

2×3=6

MONO!?

ROID«

E ↓ 35%

RAZ

SHI

KNI

ZOR
IRP
IFE

TYPEFACE	:	ABC MONUMENT GROTESK
DESIGNER	:	DINAMO & KASPER-FLORIO
LOCATION	:	BERLIN, GERMANY

		PUBLISHED BY	:	DINAMO
		CHRONOLOGY	:	N/A
		RELEASED IN	:	2018

LINK	:	HTTPS://ABCDINAMO.COM/TYPEFACES/MONUMENT-GROTESK
STYLES	:	44 STYLES, 3 FAMILIES
CREDITS	:	LARISSA KASPER & ROSARIO FLORIO/KASPER-FLORIO, ROBERT JANES & FABIOLA MEJÍA/DINAMO (DESIGN), ROBERT JANES/ DINAMO & CHI-LONG TRIEU (PRODUCTION)

ABC MONUMENT GROTESK, BORN FROM CONTOURS DISCOVERED BY SWISS DESIGN STUDIO KASPER-FLORIO IN PALMER & REY'S 1884 SPECIMEN BOOK, FEATURES LETTERFORMS WITH A COMPACT SKELETON, HIGH VERTICAL CONTRAST, AND SHARP END STROKES. DIGITISED BY KASPER-FLORIO FOR CONTEMPORARY USE, THE FONT HAS BECOME THEIR HOUSE TYPEFACE AND HAS BEEN AVAILABLE TO THE PUBLIC THROUGH DINAMO SINCE 2018. ABC MONUMENT GROTESK IS A CONFIDENTLY DISTINCTIVE FONT, CHARACTERISED BY HONEST, UNREFINED, AND IDIOSYNCRATIC SHAPES, PROVIDING A RAW AND PLEASINGLY UNPOLISHED AESTHETIC.

CAP HEIGHT   REGULAR — 270PT

X-HEIGHT

Mm

BASELINE

ABCMonument Grotesk

THE QUICK BROWN FOX
IT WOULD BE THE CHEE
IT'S A LOVELY DAY IN TH
AND THE PUNGENT ARC
PROMISE OF A SUMPTU
THINKING ABOUT THE D

The quick brown fox jumps over a lazy dog. He didn't have to, b
it would be the cheeky thing to do. After all, he had a reputation
It's a lovely day in the neighbourhood, with the sun shining, the
and the pungent aroma of fresh rubbish bins wafting through t
promise of a sumptuous meal. The sprightly fox rubs his paws t
thinking about the delicious treasures he's about to dig into. Sti
the lazy dog remains unperturbed. With her long snout, droopy
long black fur fluttering in the breeze, she is in a dreamland far
the mountains are made of beefy treats, the valleys are filled wi
and the puddles are just the right temperature. Why be in the ra
It's a dog's life, after all.

The quick brown fox jumps over a lazy dog. He didn't have to, but he thought
it would be the cheeky thing to do. After all, he had a reputation to maintain.
It's a lovely day in the neighbourhood, with the sun shining, the birds chirping, and the pungent aroma of fresh rubbish bins wafting through the air
- the promise of a sumptuous meal. The sprightly fox rubs his paws together
in glee, thinking about the delicious treasures he's about to dig into. Still in
her spot, the lazy dog remains unperturbed. With her long snout, droopy
jowls, and long black fur fluttering in the breeze, she is in a dreamland far
away - where the mountains are made of beefy treats, the valleys are filled
with tennis balls, and the puddles are just the right temperature. Why be in
the rat race? It's a dog's life, after all.

ABC MONUMENT GROTESK OWES ITS POINT DE DÉPART TO A FEW INTRIGUING CONTOURS THAT THE SWISS DESIGN STUDIO KASPER-FLORIO STUMBLED ACROSS IN AN ONLINE SCAN OF THE FOUNDRY PALMER & REY'S 1884 NEW SPECIMEN BOOK. COMPELLED BY THE LETTERFORMS' COMPACT SKELETON, HIGH VERTICAL CONTRAST, AND SURPRISINGLY SHARP END STROKES, KASPER-FLORIO DIGITIZED AND REINTERPRETED THE TYPEFACE FOR CONTEMPORARY USE. EVER SINCE, THE DESIGN HAS SERVED AS THE STUDIO'S HOUSE TYPEFACE, AND IT'S BEEN AVAILABLE TO THE PUBLIC VIA DINAMO SINCE 2018. FEATURING HONEST, UNREFINED, AND IDIOSYNCRATIC SHAPES, ABC MONUMENT GROTESK IS A DISTINCTIVELY CONFIDENT FONT WITH A RAW AND PLEASINGLY UNPOLISHED FEEL. IT'S AVAILABLE IN SEVEN DIFFERENT WEIGHTS, INCLUDING ITALIC, MONO, AND SEMI-MONO CUTS, AS WELL AS HEAVY AND BLACK WITH CORRESPONDING ITALICS.

B

MONUMENT GROTESK

DINAMO TYPEFACE

P

TYPEFACE	:	MORI
DESIGNER	:	CAIO KONDO
LOCATION	:	MONTREAL, CANADA
PUBLISHED BY	:	PANGRAM PANGRAM® FOUNDRY
CHRONOLOGY	:	N/A
RELEASED IN	:	2022
LINK	:	HTTPS://PANGRAMPANGRAM.COM/PRODUCTS/MORI
STYLES	:	16

MORI IS A GOTHIC SANS SERIF FONT INFLUENCED BY CONTEMPORARY JAPANESE DESIGN — IDEAL FOR EDITORIALS, GRAPHIC DESIGN, AND BRANDING. IT OFFERS 16 STYLES FROM EXTRALIGHT TO EXTRABOLD, FEATURING 597 GLYPHS AND VARIOUS OPENTYPE FEATURES, INCLUDING CIRCLED AND SQUARED NUMBERS, SUBSCRIPT AND SUPERSCRIPT NUMBERS, SYMBOLS, AND ALTERNATES. THE FONT STANDS OUT WITH ITS UNIQUE SHAPES AND CURVES, SUCH AS THE GEOMETRIC "R" AND DOUBLE-STORY "G". ITS OTHER NOTABLE FEATURES INCLUDE THE DISTINCTIVE "G", NUMBER "6", AND NUMBER "9". WHILE MORI'S PERSONALITY SHINES THROUGH IN ITS EXAGGERATED DIACRITICS AND PUNCTUATIONS, IT ALSO COMBINES FUNCTIONALITY WITH DISTINCTIVE DESIGN ELEMENTS, PROVIDING THE BEST OF BOTH WORLDS OR, AS SUGGESTED, THE BEST OF BOTH AGES.

CAP HEIGHT

REGULAR — 290PT

X HEIGHT

Mm

BASELINE

Mori

THE QUICK BROWN FOX JU

IT WOULD BE THE CHEEKY

IT'S A LOVELY DAY IN THE N

AND THE PUNGENT AROMA

PROMISE OF A SUMPTUOU

THINKING ABOUT THE DELI

THE LAZY DOG REMAINS U

The quick brown fox jumps over a lazy dog. He didn't

it would be the cheeky thing to do. After all, he had a

It's a lovely day in the neighbourhood, with the sun sh

and the pungent aroma of fresh rubbish bins wafting

promise of a sumptuous meal. The sprightly fox rubs

thinking about the delicious treasures he's about to d

the lazy dog remains unperturbed. With her long snou

long black fur fluttering in the breeze, she is in a drear

the mountains are made of beefy treats, the valleys a

The quick brown fox jumps over a lazy dog. He didn't have to, but he thought
it would be the cheeky thing to do. After all, he had a reputation to maintain.
It's a lovely day in the neighbourhood, with the sun shining, the birds chirping,
and the pungent aroma of fresh rubbish bins wafting through the air – the
promise of a sumptuous meal. The sprightly fox rubs his paws together in glee,
thinking about the delicious treasures he's about to dig into. Still in her spot,
the lazy dog remains unperturbed. With her long snout, droopy jowls, and
long black fur fluttering in the breeze, she is in a dreamland far away – where
the mountains are made of beefy treats, the valleys are filled with tennis balls,
and the puddles are just the right temperature. Why be in the rat race?
It's a dog's life, after all.

PP Mori

PP Mori

PP Mori

TYPEFACE	:	NEOGEO
DESIGNER	:	IAN PARTY
LOCATION	:	LAUSANNE, SWITZERLAND

	PUBLISHED BY	:	NEWGLYPH
	CHRONOLOGY	:	N/A
	RELEASED IN	:	2023

LINK	:	HTTPS://NEWGLYPH.COM/CLASSIC-COLLECTION/#FONT-NEOGEO
STYLES	:	20 STYLES + A VARIABLE FONT
CREDITS	:	IGINO MARINI (KERNING)

NEOGEO IS A CUTTING-EDGE VARIABLE FONT THAT EXQUISITELY CAPTURES THE ESSENCE OF ITS PREDECESSORS WHILE BOLDLY PROPELLING THE GEOMETRIC FONT STYLE INTO THE FUTURE.

CAP HEIGHT   REGULAR — 290PT

X-HEIGHT

BASELINE

NeoGeo

THE QUICK BROWN F

IT WOULD BE THE CHE

IT'S A LOVELY DAY IN T

AND THE PUNGENT A

PROMISE OF A SUMPT

THINKING ABOUT TH

THE LAZY DOG REMA

LONG BLACK FUR FLU

The quick brown fox jumps over a lazy dog. He didn't have
it would be the cheeky thing to do. After all, he had a reput
It's a lovely day in the neighbourhood, with the sun shining,
and the pungent aroma of fresh rubbish bins wafting throu
promise of a sumptuous meal. The sprightly fox rubs his po
thinking about the delicious treasures he's about to dig into
the lazy dog remains unperturbed. With her long snout, dro
long black fur fluttering in the breeze, she is in a dreamland

NeoGeoNeoGeoNeo
NeoGeoNeoGeoNe
NeoGeoNeoGeoNe
NeoGeoNeoGeoN
NeoGeoNeoGeo
NeoGeoNeoGe
NeoGeoNeoGe
NeoGeoNeoG
NeoGeoNeoG
NeoGeoNeo

TYPEFACE	:	NEUE MACHINA
DESIGNER	:	CAIO KONDO
LOCATION	:	MONTREAL, CANADA

PUBLISHED BY	:	PANGRAM PANGRAM
CHRONOLOGY	:	N/A
RELEASED IN	:	2019, 2022

LINK	:	HTTPS://PANGRAMPANGRAM.COM/PRODUCTS/
		NEUE-MACHINA-COLLECTION
STYLES	:	36

NEUE MACHINA IS A METICULOUSLY CRAFTED TYPEFACE WITH MONOSPACE/ GEOMETRIC FEATURES AND PRONOUNCED INKTRAPS IN ITS HEAVIER WEIGHTS. INSPIRED BY ROBOTICS AND MACHINES, IT IS TAILORED FOR THE FUTURE OF TECHNOLOGY. THE FONT IS VERSATILE, SEAMLESSLY BLENDING INTO LIGHTER DESIGNS OR ADDING PERSONALITY TO HEAVIER ONES. IT OFFERS AN INKTRAP CUT FOR SUBTLETY AND A PLAIN CUT FOR A BOLDER LOOK, EACH ACCOMPANIED BY CORRESPONDING ITALICS.

CAP HEIGHT

REGULAR — 290PT

X-HEIGHT

Nn

BASELINE

Neue Machina

THE QUICK BR

IT WOULD BE

IT'S A LOVELY

AND THE PUNG

PROMISE OF A

THINKING ABO

THE LAZY DOG

The quick brown fox jumps over a lazy dog. He didn't have to, but he thought it would be the cheeky thing to do. After all, he had a reputation to maintain. It's a lovely day in the neighbourhood, with the sun shining, the birds chirping, and the pungent aroma of fresh rubbish bins wafting through the air – the promise of a sumptuous meal. The sprightly fox rubs his paws together in glee, thinking about the delicious treasures he's about to dig into. Still in her spot, the lazy dog remains unperturbed. With her long snout, droopy jowls, and long black fur fluttering in the breeze, she is in a dreamland far away – where the mountains are made of beefy treats, the valleys are filled with tennis balls, and the puddles are just the right temperature. Why be in the rat race? It's a dog's life, after all.

NEUEMA

ACHINA

A B C

D E F

G H I

J K L

M N O

P Q R
S T U
V W X
Y Z 0
1 2 3

TYPEFACE	:	NEUE POWER	
DESIGNER	:	POWER TYPE™ FOUNDRY	
LOCATION	:	MAKASSAR, INDONESIA	

		PUBLISHED BY	:	POWER TYPE™ FOUNDRY
		CHRONOLOGY	:	2022
		RELEASED IN	:	2022

LINK	:	HTTPS://POWER-TYPE.COM/NEUE-POWER/
STYLES	:	LIGHT, REGULAR, MEDIUM, BOLD, HEAVY, ULTRA
CREDITS	:	TEGUH ARIEF

NEUE POWER IS A MODERN SANS SERIF DISPLAY FONT FAMILY FEATURING SIX WEIGHTS AND 12-DEGREE OBLIQUES. IT SUPPORTS OVER 75 LANGUAGES (LATIN BASED) AND IS WELL-SUITED FOR DIVERSE DESIGN APPLICATIONS, INCLUDING BRANDING (IDENTITY), LOGOTYPES, PRINTS, ON-SCREEN/DIGITAL READING, POSTERS, HEADLINES, CAPTIONS, AND BODY TEXTS. WITH A TOTAL OF 12 FONTS RANGING FROM LIGHT TO ULTRA, INCLUDING OBLIQUES, NEUE POWER OFFERS A VISUALLY APPEALING COMMUNICATION STYLE FOR ANY DESIGN PROJECT.

CAP HEI   REGULAR – 290PT

X-HEIGH

Nn

BASELINE

Neue Power

THE QUICK BROW

IT WOULD BE THE

ITS A LOVELY DAY

AND THE PUNGEN

PROMISE OF A SU

THINKING ABOUT

THE LAZY DOG RE

LONG BLACK FUR

THE MOUNTAINS

The quick brown fox jumps over a lazy dog. He didnt have to but he thought it would be the cheeky thing to do. After all he had a reputation to maintain. Its a lovely day in the neighbourhood with the sun shining the birds chirping and the pungent aroma of fresh rubbish bins wafting through the air the promise of a sumptuous meal. The sprightly fox rubs his paws together in glee thinking about the delicious treasures hes about to dig into. Still in her spot the lazy dog remains unperturbed. With her long snout droopy jowls and long black fur fluttering in the breeze she is in a dreamland far away where the mountains are made of beefy treats the valleys are filled with tennis balls and the puddles are just the right temperature. Why be in the rat race Its a dogs life after all.

Aa

GRINDLEZLY
VAÊSÇØÅR
METAÑOIAC
BARTEŅDEŖ

FLAMMABLE   RECYCLED
Easy To Burn   Can Be Used Again

Statement*●

A statement is a sentence that says something is true, like "Pizza is delicious." There are other kinds of statements in the worlds of the law, banking, and government.

NORMAL
NORMAL

Espresso Single 2.5$ Double 3.5$	**Cortado** Single 2.5$ Double 3.5$
Cappuccino Single 2.5$ Double 3.5$	**Drip Coffee** Single 2.5$ Double 3.5$
Flat White Single 2.5$ Double 3.5$	**Macchiato** Single 2.5$ Double 3.5$
Mocha Single 2.5$ Double 3.5$	**Americano** Single 2.5$ Double 3.5$

Culture App and the Rise of the
<CODED GAZE/>

META

OBSERVE THE STARS.

"the town has been busy stargazing as British superstars jetted in for the grand finale"

Currency *¢$$¥£¤●

$

A currency has to be derived from the Latin word "currere" which means "to run" or "to flow". On the contrary. Money has been derived from the Roman word "monere" which means "to warn" in Latin.

NEUE POWER

Culture App and the Rise of the

<CODED GAZE/>

METAVORA

OBSERVE THE STARS.

"a telescope for stargazing through a retractable roof"

"the town has been busy stargazing as British superstars jetted in for the grand finale"

EDITORIAL PAGE

Using
CANON
EOS 5D Mark IV

Madison
Wisconsin
USA

PHOTO BY

DAVE HOEFLER

HOW TO   STOP
WAR,
USING   *DESIGN.*
YEAH! MANY
PERSPECTIVES

TYPEFACE	:	MD NICHROME
DESIGNER	:	MASS-DRIVER™
LOCATION	:	THE HAGUE, THE NETHERLANDS

PUBLISHED BY	:	MASS-DRIVER™
CHRONOLOGY	:	2020 - 2021
RELEASED IN	:	2021

LINK	:	HTTPS://MASS-DRIVER.COM/TYPEFACES/MD-NICHROME
STYLES	:	16 (INFRA, INFRA OBLIQUE, THIN, THIN OBLIQUE, LIGHT, LIGHT OBLIQUE, REGULAR, REGULAR OBLIQUE, DARK, DARK OBLIQUE, BOLD, BOLD OBLIQUE, BLACK, BLACK OBLIQUE, ULTRA, ULTRA OBLIQUE)
CREDITS	:	FUTUREFONTS

MD NICHROME IS A DISPLAY TYPEFACE THAT DRAWS INSPIRATION FROM THE TYPOGRAPHY FOUND IN SCI-FI PAPERBACKS FROM THE 70'S AND EARLY 80'S. DURING THAT ERA, TYPEFACES CREATED FOR DRY TRANSFERS OR PHOTOTYPESETTING WERE NOT DIGITISED WITH THE PRECISION THEY DESERVED. THE DESIGNERS OF MD NICHROME SOUGHT TO ADDRESS THIS GAP FOR MODERN TECHNOLOGIES AND STYLES. RATHER THAN REVIVING A SPECIFIC TYPEFACE, IT CAPTURES ELEMENTS FROM VARIOUS FONTS OF THAT TIME AND GENRE.

CAP HEIGHT   REGULAR — 290PT

X-HEIGHT

Nn

BASELINE

MDNichrome

THE QUICK BROWN FOX JU

IT WOULD BE THE CHEEKY TH

IT'S A LOVELY DAY IN THE NEI

AND THE PUNGENT AROMA

PROMISE OF A SUMPTUOUS

THINKING ABOUT THE DELIC

THE LAZY DOG REMAINS UN

LONG BLACK FUR FLUTTERIN

THE MOUNTAINS ARE MADE

The quick brown fox jumps over a lazy dog. He didn't have to, but he thought it would be the che
he had a reputation to maintain. It's a lovely day in the neighbourhood, with the sun shining, the b
gent aroma of fresh rubbish bins wafting through the air - the promise of a sumptuous meal. The
together in glee, thinking about the delicious treasures he's about to dig into. Still in her spot, the
turbed. With her long snout, droopy jowls, and long black fur fluttering in the breeze, she is in a d
the mountains are made of beefy treats, the valleys are filled with tennis balls, and the puddles a
ture. Why be in the rat race? It's a dog's life, after all.

Neolithic Rit

$38.99 Tra

The Moons

Art History

& Other

Recombi

ual Studies

nsaction

of Jupiter

Lectures

Planets

nant DNA

TYPEFACE	:	TT NORMS PRO
DESIGNER	:	TYPETYPE.ORG
LOCATION	:	SAINT PETERSBURG, RUSSIA

PUBLISHED BY	:	TYPETYPE.ORG
CHRONOLOGY	:	2021 - 2023
RELEASED IN	:	2021

LINK	:	HTTPS://TYPETYPE.ORG/FONTS/TT-NORMS-PRO/
STYLES	:	102 STYLES + 2 VARIABLE FONTS

TT NORMS® PRO IS A VERSATILE GEOMETRIC SANS SERIF FONT DESIGNED AS A RELIABLE WORKHORSE. SUITABLE FOR A WIDE RANGE OF APPLICATIONS, FROM MODERN STREAMING SERVICES AND BANKING SYSTEMS TO STYLISH CLOTHING BRANDS AND THE AUTOMOTIVE INDUSTRY, IT SEAMLESSLY ADAPTS TO BOTH DIGITAL AND PRINT FORMATS. THE TYPEFACE OFFERS 11 UPRIGHT AND 11 ITALIC STYLES, EACH WITH A CLASSIC, CONDENSED, COMPACT, AND EXPANDED SUB-FAMILY. IT ALSO INCLUDES THE TT NORMS® PRO MONO SUB-FAMILY, TWO VARIABLE FONTS (TT NORMS® PRO AND TT NORMS® PRO MONO), A LARGE CHARACTER SET, SUPPORT FOR 275+ LANGUAGES, A FUNCTIONAL SET OF OPENTYPE FEATURES, AS WELL AS OTHER TOOLS FOR CREATING CLEAN AND MODERN DESIGNS.

CAP HEIGHT   REGULAR — 290PT

X-HEIGHT

Nn

BASELINE

^{TT} Norms Pro

THE QUICK BR

IT WOULD BE T

IT'S A LOVELY

AND THE PUN

PROMISE OF A

THINKING ABC

THE LAZY DOC

LONG BLACK

THE MOUNTA

Kή6ëy

Ωώ4N

Bőf

TypeType

TT Norms® Pro

TYPEFACE	:	NOUVEAU
DESIGNER	:	DDOTT
LOCATION	:	BARCELONA, SPAIN; COLOGNE, GERMANY

	PUBLISHED BY	:	DDOTT
	CHRONOLOGY	:	2017, 2023
	RELEASED IN	:	2023

LINK	:	HTTPS://DDOTT.NET/FONT/NOUVEAU-GRANDE/
STYLES	:	22 STYLES, 2 FAMILIES
CREDITS	:	DOMINIK THIEME

THE NOUVEAU FAMILY IS A MODERN SANS-SERIF FONT THAT DRAWS INSPIRATION FROM LATE 19TH-CENTURY POSTERS, INFUSING PLAYFUL FLORAL DETAILS INTO AN EARLY GROTESQUE STYLE. INITIALLY RELEASED IN 2017, IT HAS BEEN REVAMPED WITH TWO NEW WEIGHTS AND THE ADDITION OF A HIGH-CONTRAST FAMILY, NOUVEAU GRANDE. ENHANCEMENTS TO TERMINALS AND COUNTERS IMPROVED ITS LEGIBILITY AT SMALLER TEXT SIZES, WHILE SMART FEATURES, INCLUDING CASE-SENSITIVE AND CONTEXTUAL FORMS, ALONG WITH AN EXTENSIVE SELECTION OF LIGATURES AND SWASHES, WERE ALSO INCORPORATED. TODAY, IT BLENDS CONTEMPORARY AESTHETICS WITH A HINT OF CALLIGRAPHY, BRINGING ELEGANCE TO TITLES AND COPY.

CAP HEIGHT

REGULAR — 290PT

X-HEIGHT

Nn

BASELINE

Nouveau

THE QUICK BROWN FOX JUM

IT WOULD BE THE CHEEKY T

ITS A LOVELY DAY IN THE NEI

AND THE PUNGENT AROMA

PROMISE OF A SUMPTUOUS

THINKING ABOUT THE DELIC

The quick brown fox jumps over a lazy dog. He didnt have to, but he
it would be the cheeky thing to do. After all, he had a reputation to
Its a lovely day in the neighbourhood, with the sun shining, the bird
and the pungent aroma of fresh rubbish bins wafting through the a
promise of a sumptuous meal. The sprightly fox rubs his paws toge
thinking about the delicious treasures hes about to dig into. Still in
the lazy dog remains unperturbed. With her long snout, droopy jov
long black fur fluttering in the breeze, she is in a dreamland far awa
the mountains are made of beefy treats, the valleys are filled with
and the puddles are just the right temperature. Why be in the rat r
Its a dogs life, after all.

The quick brown fox jumps over a lazy dog. He didnt have to, but he thought
it would be the cheeky thing to do. After all, he had a reputation to maintain.
Its a lovely day in the neighbourhood, with the sun shining, the birds chirping,
and the pungent aroma of fresh rubbish bins wafting through the air - the
promise of a sumptuous meal. The sprightly fox rubs his paws together in glee,
thinking about the delicious treasures hes about to dig into. Still in her spot,
the lazy dog remains unperturbed. With her long snout, droopy jowls, and
long black fur fluttering in the breeze, she is in a dreamland far away - where
the mountains are made of beefy treats, the valleys are filled with tennis balls,
and the puddles are just the right temperature. Why be in the rat race
Its a dogs life, after all.

NOU

N

OU

VEAU
n

TYPEFACE	:	NUCKLE	
DESIGNER	:	HEAVYWEIGHT DIGITAL TYPE FOUNDRY	
LOCATION	:	PRAGUE, CZECH REPUBLIC	

274

PUBLISHED BY	:	HEAVYWEIGHT DIGITAL TYPE FOUNDRY
CHRONOLOGY	:	N/A
RELEASED IN	:	2021

LINK	:	HTTPS://HEAVYWEIGHT-TYPE.COM/FONTS/NUCKLE/DETAIL
STYLES	:	HAIRLINE, THIN, EXTRALIGHT, LIGHT, REGULAR, MEDIUM, SEMIBOLD, BOLD

NUCKLE, AN EARLY HEAVYWEIGHT FONT DATING BACK TO 2011, ORIGINATED AS A FUNCTIONAL GROTESQUE TO MEET SPECIFIC GRAPHIC DEMANDS. DESPITE LACKING A PRONOUNCED STYLE INITIALLY, IT DEMONSTRATED CLEAR POTENTIAL IN TEXT APPLICATIONS. THROUGH SUBSEQUENT PHASES OF DEVELOPMENT, IT AIMED TO DISTINGUISH ITSELF FROM OTHER MODERN SANS-SERIF ALPHABETS AFTER EXTENSIVE RESEARCH TO REACH AN IDEAL POSITION WITHIN THE FONT CATEGORY. THE FONT'S UNIQUE CHARACTERISTIC THAT SETS IT APART FROM THE MASS OF SIMILAR FONTS WAS A CHALLENGING ASPECT TO DEFINE DURING ITS CREATION.

CAP HEIGHT   REGULAR — 220PT

X-HEIGHT

Nn

BASELINE

Nuckle

THE QUICK BROWN FOX
IT WOULD BE THE CHEEK
ITS A LOVELY DAY IN THE
AND THE PUNGENT AROI
PROMISE OF A SUMPTUC
THINKING ABOUT THE DE
THE LAZY DOG REMAINS

The quick brown fox jumps over a lazy dog. He dic
it would be the cheeky thing to do. After all, he hac
Its a lovely day in the neighbourhood, with the sun
and the pungent aroma of fresh rubbish bins waft
promise of a sumptuous meal. The sprightly fox rl
thinking about the delicious treasures hes about t
the lazy dog remains unperturbed. With her long s
long black fur fluttering in the breeze, she is in a dr
the mountains are made of beefy treats, the valley

The quick brown fox jumps over a lazy dog. He didnt have to, but he thought
it would be the cheeky thing to do. After all, he had a reputation to maintain.
Its a lovely day in the neighbourhood, with the sun shining, the birds chirping,
and the pungent aroma of fresh rubbish bins wafting through the air the
promise of a sumptuous meal. The sprightly fox rubs his paws together in glee,
thinking about the delicious treasures hes about to dig into. Still in her spot,
the lazy dog remains unperturbed. With her long snout, droopy jowls, and
long black fur fluttering in the breeze, she is in a dreamland far away where
the mountains are made of beefy treats, the valleys are filled with tennis balls,
and the puddles are just the right temperature. Why be in the rat race
Its a dogs life, after all.

N⊖⊕⊖
N xy
a G
h

TYPEFACE	:	OFELIA
DESIGNER	:	DANIEL SABINO
LOCATION	:	SÃO PAULO, BRAZIL

		PUBLISHED BY	:	BLACKLETRA TYPE FOUNDRY
		CHRONOLOGY	:	N/A
		RELEASED IN	:	2016

LINK   : HTTPS://BLACKLETRA.COM/TYPEFACES/OFELIA-DISPLAY
STYLES   : DISPLAY: THIN, THIN ITALIC, EXTRALIGHT, EXTRALIGHT
            ITALIC, LIGHT, LIGHT ITALIC, REGULAR, ITALIC, MEDIUM,
            MEDIUM ITALIC, BOLD, BOLD ITALIC, EXTRABOLD, EXTRABOLD
            ITALIC
            TEXT: LIGHT, LIGHT ITALIC, REGULAR, ITALIC, MEDIUM, MEDIUM
            ITALIC, SEMIBOLD, SEMIBOLD ITALIC, BOLD, BOLD ITALIC

OFELIA IS A VERSATILE GEOMETRIC SANS-SERIF FONT SUITABLE FOR VARIOUS APPLICATIONS. IT COMES IN TWO OPTICAL SIZES, DISPLAY AND TEXT, STRIKING A BALANCE BETWEEN A RIGID GEOMETRIC STRUCTURE AND LETTERS WITH A GESTURAL TOUCH, SUCH AS "A", "F", AND THE COMMA. THE FONT FAMILY INCLUDES SMALL CAPS, OLD STYLE, AND TABULAR FIGURES, ALONG WITH ALTERNATES FOR "A" AND "L". OVERALL, OFELIA PERFORMS WELL IN ALMOST ANY SITUATION, OFFERING JUST THE RIGHT AMOUNT OF PERSONALITY.

CAP HEIGHT

REGULAR — 290PT

X-HEIG

BASELINE

Ofelia

IT WOULD BE TH

IT'S A LOVELY DA

AND THE PUNG

PROMISE OF A S

THINKING ABOU

THE LAZY DOG

LONG BLACK FU

THE MOUNTAIN

AND THE PUDD

IT'S A DOG'S LIFE

BRÛLURES

DÉCOLLETÉ

POTÊNCIAS

LÖFVINGIN

CALIFORNIA

PRIVILÉGIUM

BEËINDIGING

netcoördinator

retfærdiggøres

riorganizzerà

hljóðstafrófið

políticament

fotossíntese

guggenheim

TYPEFACE	:	OFFBIT
DESIGNER	:	POWER TYPE™ FOUNDRY
LOCATION	:	MAKASSAR, INDONESIA

		PUBLISHED BY	:	POWER TYPE™ FOUNDRY
		CHRONOLOGY	:	2022
		RELEASED IN	:	2022

LINK	:	HTTPS://POWER-TYPE.COM/OFFBIT/
STYLES	:	REGULAR, BOLD, DOT, DOT BOLD, 101, 101 BOLD
CREDITS	:	TEGUH ARIEF

OFFBIT IS A FONT TYPE DERIVED FROM BITMAPS WITH VARIOUS VARIATIONS FROM EACH BOX. THE TERM "BITMAP" ORIGINATES FROM COMPUTER PROGRAMMING, REPRESENTING A SPATIALLY MAPPED ARRAY OF BITS. IN THE CASE OF POWER TYPE, IT REFERS TO AN ARRAY OF PIXELS SPATIALLY MAPPED INTO SHAPES SUCH AS DOTS AND OTHER MODELS. THIS FONT ALIGNS WITH THEMES OF COMPUTING, GRAPHIC DESIGN, POSTERS, AND OTHER MEDIA, MAKING IT VERSATILE FOR COMBINED APPLICATIONS.

CAP HEIGHT

X-HEIGHT

REGULAR – 290PT

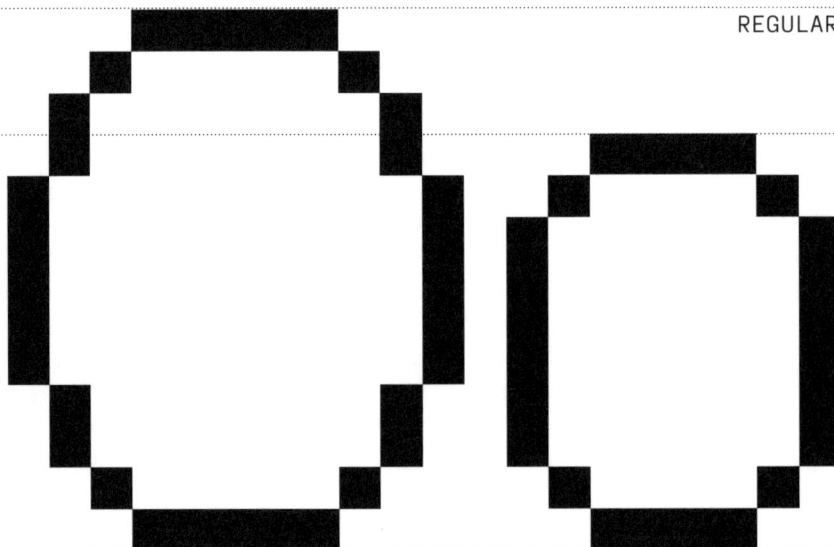

BASELINE

OffBit

THE QUICK BROW

IT WOULD BE THE

ITS A LOVELY DAY

AND THE PUNGEN

PROMISE OF A SU

THINKING ABOUT T

THE LAZY DOG R

LONG BLACK FUR

THE MOUNTAINS A

OffBit fonts

OffBit Contain 6 Styles ⬤ Bitmap & Display

<Regular, **Bold**, Dot, **Dot Bold**, 101, **101 Bold**/>

Power Type Bitmap & Display Font Collection

☀BitOFF✔/05⇡

OffBit fonts

OffBit Contain 6 Styles ⬤ Bitmap & Display

<Regular, **Bold**, Dot, **Dot Bold**, 101, **101 Bold**/>

Power Type Bitmap & Display Font Collection

☀BitOFF✔/05⇡

OffBit fonts

OffBit Contain 6 Styles ⬤ Bitmap & Display

<Regular, **Bold**, Dot, **Dot Bold**, 101, **101 Bold**/>

Power Type Bitmap & Display Font Collection

☀BitOFF✔/05⇡

Foundry-no.05 Bit-Off ✔'22

Power Type™ Foundry

AaBbCcDdEe Welcome To BitmapWorld Power type™

Foundry-no.05 Bit-Off ✔'22

www.power-type.com

AaBbCcDdEe Welcome To

SUPER BITMAP

187pt

OffBit Regular

187pt 187pt

OffBit Bold

187pt 187pt

OffBit Dot

187pt 187pt

OffBit Dot Bold

187pt 187pt

OffBit 101

187pt 187pt

OffBit 101 Bold

101
101
101

TYPEFACE   :   ONSITE
DESIGNER   :   SOCIOTYPE
LOCATION   :   LONDON, UK

                     PUBLISHED BY   :   SOCIOTYPE
                     CHRONOLOGY   :   2019 - 2022
                     RELEASED IN   :   2022

LINK   :   HTTPS://SOCIO-TYPE.COM/ONSITE
STYLES   :   42 STYLES IN TOTAL.
                     3 WIDTHS: ONSITE CONDENSED, ONSITE STANDARD,
                     ONSITE EXTENDED
                     7 WEIGHTS FOR EACH SUB-FAMILY: THIN, EXTRALIGHT, LIGHT,
                     REGULAR, MEDIUM, BOLD, EXTRABOLD + ITALICS

ONSITE BLENDS THE TIMELESS STYLE OF A MID-20TH CENTURY GROTESK WITH AN INDUSTRIAL FEEL AND A SYSTEMATIC RANGE OF WIDTHS INSPIRED BY GERMAN ROAD SIGNAGE. ITS STABLE, ROBUST FORM ENSURES FAULTLESS LEGIBILITY FOR SMALL TEXT. NOTABLY, ITS DISTINCTIVE DETAILING, INCLUDING ITS SUBTLY FLATTENED CURVES AND APEXES, DOUBLE-POINT STRUCTURE, AND ALMOST IMPERCEPTIBLY FLARED TERMINALS, BECOMES MORE PROMINENT AT LARGER DISPLAY SIZES.

CAP HEIGHT   REGULAR — 230PT

X-HEIGHT

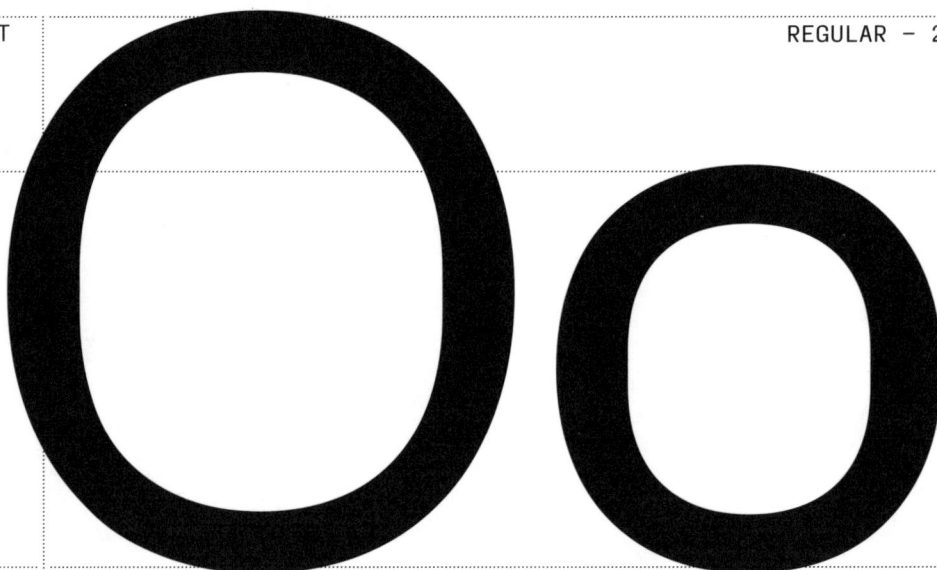

BASELINE

Onsite

THE QUICK BROWN FOX J
IT WOULD BE THE CHEEKY
IT'S A LOVELY DAY IN THE I
AND THE PUNGENT AROM
PROMISE OF A SUMPTUOU
THINKING ABOUT THE DEL
THE LAZY DOG REMAINS U
LONG BLACK FUR FLUTTE
THE MOUNTAINS ARE MAD
AND THE PUDDLES ARE JU
IT'S A DOG'S LIFE, AFTER A

The quick brown fox jumps over a lazy dog. He didn't have to, but he thought it would be the cheeky thing to do. After all, he had a reputation to maintain. It's a lovely day in the neighbourhood, with the sun shining, the birds chirping, and the pungent aroma of fresh rubbish bins wafting through the air - the promise of a sumptuous meal. The sprightly fox rubs his paws together in glee, thinking about the delicious treasures he's about to dig into. Still in her spot, the lazy dog remains unperturbed. With her long snout, droopy jowls, and long black fur fluttering in the breeze, she is in a dreamland far away - where the mountains are made of beefy treats, the valleys are filled with tennis balls, and the puddles are just the right temperature. Why be in the rat race? It's a dog's life, after all.

Aâ Żż

VERSION 1.100	3 WIDTHS	42 STYLES	765 GLYPHS PER STYLE

Onsite Extended · Bold

By 2035, it will be *Gen Z's turn.*

Onsite Standard · Medium

In June & July of 2020, there was a 126% increase in people considering properties in villages, compared with a 68% rise in searches in towns. The research, conducted by *Rightmove*, also revealed regional splits too.

Onsite Standard · Medium Italic

Casa do Penedo

Onsite Extended · Extralight

abcdefghijklmnopqrstuvwxyz
ABCDEFGHIJKLMNOPQRSTU
VWXYZ ⤷ 0123456789 .,?! *

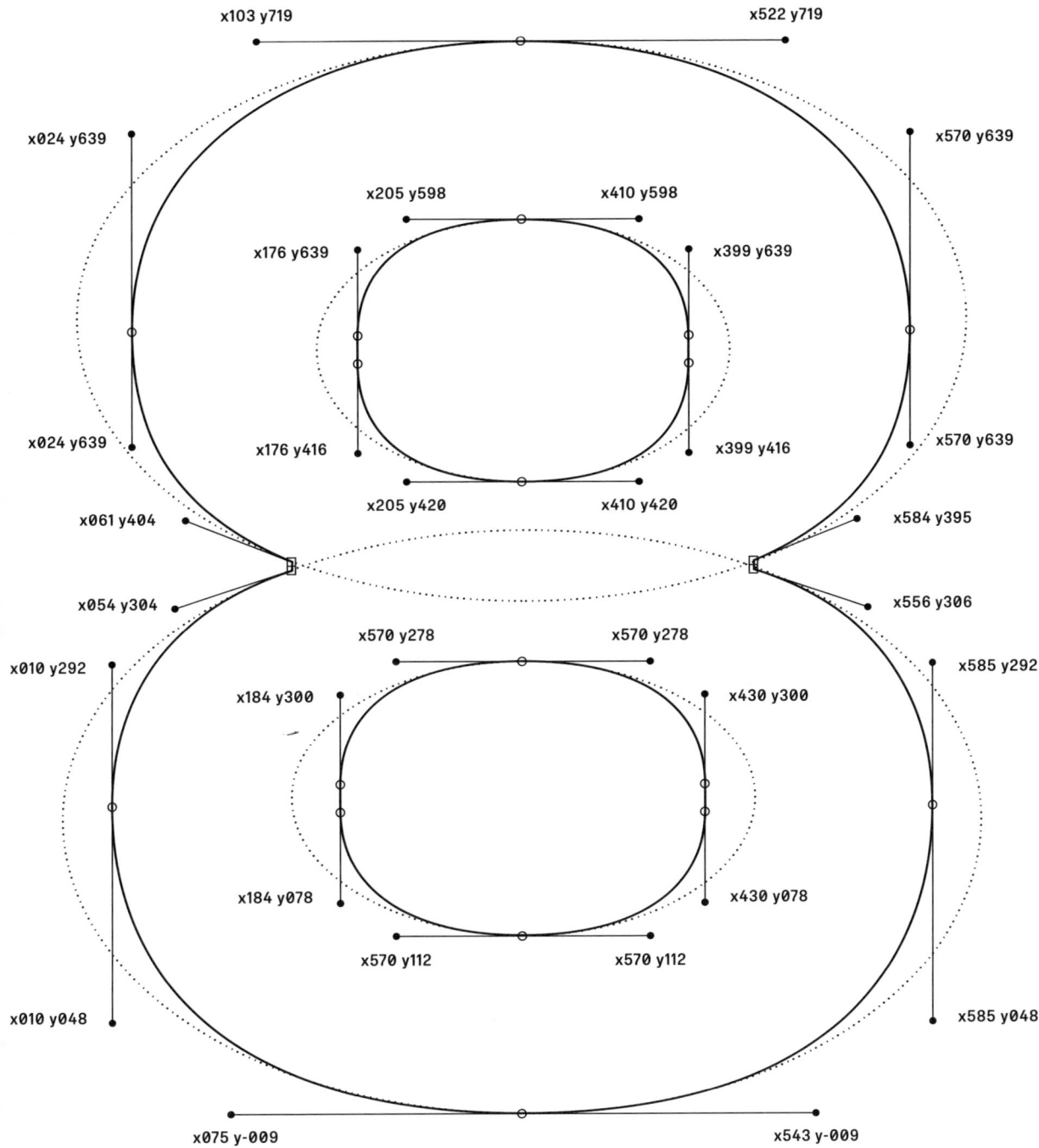

x103 y719   x522 y719

x024 y639   x570 y639

x205 y598   x410 y598

x176 y639   x399 y639

x024 y639   x570 y639

x176 y416   x399 y416

x205 y420   x410 y420

x061 y404   x584 y395

x054 y304   x556 y306

x570 y278   x570 y278

x010 y292   x585 y292

x184 y300   x430 y300

x184 y078   x430 y078

x570 y112   x570 y112

x010 y048   x585 y048

x075 y-009   x543 y-009

TYPEFACE : F37 ORACLE
DESIGNER : F37®
LOCATION : MANCHESTER, UK

PUBLISHED BY : F37®
CHRONOLOGY : 2022
RELEASED IN : 2022

LINK : HTTPS://F37FOUNDRY.COM/FONTS/F37-ORACLE
STYLES : 5 WEIGHTS WITH MATCHING OBLIQUES, TOTALLING 10 STYLES

F37 ORACLE IS UNDOUBTEDLY A GROTESQUE SANS FONT, YET SOME OF ITS QUIRKY, MANNERED COMPONENTS SEEM TO HAIL FROM ANOTHER REALM. NOTABLY, THERE ARE EXTRAVAGANT FLOURISHES ON THE "A", "G", "K", AND "Y", WHERE TERMINAL ARCHES CLOSE IN ON THEMSELVES, FORMING INTRIGUING AND CHARACTERFUL HANDWRITING-LIKE SHAPES. ADDITIONALLY, THE "C", "E", "F", "S", AND "T" FEATURE LONGER-THAN-USUAL ARCHES, MANY WITH A DISTINCTIVE OVERBITE. THESE UNIQUE DESIGN ELEMENTS CONTRIBUTE TO THE FONT'S DISTINCT AND CAPTIVATING APPEARANCE.

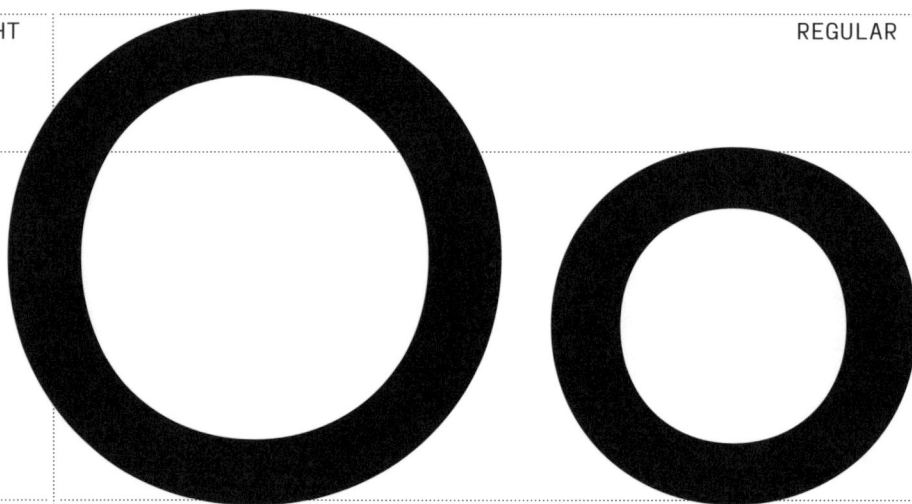

CAP HEIGHT

REGULAR — 290PT

X-HEIGHT

BASELINE

F37 Oracle

THE QUICK BROWN FO

IT WOULD BE THE CHE

IT'S A LOVELY DAY IN T

AND THE PUNGENT AR

PROMISE OF A SUMPTU

THINKING ABOUT THE

THE LAZY DOG REMAI

LONG BLACK FUR FLU

THE MOUNTAINS ARE

AND THE PUDDLES AR

The quick brown fox jumps over a lazy dog. He didn't have to, but he thought it would be the cheeky thing to do. After all, he had a reputation to maintain. It's a lovely day in the neighbourhood, with the sun shining, the birds chirping, and the pungent aroma of fresh rubbish bins wafting through the air - the promise of a sumptuous meal. The sprightly fox rubs his paws together in glee, thinking about the delicious treasures he's about to dig into. Still in her spot, the lazy dog remains unperturbed. With her long snout, droopy jowls, and long black fur fluttering in the breeze, she is in a dreamland far away - where the mountains are made of beefy treats, the valleys are filled with tennis balls, and the puddles are just the right temperature. Why be in the rat race? It's a dog's life, after all.

Light

Oracle

Light Italic

Oracle

Regular

Oracle

Regular Italic

Oracle

Medium

Oracle

Medium Italic

Oracle

Semi Bold

Oracle

Semi Bold Italic

Oracle

Bold

Oracle

Bold Italic

Oracle

TYPEFACE	:	FT PILAR
DESIGNER	:	FUERTE TYPE
LOCATION	:	DUBAI, UAE; COLONIA, URUGUAY

296

PUBLISHED BY	:	FUERTE TYPE
CHRONOLOGY	:	N/A
RELEASED IN	:	2022

| LINK | : | HTTPS://WWW.FUERTETYPE.COM/TYPEFACES/PILAR/ |
| STYLES | : | HAIR, THIN, LIGHT, REGULAR, MEDIUM, BOLD, BLACK |

PILAR IS A STRAIGHTFORWARD AND HIGHLY VERSATILE SANS-SERIF TYPEFACE DESIGNED FOR A BROAD RANGE OF PURPOSES. ITS CLEAN, SIMPLE SHAPES, TIMELESS AESTHETICS, AND HARMONIOUS TEXTURE MAKE IT WELL-SUITED FOR VARIOUS APPLICATIONS, INCLUDING LONG-FORM READING. INFLUENCED BY THE RATIONALITY OF CLASSIC SWISS NEO-GROTESQUE TYPEFACES FROM THE MID-20TH CENTURY, PILAR BALANCES TRADITIONAL ELEMENTS WITH SUBTLE QUIRKS AND DETAILS THAT ADD WARMTH AND A DISTINCT PRESENCE IN THE CONTEMPORARY LANDSCAPE OF SANS-SERIF TYPEFACES.

CAP HEIGHT

REGULAR — 290PT

X-HEIGHT

Pp

BASELINE

FTPilar

THE QUICK BRO

IT WOULD BE TH

IT'S A LOVELY DA

AND THE PUNGE

PROMISE OF A S

THINKING ABOU

THE LAZY DOG F

LONG BLACK FU

THE MOUNTAINS

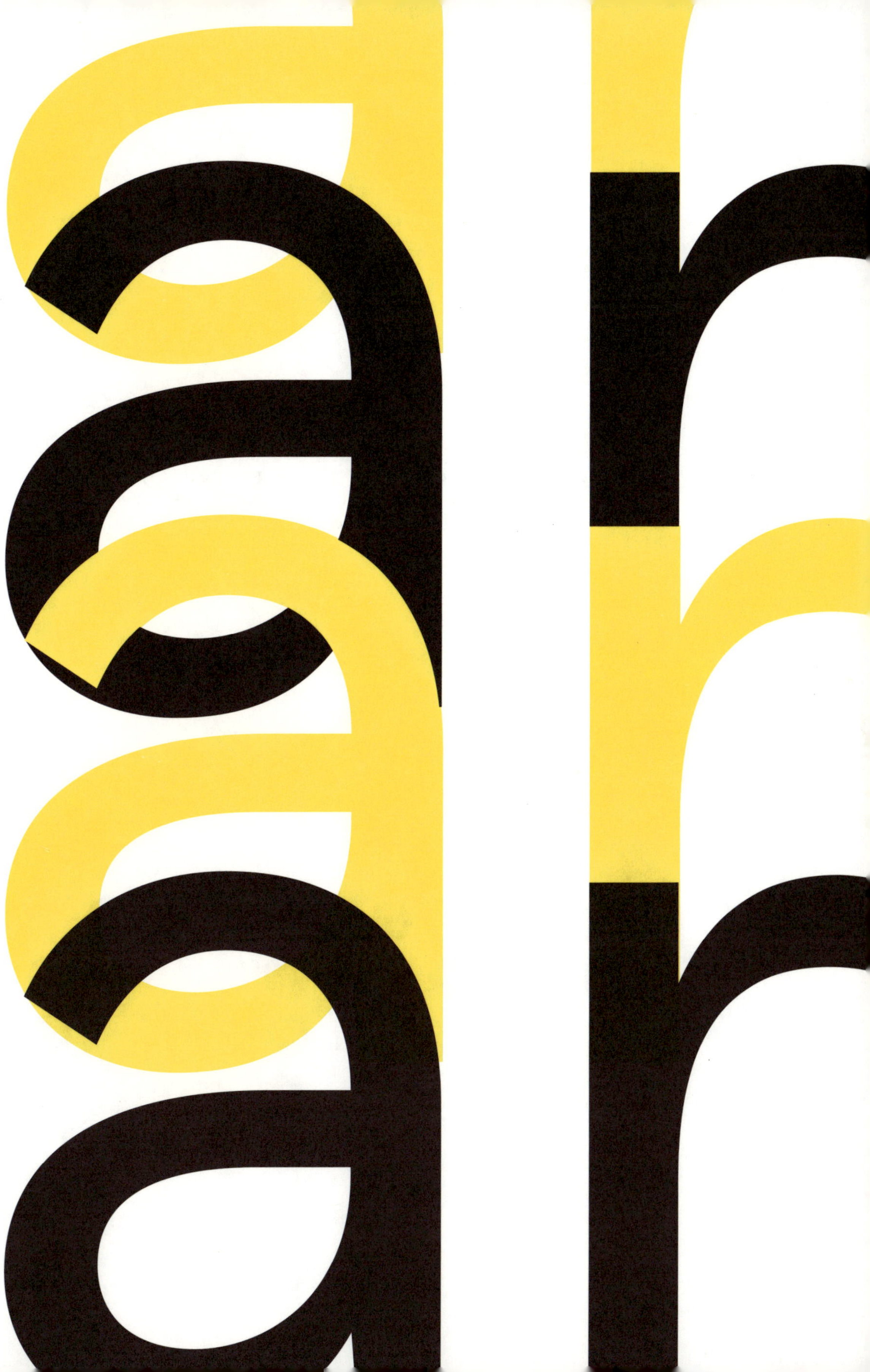

TYPEFACE	:	FOUNDRY PLEK
DESIGNER	:	THE FOUNDRY TYPES
LOCATION	:	UK

PUBLISHED BY	:	THE FOUNDRY TYPES
CHRONOLOGY	:	2002
RELEASED IN	:	2002

LINK	:	HTTPS://WWW.THEFOUNDRYTYPES.COM
STYLES	:	LIGHT, REGULAR, MEDIUM, BOLD

THE FOUNDRY PLEK FAMILY WAS CONSTRUCTED USING THE INTEGRAL DOT MATRIX GRID SYSTEM THAT DEFINES ALL ITS LETTERFORMS. ORIGINALLY CONCEIVED AS A WAY TO CREATE A DOT-MATRIX TYPEFACE USING A 5X9 GRID SYSTEM, FOUNDRY PLEK ALLOWS DOTS TO VARY IN SIZE WHILE STRICTLY ADHERING TO THE GRID. THIS FLEXIBILITY ENABLES PRECISE LAYERING OF TEXT BOXES TO BUILD VARIOUS COLOUR SCHEMES. FOUNDRY PLEK MAINTAINS ESSENTIAL LETTERFORMS AND FUNCTIONS AS A CORRESPONDENCE FONT, CREATING A "TYPEWRITER" EFFECT.

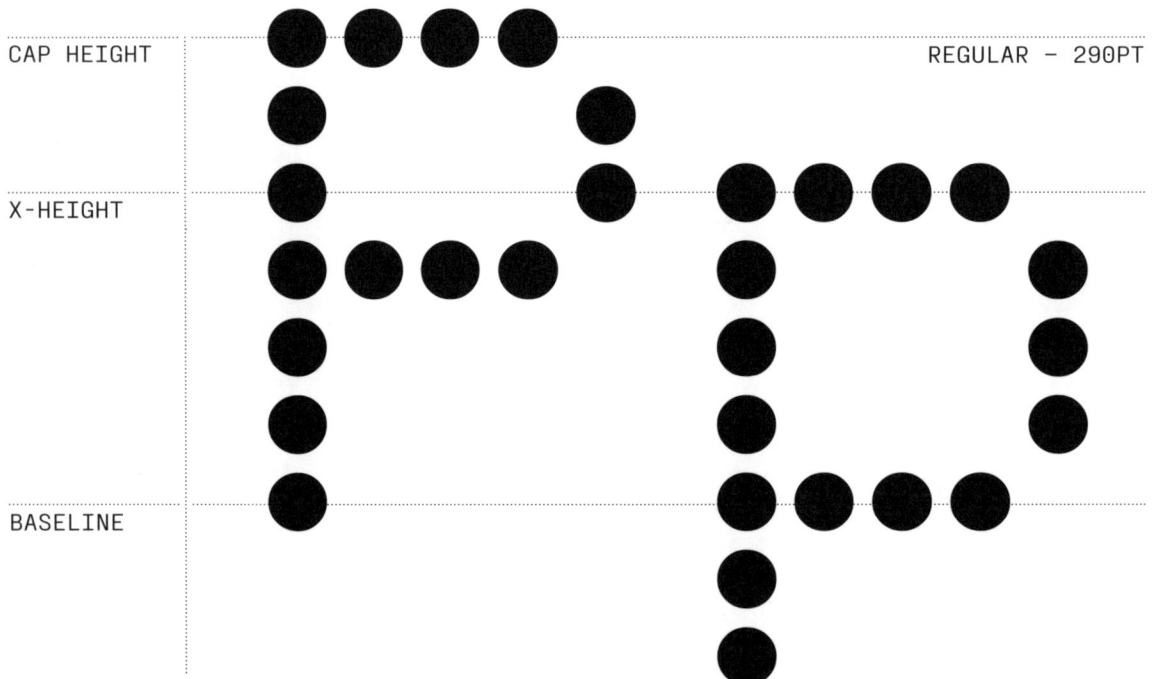

CAP HEIGHT

X-HEIGHT

REGULAR — 290PT

BASELINE

FOUNDRY Plek

THE QUICK BROWN FO

IT WOULD BE THE CHE

ITS A LOVELY DAY IN

AND THE PUNGENT AR

PROMISE OF A SUMPT

THINKING ABOUT THE

THE LAZY DOG REMAI

LONG BLACK FUR FLU

THE MOUNTAINS ARE

AND THE PUDDLES AR

The quick brown fox jumps over a lazy dog. He didn't have to, but he thought
it would be the cheeky thing to do. After all, he had a reputation to maintain.
Its a lovely day in the neighbourhood, with the sun shining, the birds chirping,
and the pungent aroma of fresh rubbish bins wafting through the air - the
promise of a sumptuous meal. The sprightly fox rubs his paws together in glee,
thinking about the delicious treasures he's about to dig into. Still in her spot,
the lazy dog remains unperturbed. With her long snout, droopy jowls, and
long black fur >uttering in the breeze, she is in a dreamland far away - where
the mountains are made of beefy treats, the valleys are <lled with tennis balls,
and the puddles are just the right temperature. Why be in the rat race?
Its a dogs life, after all.

Four

Light
Regular
Medium
Bold

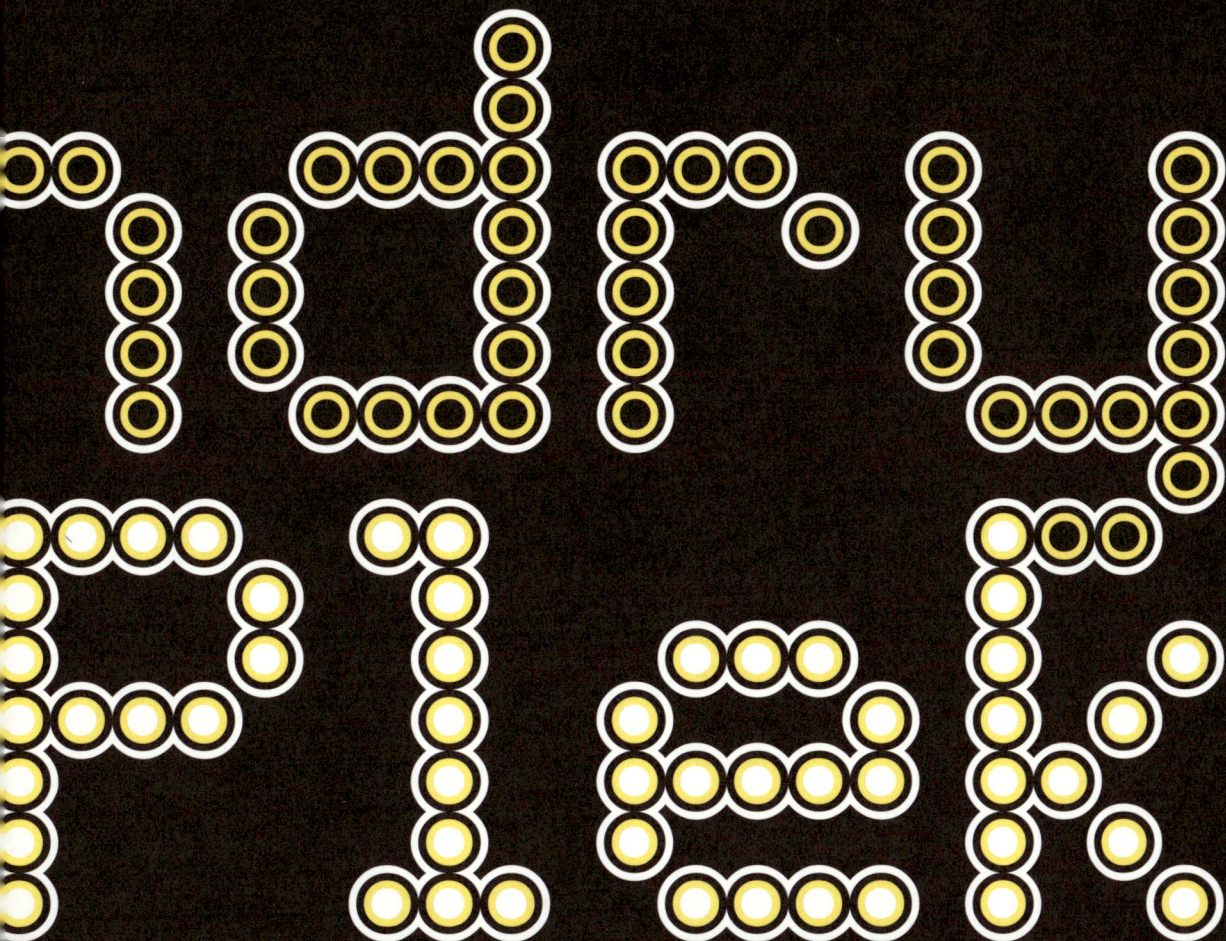
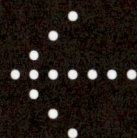

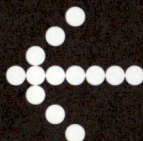

TYPEFACE	:	GT PRESSURA
DESIGNER	:	MOIRÉ
LOCATION	:	LUCERNE, SWITZERLAND; NEW YORK, US

PUBLISHED BY	:	GRILLI TYPE
CHRONOLOGY	:	N/A
RELEASED IN	:	2012, 2017, 2022

LINK	:	HTTPS://WWW.GT-PRESSURA.COM/
STYLES	:	36
CREDITS	:	MARC KAPPELER/MOIRÉ (DESIGN), DOMINIK HUBER (DESIGN & SCRIPT EXTENSIONS), PANOS HARATZO POULOS (GREEK), DONNY TRUONG (VIETNAMESE), ARPHIC (CHINESE), TYPE PROJECT (JAPANESE), SANDOLL (KOREAN)

GT PRESSURA TAKES INSPIRATION FROM THE HISTORY OF METAL TYPE PRINTING AND ENGINEERED LETTERS STAMPED ONTO SHIPPING BOXES. IT INCORPORATES THE VISUAL GESTURE OF INK SPREADING UNDER PRESSURE AS A STYLISTIC DEVICE, PROVIDING AN ALTERNATIVE TO THE MORE DELICATE TYPEFACES OF THE DIGITAL AGE. INITIALLY RELEASED IN 2012, CYRILLIC LANGUAGE SUPPORT WAS ADDED IN 2017. IN 2022, THE TYPEFACE WAS RE-RELEASED WITH EXPANDED LATIN AND VIETNAMESE SUPPORT, ALONG WITH MATCHING CHINESE, JAPANESE, AND KOREAN TYPEFACES.

CAP HEIGHT

X-HEIGHT

BASELINE

REGULAR — 290PT

Pp

GT Pressura

THE QUICK BROWN FOX JUMP

IT WOULD BE THE CHEEKY TH

IT'S A LOVELY DAY IN THE NEI

AND THE PUNGENT AROMA O

PROMISE OF A SUMPTUOUS M

THINKING ABOUT THE DELICIC

THE LAZY DOG REMAINS UNP

LONG BLACK FUR FLUTTERING

THE MOUNTAINS ARE MADE O

AND THE PUDDLES ARE JUST

The quick brown fox jumps over a lazy dog. He didn't have

it would be the cheeky thing to do. After all, he had a repu

It's a lovely day in the neighbourhood, with the sun shinin

and the pungent aroma of fresh rubbish bins wafting thro

promise of a sumptuous meal. The sprightly fox rubs his p

thinking about the delicious treasures he's about to dig in

the lazy dog remains unperturbed. With her long snout, d

long black fur fluttering in the breeze, she is in a dreamla

so what is it th...
...e type
...ew, that
conv...ea...beyond
th...it...ut

unspools a...ight...
of sorts, s...asi...
constellation of s...
and diverse pro...

THEY'RE ESSENTIAL TO OUR MIS-
...AND INFO... DESIRE TO
...THAT...

...N A VOIC...
...A COMPELLIN...
...OWN WORDS.

The studio now nu...
with colleagues dis...
across the globe. We m...
type with a point of view,
type that conveys meaning
beyond the words it spells
o...scends
...e, whic...

We make t...t...ew, type
...at con...
spells a...also tra...ds...e
...llence, which we consider a given –
...er all, if our type didn't read and p...m
...wide range of challenging...
...ts, we wouldn't be doing our j...

...a point of view,
...ype th...s m...
...he word...pells...so
transcends technica...ce,
which we consider a g...ll,
if our type didn't re...rm
well in a wide rang...
ing environments, w...be
doing our job. What...us
is this: What story...
face tell? What kind...ty
does it have? Noël...er-
ry Blancpain founde...pe
in Switzerland in l...a
collaborative avenu...
with other designers...
foundry is based in...
active on a global s...

The relationships we'...
...other c...
...rations...true...
...he won...re essenti...
...ur mi...d inf...
...re t...e...
...'s...
...W...
...o show
them a
...mpelling

But just because we're Swiss ...sn't mean we're... We mak... type... a point o... hat... ing beyond the words... anscends... which... consider a ...a... ur typ... n't read and ...in... f challenging ...ts, w... e doing our job. What matters to... is this: What story do... face t... ind ...ave...

GT Pressura
Medium
Size: 7 pt

...and Thierry Bla... ...Switzerl... ...faces ...th... ...ur...

City... ...sively ri... cheting bet... East Asia, No... ica, and Europe. The studio... eight with colleagues di... just bec... 're ne... type... ...ew... ...onveys... ...lls... ...ic des... ...ain-ing and temperament who happen to run a type foundry. The relationships we've forged with other designers are collaborations in the truest sense of the word. They're essential to our mission and inform our desire to produce useful type.

wh... our ty... wide... he... nts, we wo...

We... grap... esigners by training... empera-ment who... en to run... t... So... th oth... are collabor... tru-est sen... th... d.

GT Press...
Mono Re...
Size:

...But wait there's more! Besides... ffering retail typefaces, we're also a service provider. Our Commissions section unspools a highlight reel of sorts, showcasing a constellation of selected and diverse projects.

This also transcends technical excellence, which we consider a given, if our type didn't read and perform well in a wide range of challenging environments, we wouldn't be doing our job.

TYPEFACE	:	MD PRIMER
DESIGNER	:	MASS-DRIVER™
LOCATION	:	THE HAGUE, THE NETHERLANDS

		PUBLISHED BY	:	MASS-DRIVER™
		CHRONOLOGY	:	2021
		RELEASED IN	:	2021

LINK	:	HTTPS://MASS-DRIVER.COM/TYPEFACES/MD-PRIMER
STYLES	:	6 (LIGHT, REGULAR, MEDIUM, SEMIBOLD, BOLD, BLACK)
CREDITS	:	DAN REYNOLDS/TYPEOFF.DE

MD PRIMER IS A DIGITAL REINTERPRETATION INSPIRED BY THE FLAWS AND VARIATIONS FOUND IN EARLY GROTESQUE TYPEFACES FROM THE LATE 19TH CENTURY. CRAFTED BY SKILLED INDIVIDUALS BEFORE THE SANS-SERIF STYLE TOOK ON ITS FAMILIAR CONTEMPORARY FORMS, THESE TYPEFACES OFFER A DIVERSE RANGE THAT MAY SEEM SOMEWHAT UNREFINED TO THE MODERN EYE. MD PRIMER AIMS TO EVOKE AND CELEBRATE THESE UNIQUE CHARACTERISTICS, EMBRACING THEIR MISMATCHED PROPORTIONS AS PART OF A CONTEMPORARY DESIGN AESTHETIC.

CAP HEIGHT   REGULAR — 290PT

X-HEIGHT

BASELINE

MDPrimer

THE QUICK BROWN FO

IT WOULD BE THE CHE

IT'S A LOVELY DAY IN T

AND THE PUNGENT AF

PROMISE OF A SUMPT

THINKING ABOUT THE

THE LAZY DOG REMAI

LONG BLACK FUR FLU

THE MOUNTAINS ARE

AND THE PUDDLES AR

The quick brown fox jumps over a lazy dog. He didn't have to, but he thought it would be the cheeky thing to do. After all, he had a reputation to maintain. It's a lovely day in the neighbourhood, with the sun shining, the birds chirping, and the pungent aroma of fresh rubbish bins wafting through the air - the promise of a sumptuous meal. The sprightly fox rubs his paws together in glee, thinking about the delicious treasures he's about to dig into. Still in her spot, the lazy dog remains unperturbed. With her long snout, droopy jowls, and long black fur fluttering in the breeze, she is in a dreamland far away - where the mountains are made of beefy treats, the valleys are filled with tennis balls, and the puddles are just the right temperature. Why be in the rat race? It's a dog's life, after all.

er'sche Gieß

der, Luse & C

nes Conner's

elter & Giese

riftgießerei E

s-Driver, 's-C

erei, Frankfu

Co., Chicago

Sons, New Y

cke, Leipzig.

enjamin Kre

Gravenhage,

TYPEFACE	:	RÄDER
DESIGNER	:	VALERIO MONOPOLI
LOCATION	:	MONTREAL, CANADA

		PUBLISHED BY	:	PANGRAM PANGRAM
		CHRONOLOGY	:	N/A
		RELEASED IN	:	2022

| LINK | : | HTTPS://PANGRAMPANGRAM.COM/PRODUCTS/RADER |
| STYLES | : | 16 |

RÄDER IS A VERSATILE TYPEFACE DESIGNED FOR BOTH EXPRESSIVE DISPLAY AND READABLE EDITORIAL PURPOSES, OFFERING 16 CAREFULLY CRAFTED WEIGHTS FROM A HAIRLINE CUT TO A BOLD, DECORATIVE STYLE. INSPIRED BY VINTAGE SIGNAGE SYSTEMS, RÄDER AIMS TO REVIVE THE GRAPHIC COMPROMISE BETWEEN MESSAGE CLARITY AND VISUAL APPEAL SEEN IN EARLY URBAN WAYFINDING. IT DRAWS FROM A TURN-OF-THE-CENTURY AESTHETIC TO BRING THE CRAFT OF OLD ROAD SIGNAGE BACK TO CONTEMPORARY INDUSTRIAL GROTESQUES. ITS INNER ROUND COUNTERS PROVIDE A PRINTED TYPEFACE FEEL WITHOUT SACRIFICING ITS MODERN LOOK.

CAP HEIGHT

REGULAR — 275PT

X-HEIGHT

BASELINE

Räder

THE QUICK BROWN FOX JUMP
IT WOULD BE THE CHEEKY THI
IT'S A LOVELY DAY IN THE NEIG
AND THE PUNGENT AROMA OF
PROMISE OF A SUMPTUOUS ME
THINKING ABOUT THE DELICIO
THE LAZY DOG REMAINS UNPE

The quick brown fox jumps over a lazy dog. He didn't have to, but he t
it would be the cheeky thing to do. After all, he had a reputation to mai
It's a lovely day in the neighbourhood, with the sun shining, the birds
and the pungent aroma of fresh rubbish bins wafting through the air
promise of a sumptuous meal. The sprightly fox rubs his paws togeth
thinking about the delicious treasures he's about to dig into. Still in he
the lazy dog remains unperturbed. With her long snout, droopy jowls,
long black fur fluttering in the breeze, she is in a dreamland far away

The quick brown fox jumps over a lazy dog. He didn't have to, but he thought
it would be the cheeky thing to do. After all, he had a reputation to maintain.
It's a lovely day in the neighbourhood, with the sun shining, the birds chirping,
and the pungent aroma of fresh rubbish bins wafting through the air – the
promise of a sumptuous meal. The sprightly fox rubs his paws together in glee,
thinking about the delicious treasures he's about to dig into. Still in her spot,
the lazy dog remains unperturbed. With her long snout, droopy jowls, and
long black fur fluttering in the breeze, she is in a dreamland far away – where
the mountains are made of beefy treats, the valleys are filled with tennis balls,
and the puddles are just the right temperature. Why be in the rat race?
It's a dog's life, after all.

ai!M
@i.
#!aiⱭ
23

TYPEFACE	:	RAINER
DESIGNER	:	PHILIPP NEUMEYER
LOCATION	:	BERLIN, GERMANY

	PUBLISHED BY	:	VECTRO
	CHRONOLOGY	:	2018 - 2022
	RELEASED IN	:	2018 - 2022

LINK	:	HTTPS://VECTROTYPE.COM
STYLES	:	HAIRLINE, HAIRLINE SLANTED, THIN, THIN SLANTED, LIGHT, LIGHT SLANTED, REGULAR, REGULAR SLANTED, MEDIUM, MEDIUM SLANTED, BOLD, BOLD SLANTED

RAINER IS A COMPRESSED SANS-SERIF TYPEFACE FEATURING CLOSED APERTURES, A LARGE X-HEIGHT, SHORT ASCENDERS, AND EVEN SHORTER DESCENDERS. ITS OVERALL DESIGN IS SUBTLE, OCCASIONALLY PUNCTUATED BY LAVISH PECULIARITIES, SUCH AS A RELATIVELY HIGH WAIST IN CERTAIN LETTERS. RAINER CONSISTS OF 12 STYLES IN SIX WEIGHTS, INCLUDING UPRIGHT AND SLANTED VERSIONS, AND OFFERS EXTENDED LANGUAGE SUPPORT, COVERING LATIN, CYRILLIC, GREEK, VARIOUS ARROWS, AND SELECTED SYMBOLS. IT SERVES AS A VERSATILE WORKHORSE, PARTICULARLY SUITED FOR TIGHT HEADLINES AND LARGE TYPESETTING APPLICATIONS.

CAP HEIGHT

REGULAR — 290PT

X-HEIGHT

Rr

BASELINE

Rainer

THE QUICK BROWN FOX JUMPS OVER A LAZY DOG. HE DIDN'T HAVE TO, BUT HE

IT WOULD BE THE CHEEKY THING TO DO. AFTER ALL, HE HAD A REPUTATION TO

IT'S A LOVELY DAY IN THE NEIGHBOURHOOD, WITH THE SUN SHINING, THE BIR

AND THE PUNGENT AROMA OF FRESH RUBBISH BINS WAFTING THROUGH THE

PROMISE OF A SUMPTUOUS MEAL. THE SPRIGHTLY FOX RUBS HIS PAWS TOGE

THINKING ABOUT THE DELICIOUS TREASURES HE'S ABOUT TO DIG INTO. STILL

THE LAZY DOG REMAINS UNPERTURBED. WITH HER LONG SNOUT, DROOPY JOW

LONG BLACK FUR FLUTTERING IN THE BREEZE, SHE IS IN A DREAMLAND FAR AV

THE MOUNTAINS ARE MADE OF BEEFY TREATS, THE VALLEYS ARE FILLED WITH

The quick brown fox jumps over a lazy dog. He didn't have to, but he thought it would be the cheeky thing to do. After all, he had a reputation to maintain. It's a lovely day in the neighbourhood, with the sun shining, the birds chirping, and the pungent aroma of fresh rubbish bins wafting through the air - the promise of a sumptuous meal. The sprightly fox rubs his paws together in glee, thinking about the delicious treasures he's about to dig into. Still in her spot, the lazy dog remains unperturbed. With her long snout, droopy jowls, and long black fur fluttering in the breeze, she is in a dreamland far away - where the mountains are made of beefy treats, the valleys are filled with tennis balls, and the puddles are just the right temperature. Why be in the rat race?

Raï

TYPEFACE	:	REWORK
DESIGNER	:	SOCIOTYPE
LOCATION	:	LONDON, UK

		PUBLISHED BY	:	SOCIOTYPE
		CHRONOLOGY	:	2019 - 2023
		RELEASED IN	:	2023

LINK	:	HTTPS://SOCIO-TYPE.COM/REWORK
STYLES	:	48 STYLES IN TOTAL.
		4 SUB-FAMILIES: REWORK MICRO, REWORK TEXT,
		REWORK HEADLINE, REWORK DISPLAY
		6 WEIGHTS FOR EACH SUB-FAMILY: THIN, EXTRALIGHT,
		LIGHT, REGULAR, SEMIBOLD, BOLD + ITALICS

REWORK IS A HISTORICAL HYBRID FONT, TRACING ITS ROOTS BACK TO A ROBUST, GEOMETRIC SANS-SERIF STYLE THAT SPANS FROM ANCIENT GREEK STONE INSCRIPTIONS TO MODERN TIMES. IT DRAWS INFLUENCE FROM 19TH-CENTURY ARCHITECTURAL LETTERING, EARLY PRINTED GROTESQUES, COPPERPLATE ENGRAVING, AND 20TH-CENTURY PHOTOTYPESETTING. WITH 48 STYLES AND FOUR OPTICAL SIZES, INCLUDING A MICRO FAMILY, REWORK SERVES AS A MODERN WORKHORSE DESIGNED TO PERFORM IMPECCABLY AT ANY SCALE, FROM MONUMENTAL TO MINUSCULE.

CAP HEIGHT

REGULAR — 290PT

X-HEIGHT

Rr

BASELINE

Rework

THE QUICK BROWN FC
IT WOULD BE THE CHE
IT'S A LOVELY DAY IN 7
AND THE PUNGENT AI
PROMISE OF A SUMPT
THINKING ABOUT THE
THE LAZY DOG REMAI

The quick brown fox jumps over a lazy dog. He
it would be the cheeky thing to do. After all, he
It's a lovely day in the neighbourhood, with the
and the pungent aroma of fresh rubbish bins v
promise of a sumptuous meal. The sprightly fo
thinking about the delicious treasures he's abo
the lazy dog remains unperturbed. With her lo
long black fur fluttering in the breeze, she is in

The quick brown fox jumps over a lazy dog. He didn't have to, but he thought
it would be the cheeky thing to do. After all, he had a reputation to maintain.
It's a lovely day in the neighbourhood, with the sun shining, the birds chirping,
and the pungent aroma of fresh rubbish bins wafting through the air - the
promise of a sumptuous meal. The sprightly fox rubs his paws together in glee,
thinking about the delicious treasures he's about to dig into. Still in her spot,
the lazy dog remains unperturbed. With her long snout, droopy jowls, and
long black fur fluttering in the breeze, she is in a dreamland far away - where
the mountains are made of beefy treats, the valleys are filled with tennis balls,
and the puddles are just the right temperature. Why be in the rat race?
It's a dog's life, after all.

REWORK MICRO
Recommended Use: 5 → 10pt
①

REWORK TEXT
Recommended Use: 8 → 30pt
②

REWORK HEADLINE
Recommended Use: 24 → 72pt
③

REWORK DISPLAY
Recommended Use: 72pt+
④

①

Rework Display Thin

Rework Display Thin Italic

Rework Display Extralight

Rework Display Extralight Italic

Rework Display Light

Rework Display Light Italic

Rework Display Regular

Rework Display Regular Italic

Rework Display Semibold

Rework Display Semibold Italic

Rework Display Bold

Rework Display Bold Italic

②

Rework Headline Thin

Rework Headline Thin Italic

Rework Headline Extralight

Rework Headline Extralight Italic

Rework Headline Light

Rework Headline Light Italic

Rework Headline Regular

Rework Headline Regular Italic

Rework Headline Semibold

Rework Headline Semibold Italic

Rework Headline Bold

Rework Headline Bold Italic

③ Rework Text Thin
Rework Text Thin Italic
Rework Text Extralight
Rework Text Extralight Italic
Rework Text Light
Rework Text Light Italic
Rework Text Regular
Rework Text Regular Italic
Rework Text Semibold
Rework Text Semibold Italic
Rework Text Bold
Rework Text Bold Italic

④ Rework Micro Thin
Rework Micro Thin Italic
Rework Micro Extralight
Rework Micro Extralight Italic
Rework Micro Light
Rework Micro Light Italic
Rework Micro Regular
Rework Micro Regular Italic
Rework Micro Semibold
Rework Micro Semibold Italic
Rework Micro Bold
Rework Micro Bold Italic

A*

REWORK MICRO: Ascender   748

REWORK DISPLAY: Ascender   676

ayef

A*

REWORK DISPLAY: Descender   -140

REWORK MICRO: Descender   -220

Thin
Italic

The sun–soaked scenes of freedom and rebellion

32

Extra
light

9/11's Memorial: "Wall of Hope & Remembrance"

32

Light
Italic

Desire paths; our oldest marks on the landscape

32

Regular

EXTINCTION REBELLION uses Occupy's methods

32

Semibold
Italic

Tinned food or crates of anti—bacterial hand gel

32

Bold

A Nuclear Household's Resident Indiana Jones

32

Thin
&
Thin
Italic

CREATIVITY is capable of flourishing in *confinement*

Whether it's flowers, cans, bicycles or even sagging balloons, "improv shrines" embody community's grief. They could sacralise ground that would have otherwise just be seen as just "the side of the road".

Extralight
&
Extralight
Italic

Impromptu shrines started to spring up across New York in the wake of 9/11. In the days following the terrorist attack, there was not a clear statistic of the number of casualties.

Survivalism intersects with the politics of identity – figures like Alex Jones, Milo Yiannopolis, even Jordan Peterson have taken mantles from *Bonds and Bauers* in the battle for our continued existence. Whether we would term their theories hateful or pertinent, I'm afraid — is truly beside the point.

Light
&
Light
Italic

IF THE PSYCHOLOGICAL APPEAL of prison tattoos is deeply earthbound – signalling individuality, or gang belonging – other forms of creativity wield much heavier mantles of significance. Alexei Leonov, for instance, was the first person to make a work of art in outer space[01]. While the artefact he produced is a fairly modest object, the coloured-crayon depiction of an *orbital sunrise* represented a first in history.

→ 01 ▷ Alexei A. Leonov (30th May 1934 – 11th October 2019) was a Soviet and Russian cosmonaut, Air Force major general, writer, and artist. On 18th March 1965, he became the first person to spacewalk, exiting the capsule during the Voskhod 2 mission for 12 minutes and 9.5 seconds. He was also selected to be the first Soviet person to land on the Moon although the project was cancelled. In July 1975, Leonov commanded th Soyuz–Apollo mission, which docked in space for two days with a US Apollo capsule.

Regular
&
Regular
Italic

When Leonov put pencil to paper on board the *Vokshod 2* in 1965, he was contending with zero gravity, wedged into a tiny capsule with astronaut PAVEL BELYAYEV and wearing a bulky suit – hard to imagine a more physically constraining situation, or a more intellectually stimulating one. We make art to make sense of the world (or in Leonov's case, of the world's place in the universe)[②].

② SELECTED NOVELS BY Alexander Romanovich Belyaev:
• *Professor Dowell's Head*: Short story (1924), NYC
• *The Ruler of the World* (1926-1929), SAINT PETERSBURG
• *Shipwreck Island* (1931-1936), ISBN 5-05-000659-7
• *Last Man from Atlantis* (1941), Raduga Publisher, 1986
• KETs Star (1944). The Initials of Konstantin Tsiolkovsky.
• The Man Who Found His Face, ISBN 5-08-023643-8
• The Amphibian Man (1948): Prof Dowell's Testament
• Jump into the Void (1951): ISBN 6-02-120008-2

Semibold
&
Semibold
Italic

CULTURAL OUTPUT excels during trying times, despite the fact that austere political climates tend to retract governmental funding from the organisations which support it*. In much the same way as some of the world's best poetry is born from personal heartbreak (*Pablo Neruda* would pack half the punch if he'd written when cheerful), people produce work from negative stimuli.

* Neruda ▸ ALSO KNOWN AS *Ricardo Neftalí Rey Basoalto* Chilean poet-diplomat and politician who won the Nobel Prize for Literature in 1971. Neruda became known as a poet when he was 13 years old, and wrote in a variety of styles, including surrealist poems and historical epics. Neruda occupied many diplomatic positions in various countries during his lifetime and served a term as a Senator for the Communist Party, when President Gabriel González Videla outlawed communism in Chile in 1948.

Bold
&
Bold
Italic

From film and television to visual arts and music, trying times can birth our very best; Jon Kelly cites a veritable roster of creative greats, toiling under societal pressure: 'Vincent van Gogh, starving as he slaves over his masterpieces. Johnny Rotten, sneering at the wreckage of 1970s Britain[†]. George Orwell, finding his voice amid the poverty and despair of the Great Depression.'

† Warren Smith (2002). "Lydon, John [Johnny Rotten]". Celebrities in Hell. Chelsea press. p. 74. ISBN 978156021. On the liner notes of a 1992 single "Cruel" Lydon said, *"Where is God? I can't see no evidence of God. God is probably Barry Manilow."* (A Quietus Interview)
‡ Lydon, John (2020) I Could Be Wrong, I Could Be Right. A Way With Media, with a limited print run of 10,000 by and by mail order only. (East London Press, Bethnal Green) ISBN 978-1471137198. Lydon, John ©

TYPEFACE	:	RM MONO
DESIGNER	:	COTYPE FOUNDRY
LOCATION	:	LONDON, UK

	PUBLISHED BY	:	COTYPE FOUNDRY	
	CHRONOLOGY	:	13TH TYPEFACE RELEASE	
	RELEASED IN	:	2023	

LINK	:	HTTPS://COTYPEFOUNDRY.COM/OUR-FONTS/RM-MONO/
STYLES	:	5 WEIGHTS: LIGHT, REGULAR, SEMIBOLD, BOLD, BLACK
CREDITS	:	HOLOGRAPHIK (SPECIMEN POSTER DESIGN)

RM MONO IS THE MONOSPACED COUNTERPART OF RM NEUE, WITH EACH CHARACTER FITTING WITHIN A BOX OF THE SAME WIDTH (600 UNITS). IT COMES IN FIVE WEIGHTS, RANGING FROM LIGHT TO BLACK, MATCHING THE WEIGHTS OF ITS SISTER FAMILY. WITH EXTENSIVE LANGUAGE SUPPORT, RM MONO ENABLES TYPE TO BE SET IN MOST EUROPEAN LANGUAGES USING THE LATIN SCRIPT. WHEN PAIRED WITH RM NEUE, IT CREATES A UNIQUE HOUSE STYLE SUITABLE FOR VARIOUS BUSINESSES, OFFERING INTERESTING TYPOGRAPHIC HIERARCHIES SIMILAR TO THE COMBINATION SEEN WITH AEONIK AND AEONIK MONO.

CAP HEIGHT

REGULAR — 290PT

X-HEIGHT

Rr

BASELINE

RM Mono

THE QUICK BROWN FOX
IT WOULD BE THE CHEE
IT'S A LOVELY DAY IN
AND THE PUNGENT AROM
PROMISE OF A SUMPTUO
THINKING ABOUT THE D
THE LAZY DOG REMAINS

The quick brown fox jumps over a lazy do
it would be the cheeky thing to do. Afte
It's a lovely day in the neighbourhood,
and the pungent aroma of fresh rubbish b
promise of a sumptuous meal. The spright
thinking about the delicious treasures h
the lazy dog remains unperturbed. With h
long black fur fluttering in the breeze,

The quick brown fox jumps over a lazy dog. He didn't have to, but he thought
it would be the cheeky thing to do. After all, he had a reputation to maintain.
It's a lovely day in the neighbourhood, with the sun shining, the birds chirping,
and the pungent aroma of fresh rubbish bins wafting through the air - the
promise of a sumptuous meal. The sprightly fox rubs his paws together in glee,
thinking about the delicious treasures he's about to dig into. Still in her spot,
the lazy dog remains unperturbed. With her long snout, droopy jowls, and
long black fur fluttering in the breeze, she is in a dreamland far away - where
the mountains are made of beefy treats, the valleys are filled with tennis balls,
and the puddles are just the right temperature. Why be in the rat race?
It's a dog's life, after all.

RM MON

LIGHT

RM RM MO

REGULAR

RM SEMIBOLD M

RM BO

RM

NO
ONO
MONO
MONO
MONO
BLACK

TYPEFACE	:	RM NEUE
DESIGNER	:	COTYPE FOUNDRY
LOCATION	:	LONDON, UK

PUBLISHED BY	:	COTYPE FOUNDRY
CHRONOLOGY	:	1ST TYPEFACE RELEASE
RELEASED IN	:	2019

LINK	:	HTTPS://COTYPEFOUNDRY.COM/OUR-FONTS/RM-NEUE/
STYLES	:	5 WEIGHTS, 10 STYLES: LIGHT, REGULAR, SEMIBOLD, BOLD, BLACK, EACH WITH MATCHING OBLIQUE ITALICS + A VARIABLE FONT

INSPIRED BY UTILITARIAN NEO-GROTESQUES, RM NEUE FEATURES COMPACT PROPORTIONS AND A LOW-CONTRAST DESIGN, OFFERING IMMEDIATE FAMILIARITY WITHOUT THE EXPECTED STERILITY OF A TYPICAL GROTESQUE FONT. WITH A CHARACTER SET SPANNING THE LATIN EXTENDED UNICODE RANGE, COVERING MOST LANGUAGES IN THE LATIN SCRIPT, RM NEUE IS VISUALLY STRIKING AT DISPLAY SIZES AND HIGHLY LEGIBLE AS A TEXT FACE. IT SERVES AS THE PERFECT CHOICE FOR PROFESSIONALS SEEKING A VERSATILE SANS SERIF FONT FOR VARIOUS DESIGN ENVIRONMENTS.

CAP HEIGHT

REGULAR — 290PT

X-HEIGHT

BASELINE

Rr

RM Neue

THE QUICK BRO

IT WOULD BE TH

IT'S A LOVELY DA

AND THE PUNGE

PROMISE OF A S

THINKING ABOU

THE LAZY DOG

LONG BLACK FU

THE MOUNTAINS

5

Weights

Light
+ Italic

aa

Regular
+ Italic

aa

SemiBold
+ Italic

aa

Bold
+ Italic

aa

Black
+ Italic

aa

TYPEFACE	:	ABC ROM
DESIGNER	:	SEB MCLAUCHLAN
LOCATION	:	BERLIN, GERMANY

PUBLISHED BY	:	DINAMO
CHRONOLOGY	:	N/A
RELEASED IN	:	2023

LINK	:	HTTPS://ABCDINAMO.COM/TYPEFACES/ROM
STYLES	:	6 FAMILIES, 84 STYLES
CREDITS	:	IGINO MARINI (SPACING & KERNING), ROBERT JANES/DINAMO (PRODUCTION)

ABC ROM IS A ROBUST AND CONFIDENT FUSION OF CLASSIC GROTESK AND GOTHIC TYPEFACE STYLES. IT SEAMLESSLY COMBINES THE RATIONALISED LINES OF THE FORMER WITH RAW DETAILS FROM THE LATTER, CREATING MOMENTS THAT ARE BOTH BEAUTIFUL AND DISSONANT. DRAWING INSPIRATION FROM TYPEFACE APPLICATIONS IN CONCEPTUAL ART CATALOGUES FROM THE 60'S AND 70'S, ABC ROM EXHIBITS WIDE AND GENEROUS PROPORTIONS IN CAPS, WHILE ITS LOWERCASE CHARACTERS ARE NARROW AND ELEGANT.

CAP HEIGHT

X-HEIGHT

BASELINE

REGULAR — 290PT

Rr

ABCRom

THE QUICK BROWN FOX J
IT WOULD BE THE CHEEK
IT'S A LOVELY DAY IN THE
AND THE PUNGENT ARON
PROMISE OF A SUMPTUO
THINKING ABOUT THE DE
THE LAZY DOG REMAINS

The quick brown fox jumps over a lazy dog. He didn't h
it would be the cheeky thing to do. After all, he had a re
It's a lovely day in the neighbourhood, with the sun shir
and the pungent aroma of fresh rubbish bins wafting th
promise of a sumptuous meal. The sprightly fox rubs hi
thinking about the delicious treasures he's about to dig
the lazy dog remains unperturbed. With her long snout
long black fur fluttering in the breeze, she is in a dream

The quick brown fox jumps over a lazy dog. He didn't have to, but he thought
it would be the cheeky thing to do. After all, he had a reputation to maintain.
It's a lovely day in the neighbourhood, with the sun shining, the birds chirping,
and the pungent aroma of fresh rubbish bins wafting through the air - the
promise of a sumptuous meal. The sprightly fox rubs his paws together in glee,
thinking about the delicious treasures he's about to dig into. Still in her spot,
the lazy dog remains unperturbed. With her long snout, droopy jowls, and
long black fur fluttering in the breeze, she is in a dreamland far away - where
the mountains are made of beefy treats, the valleys are filled with tennis balls,
and the puddles are just the right temperature. Why be in the rat race?
It's a dog's life, after all.

ROM

ROM LIGHT

ABCDEFGHIJKLMNOPQRSTUVWXYZ
abcdefghijklmnopqrstuvwxyz
1234567890

ROM REGULAR

ABCDEFGHIJKLMNOPQRSTUVWXYZ
abcdefghijklmnopqrstuvwxyz
1234567890

ROM BOOK

ABCDEFGHIJKLMNOPQRSTUVWXYZ
abcdefghijklmnopqrstuvwxyz
1234567890

ROM BOLD

ABCDEFGHIJKLMNOPQRSTUVWXYZ
abcdefghijklmnopqrstuvwxyz
1234567890

ROM BLACK

ABCDEFGHIJKLMNOPQRSTUVWXYZ
abcdefghijklmnopqrstuvwxyz
1234567890

TYPEFACE	:	RULES
DESIGNER	:	LÉON HUGUES
LOCATION	:	PARIS, FRANCE

	PUBLISHED BY	:	BLAZE TYPE
	CHRONOLOGY	:	2022
	RELEASED IN	:	2022

LINK	:	HTTPS://BLAZETYPE.EU/TYPEFACES/RULES
STYLES	:	12 STYLES, 6 WEIGHTS, 2 SLANTS
CREDITS	:	MATTHIEU SALVAGGIO/BLAZE TYPE (COLLABORATION)

THE RULES FONT IS A CONTEMPORARY INTERPRETATION OF THE NEO-GROTESQUE FONT ERA, INFUSED WITH A DISTINCTIVE EDGE. ROOTED IN SWISS MODERN TYPE INSPIRATION, IT UPHOLDS A STRONG STRUCTURE THAT DRAWS FROM TYPE DESIGN TRADITION. FEATURING MODERN CAPITALS WITH OPTICALLY-MATCHING WIDTHS, MINIMAL CONTRAST IN COUNTER-FORMS, CLOSED-EDGED TERMINALS, AND AN ELEGANT TWIST, THE RULES FONT INTRODUCES A COLOURFUL ASPECT TO OPTICAL GRAY IN TEXT LAYOUTS. THE FONT FAMILY IS UNIFIED WITH SQUARED ENDINGS, PROVIDING A DYNAMIC PACE. TAILORED FOR BODY TEXTS IN PRINT, WEB, AND APP MEDIUMS, IT ALSO EXCELS AS A MAIN HEADLINE OR DISPLAY FONT FOR POSTERS AND SIGNAGE SYSTEMS.

CAP HEIGHT

EXTRALIGHT — 290PT

X-HEIGHT

BASELINE

Rules

THE QUICK BROWN FOX
IT WOULD BE THE CHEE
IT'S A LOVELY DAY IN TH
AND THE PUNGENT ARC
PROMISE OF A SUMPTU
THINKING ABOUT THE D
THE LAZY DOG REMAIN

The quick brown fox jumps over a lazy dog. He didn't
it would be the cheeky thing to do. After all, he had a
It's a lovely day in the neighbourhood, with the sun sh
and the pungent aroma of fresh rubbish bins wafting
promise of a sumptuous meal. The sprightly fox rubs
thinking about the delicious treasures he's about to d
the lazy dog remains unperturbed. With her long sno
long black fur fluttering in the breeze, she is in a drea

The quick brown fox jumps over a lazy dog. He didn't have to, but he thought
it would be the cheeky thing to do. After all, he had a reputation to maintain.
It's a lovely day in the neighbourhood, with the sun shining, the birds chirping,
and the pungent aroma of fresh rubbish bins wafting through the air - the
promise of a sumptuous meal. The sprightly fox rubs his paws together in glee,
thinking about the delicious treasures he's about to dig into. Still in her spot,
the lazy dog remains unperturbed. With her long snout, droopy jowls, and
long black fur fluttering in the breeze, she is in a dreamland far away - where
the mountains are made of beefy treats, the valleys are filled with tennis balls,
and the puddles are just the right temperature. Why be in the rat race?
It's a dog's life, after all.

RULES

IKEO™

Speeder.©

DeWOLT

LuEDis™

Beennz

Nº

9

TYPEFACE   :   SANS PLOMB
DESIGNER   :   JOHAN MOSSÉ & QUENTIN BERTHELOT/IMAGEFORMAT
COUNTRY   :   MONTPELLIER, FRANCE

                  PUBLISHED BY   :   LIFT TYPE
                  CHRONOLOGY   :   N/A
                  RELEASE   :   2022

LINK   :   HTTPS://WWW.LIFT-TYPE.FR/SHOP/TYPOGRAPHY/SANS-PLOMB/
STYLES   :   95 - 98 - SUPER - 95 OBLIQUE - 98 OBLIQUE -
                  SUPER OBLIQUE

SANS PLOMB IS A GROTESQUE FONT FAMILY INSPIRED BY FRENCH ROADS AND THE AUTOMOTIVE WORLD OF THE 80'S. DRAWING FROM GAS STATION SIGNS TO SPARE PART BRANDS, THIS FONT CAPTURES THE IMPERFECT YET BEAUTIFUL CHARM OF TYPEFACES FROM THAT ERA. WITH A COMPRESSED WIDTH AND VERY SHORT ASCENDANTS AND DESCENDANTS, SANS PLOMB IS IDEAL FOR LARGE DISPLAY TITLES. ITS DISTINCTIVENESS IS FURTHER ENHANCED BY CROPPED DIACRITICS AND REVERSED INKTRAPS, AS SEEN IN CHARACTERS LIKE "I".

CAP HEIGHT   95 — 290PT

X-HEIGHT

Ss

BASELINE

Sans Plomb

THE QUICK BROWN FOX JU

IT WOULD BE THE CHEEKY T

IT'S A LOVELY DAY IN THE N

AND THE PUNGENT AROMA

PROMISE OF A SUMPTUOUS

THINKING ABOUT THE DELIC

THE LAZY DOG REMAINS UN

The quick brown fox jumps over a lazy dog. He didn't have to, but he thought it would be the cheeky thing to do. After all, he had a reputation to maintain. It's a lovely day in the neighbourhood, with the sun shining, the birds chirping, and the pungent aroma of fresh rubbish bins wafting through the air - the promise of a sumptuous meal. The sprightly fox rubs his paws together in glee, thinking about the delicious treasures he's about to dig into. Still in her spot, the lazy dog remains unperturbed. With her long snout, droopy jowls, and long black fur fluttering in the breeze, she is in a dreamland far away - where the mountains are made of beefy treats, the valleys are filled with tennis balls, and the puddles are just the right temperature. Why be in the rat race? It's a dog's life, after all.

Nationale № 7
→ 996 km
Paris-Menton
⑤On The Way!!

⑧
[128.8 km]
(via A7D560N)

Marseille ⟷ Avignon

NORTH
EAST
SOUTH
WEST

7  9

TYPEFACE	:	SCANDIUM
DESIGNER	:	COTYPE FOUNDRY
LOCATION	:	LONDON, UK

		PUBLISHED BY	:	COTYPE FOUNDRY
		CHRONOLOGY	:	9TH TYPEFACE RELEASE
		RELEASED IN	:	2021

LINK	:	HTTPS://COTYPEFOUNDRY.COM/OUR-FONTS/SCANDIUM/
STYLES	:	14 STYLES, 7 WEIGHTS: THIN, EXTRALIGHT, LIGHT, REGULAR, SEMIBOLD, BOLD, BLACK WITH MATCHING ITALICS + A VARIABLE FONT
CREDITS	:	SEMIOTIK DESIGN (SPECIMEN BOOK DESIGN)

SCANDIUM IS A CONTEMPORARY SANS-SERIF FONT WITH OPEN SHAPES AND A TECHNICAL VIBE, DESIGNED TO MEET THE NEEDS OF THE AUTOMOTIVE INDUSTRY. ITS MODESTLY SQUARED CURVES, HIGH X-HEIGHT, AND VERTICAL TERMINALS COMBINE PERFORMANCE WITH PURPOSE. SCANDIUM ALSO FEATURES A COMPREHENSIVE SET OF ICONS, CATERING TO IN-CAR ENTERTAINMENT SYSTEMS. THESE ICONS AND SYMBOLS ARE VERSATILE, SUITABLE FOR VARIOUS ENVIRONMENTS SUCH AS WEB UI, DIGITAL MEDIA PLAYERS, ELECTRIC VEHICLES, AND NAVIGATION SYSTEMS. ADDITIONALLY, THE FONT INCLUDES A PLAYFUL SET OF EMOJIS TO INJECT A SENSE OF FUN INTO ANY DESIGN.

CAP HEIGHT

REGULAR – 220PT

X-HEIGHT

Ss

BASELINE

Scandium

THE QUICK BROWN FOX JU
IT WOULD BE THE CHEEKY
ITS A LOVELY DAY IN THE N
AND THE PUNGENT AROM
PROMISE OF A SUMPTUOL
THINKING ABOUT THE DEL
THE LAZY DOG REMAINS L

The quick brown fox jumps over a lazy dog. He didnt h
it would be the cheeky thing to do. After all, he had a
Its a lovely day in the neighbourhood, with the sun sh
and the pungent aroma of fresh rubbish bins wafting
promise of a sumptuous meal. The sprightly fox rubs
thinking about the delicious treasures hes about to di
the lazy dog remains unperturbed. With her long sno
long black fur fluttering in the breeze, she is in a drea
the mountains are made of beefy treats, the valleys a

The quick brown fox jumps over a lazy dog. He didnt have to, but he thought
it would be the cheeky thing to do. After all, he had a reputation to maintain.
Its a lovely day in the neighbourhood, with the sun shining, the birds chirping,
and the pungent aroma of fresh rubbish bins wafting through the air the
promise of a sumptuous meal. The sprightly fox rubs his paws together in glee,
thinking about the delicious treasures hes about to dig into. Still in her spot,
the lazy dog remains unperturbed. With her long snout, droopy jowls, and
long black fur fluttering in the breeze, she is in a dreamland far away where
the mountains are made of beefy treats, the valleys are filled with tennis balls,
and the puddles are just the right temperature. Why be in the rat race
Its a dogs life, after all.

A

Scandium
Regular 230pt

S

Scandium
Bold Italic 230pt

L

Scandium
SemiBold 230pt

B

Scandium
Thin 230pt

Z

Scandium
Regular 230pt

X

Scandium
Black 230pt

F

Scandium
Regular Italic 230pt

V

Scandium
Regular 230pt

N

Scandium
Light Italic 230pt

M

Scandium
Thin 230pt

P

Scandium
Regular 230pt

&

Scandium
SemiBold 230pt

TYPEFACE : SHAPE
DESIGNER : CHRISTOPH YORK
LOCATION : NEW ZEALAND

PUBLISHED BY : THE DESIGNERS FOUNDRY
CHRONOLOGY : N/A
RELEASED IN : 2019

LINK : HTTPS://THEDESIGNERSFOUNDRY.COM/SHAPE
STYLES : 18

SHAPE IS A CONTEMPORARY GEOMETRIC TYPE FAMILY COMPRISING 18 STYLES. DESIGNED WITH PRECISION, SIMPLICITY, AND A SUBTLE WARMTH, IT PRIORITISES FLEXIBILITY AS ITS FOUNDING PRINCIPLE. THE FAMILY REVOLVES AROUND AN OPEN AND ACCESSIBLE AESTHETIC, EMPHASISING CLARITY AND PURITY TO CONVEY INFORMATION EFFECTIVELY. SHAPE IS CRAFTED AS THE PERFECT MEDIUM FOR PUTTING CONTENT FIRST, MAKING IT AN IDEAL CHOICE FOR VARIOUS DESIGN CONTEXTS.

CAP HEIGHT   REGULAR — 290PT

X-HEIGHT

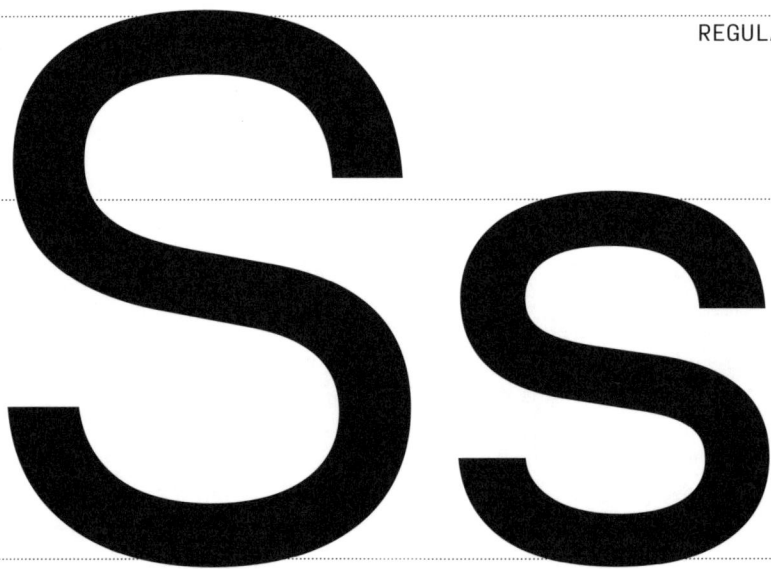

BASELINE

Shape

THE QUICK BR

IT WOULD BE T

ITS A LOVELY D

AND THE PUNC

PROMISE OF A

THINKING ABC

THE LAZY DOC

LONG BLACK F

THE MOUNTAI

Bold **Black**

Medium

Hairline

Light

Regular

Italics

Thin

Super

Semibold

Quaternions

Interceptors

Diversionary

Superseding

Whisperings

Geometrical

Recantation

Subversively

Indisputable

TYPEFACE	:	OR SIMILAR	354
DESIGNER	:	OR TYPE	
LOCATION	:	REYKJAVÍK, ICELAND; BRUSSELS, BELGIUM	

PUBLISHED BY	:	OR TYPE
CHRONOLOGY	:	N/A
RELEASED IN	:	2022

LINK	:	HTTPS://ORTYPE.IS/SPECIMEN/SIMILAR
STYLES	:	14

SIMILAR DRAWS INSPIRATION FROM THE BORDERS OF THE VAST HISTORY OF NEO-GROTESQUES. THE TYPEFACE VENTURES INTO NEW, UNEXPLORED TERRITORIES WITHIN THE GENRE, CHALLENGING PERCEPTIONS OF GROTESQUE FONTS. ITS MAIN DESIGN FEATURES INCLUDE STEEP SHOULDERS, SHORT ARCS, AND CURVY TO STRAIGHT LEGS, GUIDING THE STYLE TOWARD A HAND-DRAWN AESTHETIC RATHER THAN AN INDUSTRIAL ONE. WITH 14 STYLES AND SUBTLE CHARACTER, SIMILAR EXHIBITS VERSATILE QUALITIES. IT HAS BEEN CRAFTED AS A WORKHORSE, SUITABLE FOR BOTH LONG AND SHORT BODY COPY, WHILE ITS DISTINCTIVE FEATURES MAKE IT WELL-SUITED FOR PROMINENT USE IN BIG TITLES, POSTERS, LOGOTYPES, AND MORE. ADDITIONALLY, THE TYPEFACE IS AVAILABLE IN A FULLY VARIABLE FONT.

CAP HEIGHT

REGULAR — 290PT

X-HEIGHT

Ss

BASELINE

ORSimilar

THE QUICK BROWN FOX JU

IT WOULD BE THE CHEEKY

IT'S A LOVELY DAY IN THE

AND THE PUNGENT AROM

PROMISE OF A SUMPTUOU

THINKING ABOUT THE DE

THE LAZY DOG REMAINS U

The quick brown fox jumps over a lazy dog. He didn't ha
it would be the cheeky thing to do. After all, he had a re
It's a lovely day in the neighbourhood, with the sun shir
and the pungent aroma of fresh rubbish bins wafting th
promise of a sumptuous meal. The sprightly fox rubs h
thinking about the delicious treasures he's about to dig
the lazy dog remains unperturbed. With her long snout
long black fur fluttering in the breeze, she is in a dream

The quick brown fox jumps over a lazy dog. He didn't have to, but he thought
it would be the cheeky thing to do. After all, he had a reputation to maintain.
It's a lovely day in the neighbourhood, with the sun shining, the birds chirping,
and the pungent aroma of fresh rubbish bins wafting through the air - the
promise of a sumptuous meal. The sprightly fox rubs his paws together in glee,
thinking about the delicious treasures he's about to dig into. Still in her spot,
the lazy dog remains unperturbed. With her long snout, droopy jowls, and
long black fur fluttering in the breeze, she is in a dreamland far away - where
the mountains are made of beefy treats, the valleys are filled with tennis balls,
and the puddles are just the right temperature. Why be in the rat race?
It's a dog's life, after all.

I Copy Therefore I Paste

Looking in a Mirror

Evil Twin

or Double Walker

Walker

Similar But Quite Different

```
TYPEFACE    :    SNEAK
DESIGNER    :    FABIAN FOHRER
LOCATION    :    GERMANY

                 PUBLISHED BY       :    TIGHTYPE
                 CHRONOLOGY         :    N/A
                 RELEASED IN        :    2019

LINK        :    HTTPS://TIGHTYPE.COM/TYPEFACES/SNEAK
STYLES      :    LIGHT, LIGHT ITALIC, REGULAR, REGULAR ITALIC, MEDIUM,
                 MEDIUM ITALIC, BOLD, BOLD ITALIC, BLACK, BLACK ITALIC,
                 MONO
```

SNEAK IS A NEO-GROTESQUE TYPEFACE FEATURING SEVERAL REVERSED CHARACTERS, SUCH AS ITS DISTINCTIVE "S". IT IS AVAILABLE IN FIVE WEIGHTS WITH CORRESPONDING ITALICS AS WELL AS A MONOSPACED STYLE.

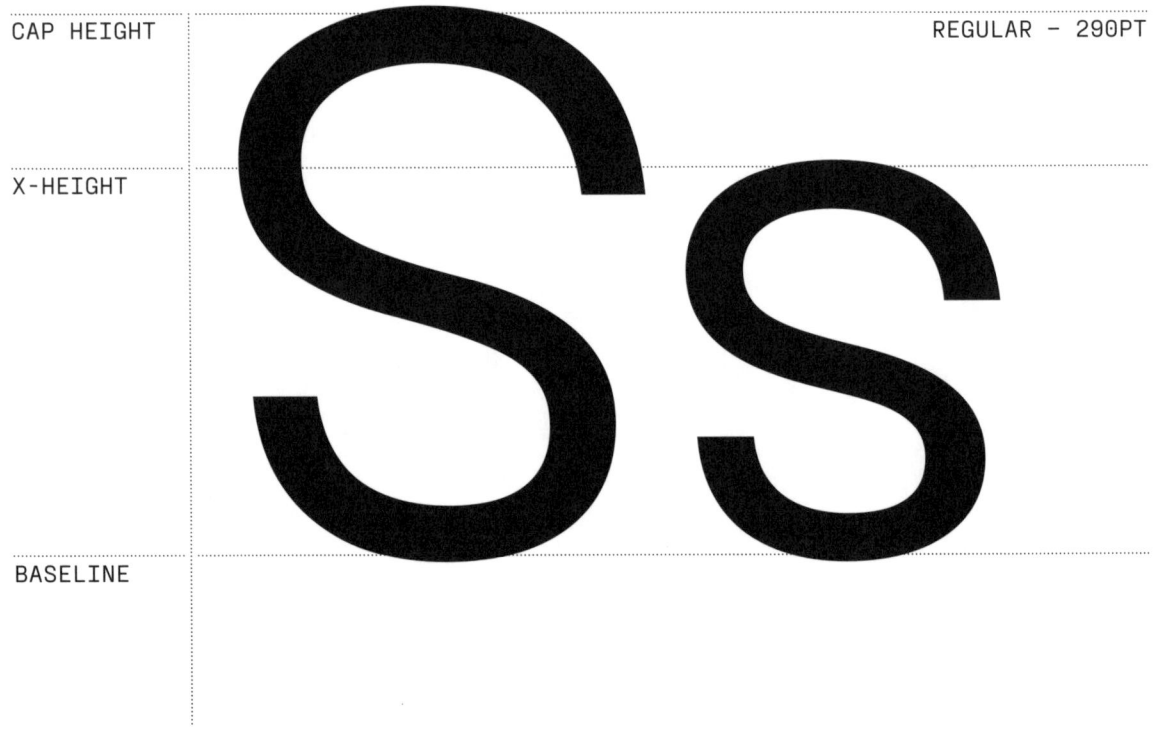

CAP HEIGHT   REGULAR — 290PT

X-HEIGHT

Ss

BASELINE

Sneak

THE QUICK BROWN FO

IT WOULD BE THE CHE

IT'S A LOVELY DAY IN T

AND THE PUNGENT AR

PROMISE OF A SUMPT

THINKING ABOUT THE

THE LAZY DOG REMAI

LONG BLACK FUR FLU

THE MOUNTAINS ARE

AND THE PUDDLES AR

The quick brown fox jumps over a lazy dog. He didn't have to, but he thought
it would be the cheeky thing to do. After all, he had a reputation to maintain.
It's a lovely day in the neighbourhood, with the sun shining, the birds chirping,
and the pungent aroma of fresh rubbish bins wafting through the air – the
promise of a sumptuous meal. The sprightly fox rubs his paws together in glee,
thinking about the delicious treasures he's about to dig into. Still in her spot,
the lazy dog remains unperturbed. With her long snout, droopy jowls, and
long black fur fluttering in the breeze, she is in a dreamland far away – where
the mountains are made of beefy treats, the valleys are filled with tennis balls,
and the puddles are just the right temperature. Why be in the rat race?
It's a dog's life, after all.

inside

Up

Upsid

e

Down

Down

TYPEFACE   :   SOLARIS
DESIGNER   :   SM FOUNDRY
LOCATION   :   APELDOORN, THE NETHERLANDS

               PUBLISHED BY   :   SM FOUNDRY
               CHRONOLOGY   :   N/A
               RELEASED IN   :   2019

LINK   :   HTTPS://S-M.NU/TYPEFACES/SOLARIS
STYLES   :   LIGHT, REGULAR, ITALIC

SOLARIS IS A HIGH CONTRAST NEO-GROTESK TYPEFACE WITH A SLEEK AND SOPHISTICATED LOOK IN LARGE SIZES, REMAINING NEUTRAL AND LEGIBLE IN SMALL SIZES. THE EMPHASISED CONTRAST IN THE CHARACTER IS FIXED ON THE CENTRE, CREATING A CONSISTENT RHYTHM OF SHAPES IN SENTENCES.

CAP HEIGHT

X-HEIGHT

BASELINE

REGULAR — 290PT

Ss

Solaris

THE QUICK BROWN

IT WOULD BE THE C

ITS A LOVELY DAY

AND THE PUNGENT

PROMISE OF A SUN

THINKING ABOUT T

THE LAZY DOG RE

LONG BLACK FUR

THE MOUNTAINS A

AND THE PUDDLES

ITS A DOGS LIFE, A

Solaris
FAMILY

Solaris Light

Light, 45 pt / 50 pt.

Aa Bb Cc Dd Ee Ff Gg Hh Ii Jj
Kk Ll Mm Nn Oo Pp Qq Rr Ss Tt
Uu Vv Ww Xx Yy Zz & Æ ß @
0 1 2 3 4 5 6 7 8 9 :;., !?

Solaris Light

14 pt International Monument Foundation Structuralist Bureau Retrospective

24 pt Olympic Metabolism Expression After Jazz

34 pt Rational Thoughts Utilize Format

44 pt Offices For The Generation

54 pt Wealth Reflects Phrases

64 pt Futurist Institute Tasks

74 pt Artificial Manifesting

84 pt Globalize Objective

94 pt Villager Associates

Ascender 869

Cap Height 706

X Height 518

Baseline 0

Descender -187

Character Overview

Uppercase Characters

A B C D E F G H I J K L M N O P Q R S T U V W X Y Z

Uppercase Accents

Á Ă Â Ä À Ā Ą Å Ã Ć Č Ç Ċ Đ Ď É Ě Ê Ë Ė È Ē Ę Ğ Ģ Ġ
Ħ Í Î Ï Ì İ Į Ķ Ĺ Ľ Ļ Ł Ń Ň Ņ Ŋ Ñ Ó Ô Ö Ò Ő Ō Ø Õ Ŕ Ř Ŗ
Ś Š Ş Ş Ŧ Ť Ţ Ţ Ú Û Ü Ù Ű Ū Ų Ů Ẃ Ŵ Ẅ Ẁ Ý Ŷ Ÿ Ỳ Ź Ž Ż

Lowercase Characters

a b c d e f g h i j k l m n o p q r s t u v w x y z

Lowercase Accents

á ă â ä à ā ą å ã ć č ç ċ ď đ é ě ê ë ė è ē ę ğ ģ ġ ħ í î í
ï ì į j ķ ĺ ľ ļ ł ń ň ņ ŋ ñ ó ô ö ò ő ō ø õ ŕ ř ŗ ś š ş ş ŧ ť ţ ţ ú
û ü ù ű ū ų ů ẃ ŵ ẅ ẁ ý ŷ ÿ ỳ ź ž ż

Additional Characters

Æ æ Œ œ Þ þ ß ð

Numbers

0 1 2 3 4 5 6 7 8 9 0 1 2 3 4 5 6 7 8 9

Punctuation Marks

: : . , . . . ! ¡ ? ¿ – — - ([{ }]) ' "

Symbols

@ & § ø # • • ∞ ↑ ↗ → ↘ ↓ ↙ ← ↖ ⇆ ♯ ∫ ∂ ◊ © ® ﹐ _ ˍ ˌ
" ' ˚ ^ / | ¦ \ « ‹ ‹ › ≥ » ¶ ‡ †

Currency

$ € £ ¥ ¢ ¤

Mathematical Symbols

× − + ÷ = ≠ ± ≈ ~ ∏ √ ∑ % ‰

TYPEFACE	:	F37 SONIC
DESIGNER	:	F37®
LOCATION	:	MANCHESTER, UK
PUBLISHED BY	:	F37®
CHRONOLOGY	:	2023
RELEASED IN	:	2023
LINK	:	HTTPS://F37FOUNDRY.COM/FONTS/F37-SONIC
STYLES	:	7 WEIGHTS WITH MATCHING OBLIQUES, TOTALLING 14 STYLES

F37 SONIC IS AN UNCONVENTIONAL GEOMETRIC SANS-SERIF DESIGNED TO AMPLIFY MESSAGES WITH SHARP, STRIKING, AND IMPACTFUL VISUALS THAT DEMAND ATTENTION. WHILE TECHNICALLY A GEOMETRIC SANS, ITS CONSTRUCTION DEVIATES FROM THE TYPICAL, SHOWCASING A UNIQUE APPEARANCE. UNLIKE TRADITIONAL APPROACHES, SONIC DERIVES ITS CIRCULAR GEOMETRY NOT FROM THE EXTERIOR BUT FROM THE COUNTERS OF THE LETTERFORMS. THIS INTENTIONAL DESIGN CHOICE RESULTS IN A PRONOUNCED JUXTAPOSITION BETWEEN NARROW, STRAIGHT LETTERS (E.G., "N", "T", AND "F") AND WIDE DIAGONAL AND ROUNDED LETTERS (E.G., "O", "A", AND "V").

CAP HEIGHT

REGULAR — 290PT

X-HEIGHT

BASELINE

Ss

F37Sonic

THE QUICK BROWN
IT WOULD BE THE CH
IT'S A LOVELY DAY IN
AND THE PUNGENT A
PROMISE OF A SUMP
THINKING ABOUT TH

The quick brown fox jumps over a lazy dog. He didn't have to, but he thought it would be the cheeky thing to do. After all, he had a reputation to maintain. It's a lovely day in the neighbourhood, with the sun shining, the birds chirping, and the pungent aroma of fresh rubbish bins wafting through the air - the promise of a sumptuous meal. The sprightly fox rubs his paws together in glee, thinking about the delicious treasures he's about to dig into. Still in her spot, the lazy dog remains unperturbed. With her long snout, droopy jowls, and long black fur fluttering in the breeze, she is in a dreamland far away - where the mountains are made of beefy treats, the valleys are filled with tennis balls, and the puddles are just the right temperature. Why be in the rat race?
It's a dog's life, after all.

The quick brown fox jumps over a lazy dog. He didn't have to, but he thought it would be the cheeky thing to do. After all, he had a reputation to maintain. It's a lovely day in the neighbourhood, with the sun shining, the birds chirping, and the pungent aroma of fresh rubbish bins wafting through the air - the promise of a sumptuous meal. The sprightly fox rubs his paws together in glee, thinking about the delicious treasures he's about to dig into. Still in her spot, the lazy dog remains unperturbed. With her long snout, droopy jowls, and long black fur fluttering in the breeze, she is in a dreamland far away - where the mountains are made of beefy treats, the valleys are filled with tennis balls, and the puddles are just the right temperature. Why be in the rat race?
It's a dog's life, after all.

So

Uncompr

Magneto

Conceptu

Radioastr

Internatio

Telecomn

nie

UltraBlack

omisable

Black

dynamics

ExtraBold

ualisation

Bold

onomical

Medium

nalisation

Regular

unication

Light

TYPEFACE	:	FAIRE SPRIG SANS
DESIGNER	:	FAIRE TYPE
LOCATION	:	NEW YORK, US

		PUBLISHED BY	:	FAIRE TYPE
		CHRONOLOGY	:	2023
		RELEASED IN	:	2023

LINK	:	HTTPS://WWW.FAIRETYPE.COM/FONTS/SPRIG-SANS
STYLES	:	HAIRLINE, THIN, LIGHT, REGULAR, MEDIUM, BOLD, BLACK, SUPER, HAIRLINE ITALIC, THIN ITALIC, LIGHT ITALIC, REGULAR ITALIC, MEDIUM ITALIC, BOLD ITALIC, BLACK ITALIC, SUPER ITALIC

SPRIG SANS IS A GEOMETRIC, GROTESQUE SANS-SERIF TYPEFACE WITH A FRIENDLY DEMEANOUR, SERVING AS THE SANS-SERIF COUNTERPART TO THE CHELTENHAM-INSPIRED SERIF TYPEFACE, SPRIG. IT RETAINS THE DISTINCTIVE FEATURES OF SPRIG, INCLUDING ROUND, ORGANIC LETTERFORMS, WITH MATCHING WEIGHTS AND LETTERFORM PROPORTIONS. THE RESULT IS A GROTESQUE SANS-SERIF FONT THAT COMBINES THE FLEXIBILITY OF A CLASSIC WORKHORSE SANS WITH UNIQUE AND INSPIRED CHARACTERS AND DETAILS. TO ESTABLISH A STRONG CONNECTION BETWEEN THE SPRIG SANS AND SERIF FAMILIES, A VARIETY OF OPENTYPE FEATURES ARE AVAILABLE, OFFERING ACCESS TO SPECIAL CHARACTERS LIKE SWASH CAPS, LIGATURES, AND ALTERNATE GLYPHS.

CAP HEIGHT

REGULAR — 290PT

X-HEIGHT

Ss

BASELINE

FAIRE Sprig Sans

THE QUICK BROWN FO>
IT WOULD BE THE CHEE
IT'S A LOVELY DAY IN TH
AND THE PUNGENT AR(
PROMISE OF A SUMPTU
THINKING ABOUT THE [

The quick brown fox jumps over a lazy dog. He didn't have t
it would be the cheeky thing to do. After all, he had a reputa
It's a lovely day in the neighbourhood, with the sun shining
and the pungent aroma of fresh rubbish bins wafting throu
promise of a sumptuous meal. The sprightly fox rubs his pa
thinking about the delicious treasures he's about to dig int
the lazy dog remains unperturbed. With her long snout, dro
long black fur fluttering in the breeze, she is in a dreamland
the mountains are made of beefy treats, the valleys are fille
and the puddles are just the right temperature. Why be in t
It's a dog's life, after all.

The quick brown fox jumps over a lazy dog. He didn't have to, but he thought
it would be the cheeky thing to do. After all, he had a reputation to maintain.
It's a lovely day in the neighbourhood, with the sun shining, the birds chirping,
and the pungent aroma of fresh rubbish bins wafting through the air - the
promise of a sumptuous meal. The sprightly fox rubs his paws together in glee,
thinking about the delicious treasures he's about to dig into. Still in her spot,
the lazy dog remains unperturbed. With her long snout, droopy jowls, and
long black fur fluttering in the breeze, she is in a dreamland far away - where
the mountains are made of beefy treats, the valleys are filled with tennis balls,
and the puddles are just the right temperature. Why be in the rat race?
It's a dog's life, after all.

st

FAI
SPRIG

Café robusta
Kokafamilien
Larix laricina
Buffel grass
Ail des bois

20

BKLYN
NYC

swash

RE
SANS

dog

©

hundredPointsSymbol

23

Acting

Offline

Mystic

Hairline
Thin
Light
Regular
Medium
Bold
Black
2023 Super

TYPEFACE	:	SURT
DESIGNER	:	BLAZE TYPE
LOCATION	:	MARSEILLE, FRANCE

PUBLISHED BY	:	BLAZE TYPE
CHRONOLOGY	:	2018 - 2023
RELEASED IN	:	2020

LINK	:	HTTPS://BLAZETYPE.EU/TYPEFACES/SURT
STYLES	:	SANS, DISPLAY, TEXT, NORMAL, EXPANDED, EXTENDED, UPRIGHT, ITALIC

THE SURT TYPEFACE FAMILY, INSPIRED BY NORSE MYTHOLOGY AND SCANDINAVIAN ARCHITECTURE, COMBINES ELEMENTS OF A GEOMETRIC SANS WITH A HUMAN TOUCH IN ITS OVERALL DESIGN TO INTRODUCE A UNIQUE QUIRKINESS TO TEXT LAYOUTS, MAKING IT DISTINCT AND COMFORTABLE TO READ. THE ROUNDED NORSE-INSPIRED GLYPHS CREATE A SUBTLE DISRUPTION IN THE TEXT'S RHYTHM. SURT ALSO TAKES INSPIRATION FROM GEOMETRIC SHAPES FOUND IN GEOMETRIC FONTS, BUT ITS INFLUENCE LEANS MORE TOWARDS CONTEMPORARY BRUTALIST ARCHITECTURE RATHER THAN HISTORICAL GEOMETRIC OR NEO-GROTESQUE FONTS, PROVIDING A MODERN TWIST TO ITS DESIGN.

CAP HEIGHT

REGULAR — 290PT

X-HEIGHT

Ss

BASELINE

Surt

THE QUICK BR

IT WOULD BE T

IT'S A LOVELY

AND THE PUNC

PROMISE OF A

THINKING ABO

THE LAZY DOC

LONG BLACK F

THE MOUNTAI

TYPEFACE	:	NB TELEVISION™ PRO
DESIGNER	:	STEFAN GANDL
LOCATION	:	BERLIN, GERMANY

		PUBLISHED BY	:	NEUBAU
		CHRONOLOGY	:	2020 – 2022
		RELEASED IN	:	2022

LINK	:	HTTPS://NEUBAULADEN.COM/PRODUCT/NB-TELEVISION-PRO-EDITION/
STYLES	:	REGULAR, 2D, 3D, MONO, MONO 2D, MONO 3D

NB TELEVISION™ PRO WAS INSPIRED BY THE POPULAR TYPEFACES OF THE "CATHODE RAY TUBE" OR CRT ERA. EACH GLYPH WAS METICULOUSLY CRAFTED WITH PIXEL-PERFECT PRECISION AS AN HOMAGE TO ANALOGUE CRT GRID-BASED, SOFT-EDGED TYPESETS, BUT TRANSLATED FOR THE DIGITAL AGE. THE FONT EXUDES WARMTH WHEN USED IN SMALL SIZES VERSUS ITS CRISP, PIXEL-DOMINATED, MODERN NEO-GROTESQUE WHEN APPLIED IN LARGE SIZES – MAKING IT IDEAL FOR BOTH PRINT AND DIGITAL MEDIA.

CAP HEIGHT

REGULAR – 290PT

X-HEIGHT

BASELINE

NB Television™ Pro

THE QUICK BROW

IT WOULD BE THE

IT'S A LOVELY DA

AND THE PUNGEI

PROMISE OF A SU

THINKING ABOUT

THE LAZY DOG RE

LONG BLACK FUI

THE MOUNTAINS

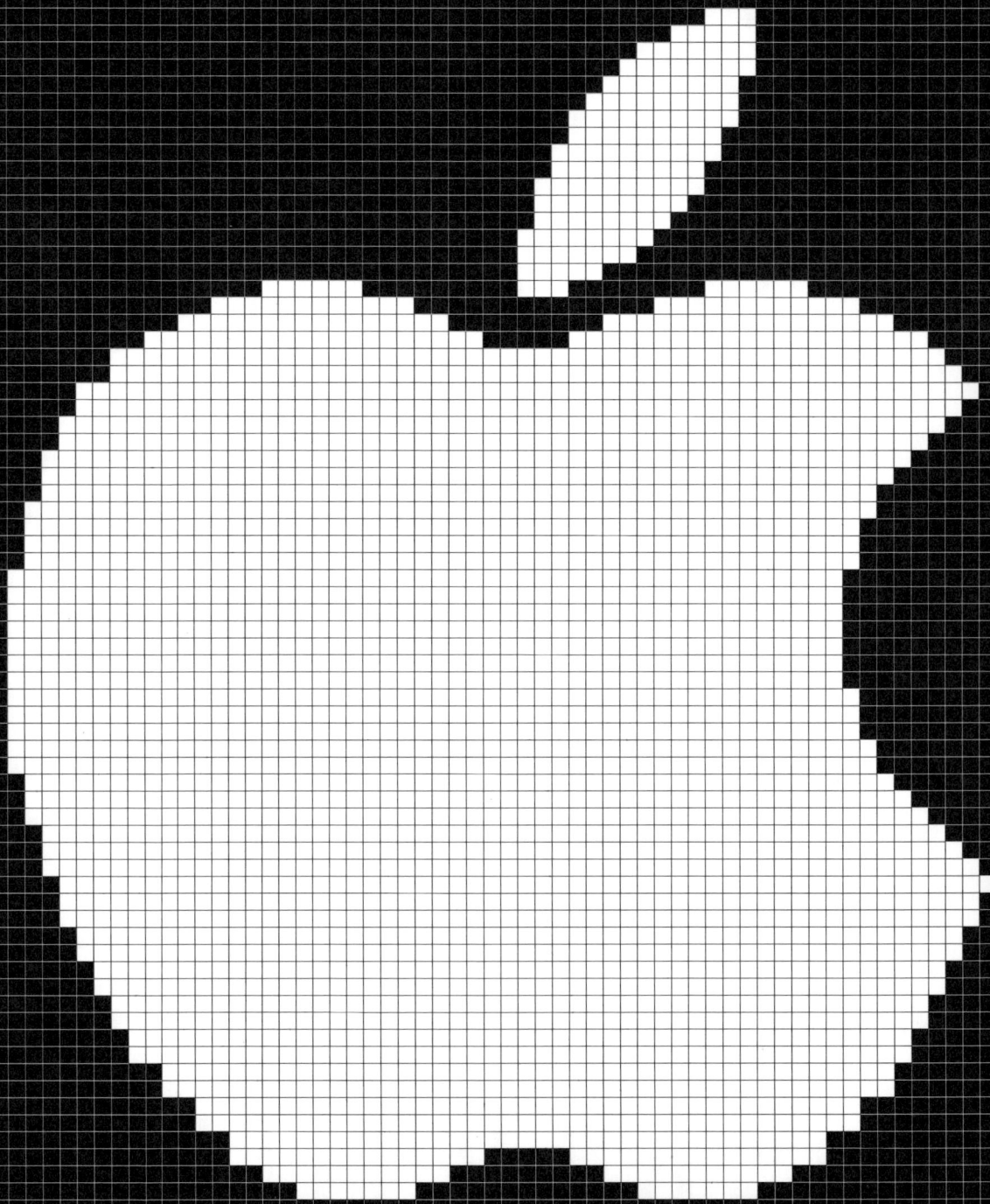

Neubau
Television™ Pro
R[1] 2D[2] 3D[3]
M[4] M2D[5] M3D[6]

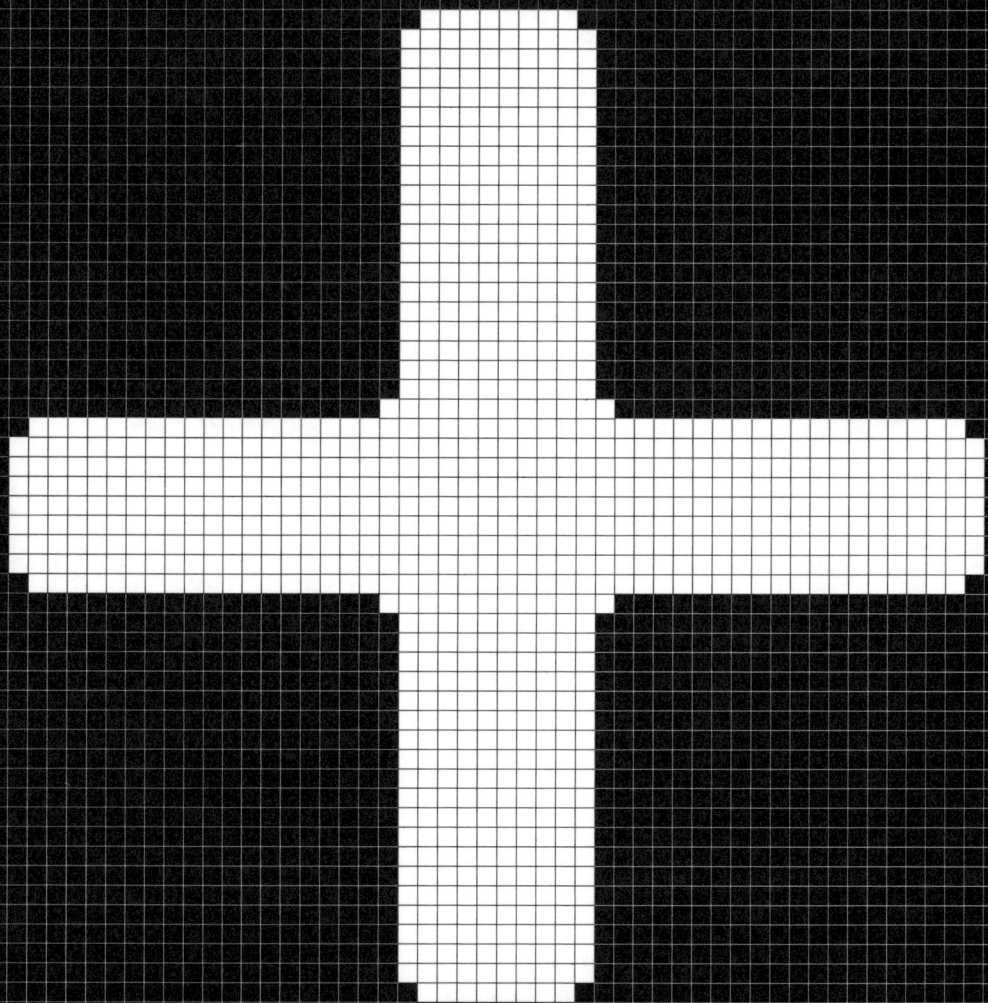

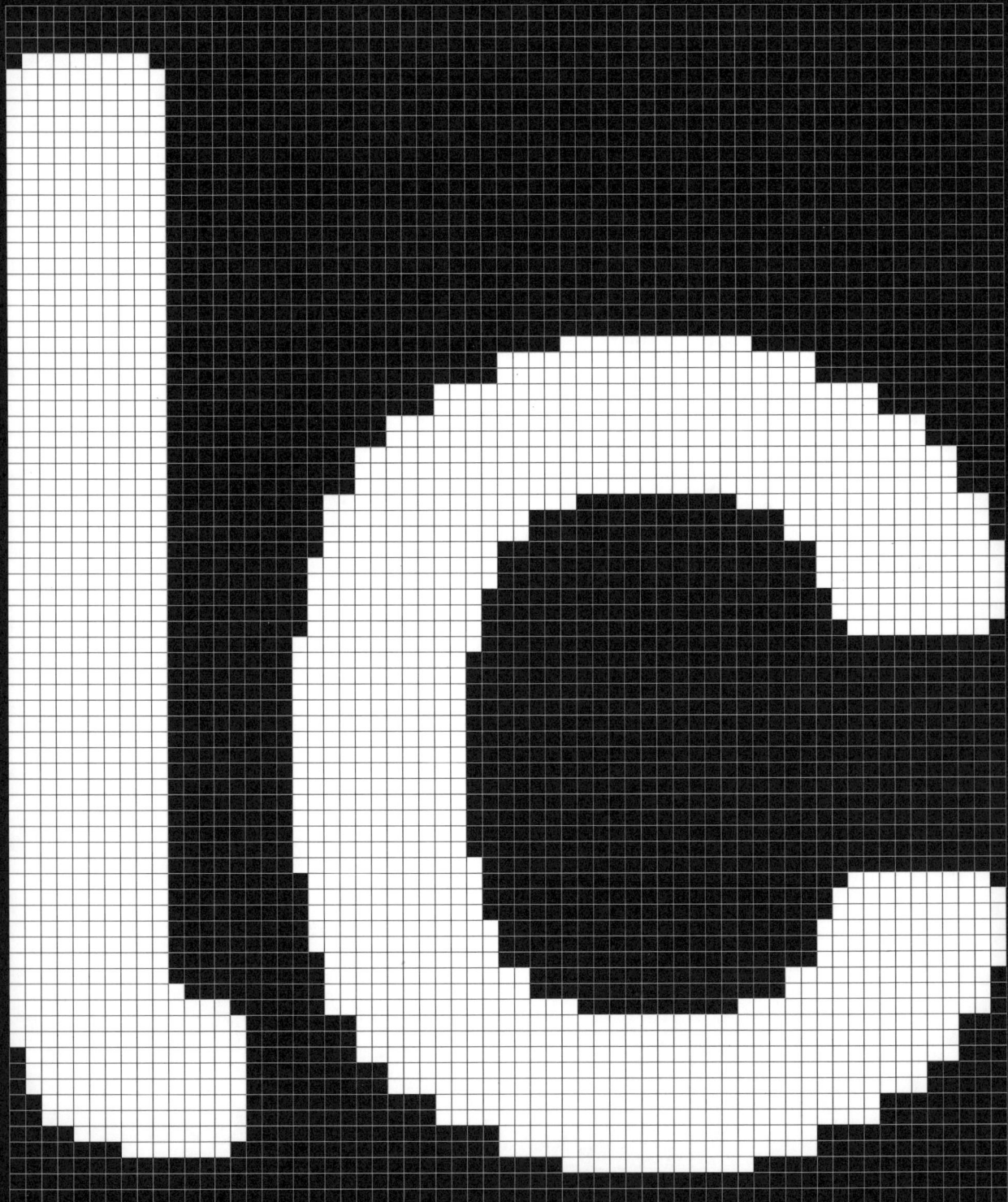

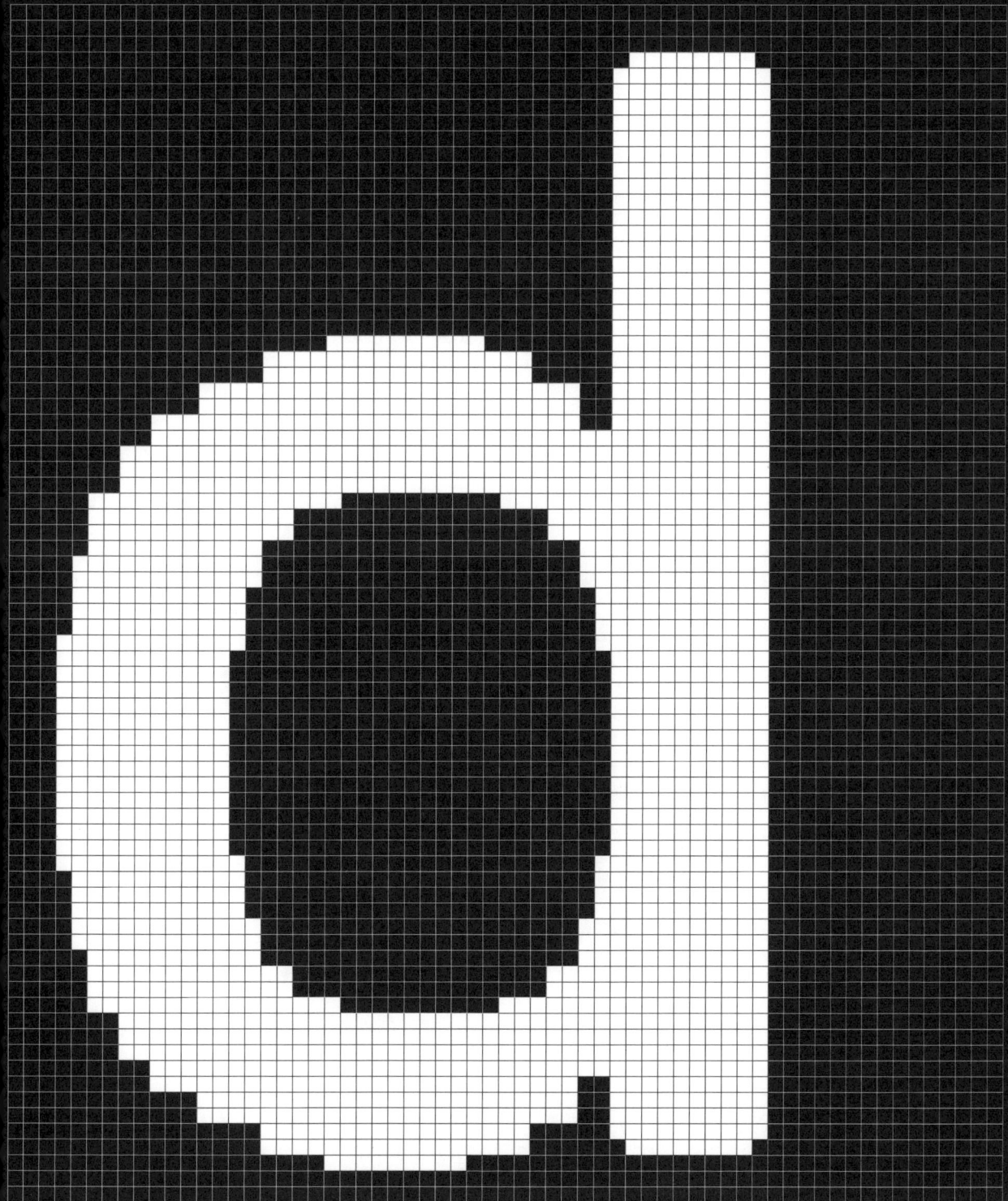

TYPEFACE	:	TOMATO GROTESK
DESIGNER	:	ANDREA BIGGIO
LOCATION	:	NEW ZEALAND

PUBLISHED BY	:	THE DESIGNERS FOUNDRY
CHRONOLOGY	:	N/A
RELEASED IN	:	2020

LINK	:	HTTPS://THEDESIGNERSFOUNDRY.COM/TOMATO-GROTESK
STYLES	:	18 STYLES + A VARIABLE FONT

TOMATO GROTESK IS A MODERN GROTESQUE FONT FAMILY WITH A BOLD DISPLAY PERSONALITY, FEATURING SIMPLE GEOMETRIC SHAPES AND ACCENTUATED CONTRAST. DESIGNED FOR VERSATILITY, IT EXCELS IN BOTH SMALL AND LARGE SIZES, WITH HIGH CONTRAST, TIGHT SPACING, AND INKTRAPS. ITS EXTENDED OPENTYPE FEATURES OFFER ADDITIONAL DESIGN OPTIONS, INCLUDING ALTERNATE GLYPHS, LIGATURES, FRACTIONS, AND VARIOUS SYMBOLS. THE FAMILY CONSISTS OF 9 WEIGHTS (LIGHT TO BLACK) WITH SLANTED VERSIONS, TOTALLING 18 STYLES, AND INCLUDES A VARIABLE VERSION FOR ADDED FLEXIBILITY.

CAP HEIGHT

REGULAR — 290PT

X-HEIGHT

Tt

BASELINE

Tomato Grotesk

THE QUICK BROW

HAVE TO, BUT HE

IT WOULD BE THI

REPUTATION TO

IT'S A LOVELY DA

SHINING, THE BIF

AND THE PUNGE

THROUGH THE A

The quick brown fox jumps over a lazy dog. He didn't have to, but he thought it would be the cheeky thing to do. After all, he had a reputation to maintain. It's a lovely day in the neighbourhood, with the sun shining, the birds chirping, and the pungent aroma of fresh rubbish bins wafting through the air - the promise of a sumptuous meal. The sprightly fox rubs his paws together in glee, thinking about the delicious treasures he's about to dig into. Still in her spot, the lazy dog remains unperturbed. With her long snout, droopy jowls, and long black fur fluttering in the breeze, she is in a dreamland far away - where the mountains are made of beefy treats, the valleys are filled with tennis balls, and the puddles are just the right temperature. Why be in the rat race? It's a dog's life, after all.

Thin

Extralight Light

Regular Medium

Semibold Bold

Extrabold

Black

tftttw
mm
gg

Répartir le beurre mou et le miel sur un moule en tôle (Ø env. 30 cm) chemisé exactement de papier cuisson. Couper les ✱s en rondelles d'env. 1 cm d'épaisseur, disposer dessus en les faisant se chevaucher, saler. Couper les oignons fanes en rouelles, répartir dessus. Piquer la pâte à la fourchette, déposer sans tasser sur les oignons. **Rentrer le bord de la pâte entre les tomates et le bord du moule. Cuisson: env. 20 min au milieu du four préchauffé à 220°C. Retirer la tarte, laisser reposer env. 2 min, retourner sur un plat. Couper le basilic en fines lanières, parsemer de fleur de sel ☺✱☺.**

Idroponica
Ebb&Flow
Potatura
Coltura
Maggio
Indoor

San Marzano
Costoluto
Pizzutello
Ciliegino
Datterini
Pachino

TOMATOES
GENERALLY COME
IN TWO DIFFERENT
GROWTH HABITS:
CORDON (OR
INDETERMINATE)
TOMATOES GROW
TALL, REACHING UP
TO 1.8M (6FT) AND
REQUIRE SUPPORT.

WWW
lätkē
♡
RRR

TYPEFACE   :   TT TRAILERS
DESIGNER   :   TYPETYPE.ORG
LOCATION   :   SAINT PETERSBURG, RUSSIA

PUBLISHED BY   :   TYPETYPE.ORG
CHRONOLOGY   :   2019 - 2022
RELEASED IN   :   2019

LINK   :   HTTPS://TYPETYPE.ORG/FONTS/TT-TRAILERS/
STYLES   :   19 STYLES + A VARIABLE FONT

TT TRAILERS IS A MODERN HUMANIST SANS SERIF THAT IS PART OF A NEW GENERATION OF NARROW TYPEFACES. IT WAS INSPIRED BY THE FILM INDUSTRY AND WAS MEANT TO POP ON TITLES AND POSTERS. ITS SLEEK AND VERSATILE NATURE ALSO MAKES IT SUITABLE FOR PACKAGING DESIGN AND BRAND IDENTITIES, ADDING A FRIENDLY AND CREATIVE VIBE TO ANY DESIGN.

CAP HEIGHT

X-HEIGHT

REGULAR — 290PT

BASELINE

^{TT}Trailers

THE QUICK BROWN FOX JUMPS OVER A LAZY DOG. HE D

IT WOULD BE THE CHEEKY THING TO DO. AFTER ALL, HE

IT'S A LOVELY DAY IN THE NEIGHBOURHOOD, WITH THE

AND THE PUNGENT AROMA OF FRESH RUBBISH BINS WA

PROMISE OF A SUMPTUOUS MEAL. THE SPRIGHTLY FOX

THINKING ABOUT THE DELICIOUS TREASURES HE'S ABO

THE LAZY DOG REMAINS UNPERTURBED. WITH HER LON

LONG BLACK FUR FLUTTERING IN THE BREEZE, SHE IS I

THE MOUNTAINS ARE MADE OF BEEFY TREATS, THE VALL

AND THE PUDDLES ARE JUST THE RIGHT TEMPERATURE.

IT'S A DOG'S LIFE. AFTER ALL

TT TRAILS
HUMANIST
DISPLAY
SANS SERIF

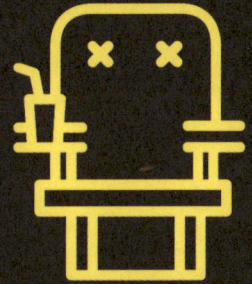

TYPEFACE	:	KOMETA UNIFORMA
DESIGNER	:	KOMETA TYPEFACES
LOCATION	:	BRNO, CZECH REPUBLIC

	PUBLISHED BY	:	KOMETA TYPEFACES
	CHRONOLOGY	:	2021 - PRESENT
	RELEASED IN	:	2022

| LINK | : | HTTPS://WWW.KOMETA.XYZ/TYPEFACES/UNIFORMA/ |
| STYLES | : | HAIRLINE-BLACK IN ROMAN & ITALIC (TOTALLING 18 STYLES) |

UNIFORMA IS A TYPEFACE THAT NAVIGATES THE BALANCE BETWEEN DISPLAY AND TEXT CONSIDERATIONS. WITH 9 WEIGHTS IN BOTH UPRIGHT AND IMPRESSIVE -28° ITALIC STYLES, IT OFFERS A VERSATILE RANGE FOR EXPRESSIVE YET RESOLUTE TYPOGRAPHY. AVAILABLE IN 18 STYLES, IT MANAGES TO AVOID APPEARING IMPERIOUS WHILE PROVIDING A DISTINCTIVE AESTHETIC.

CAP   REGULAR — 290PT

X-HE

BASELINE

KOMETA Uniforma

THE QUICK B

THOUGHT IT

TION TO MA

SHINING, TH

WAFTING TH

SPRIGHTLY F

CIOUS TREA

MAINS UNRE

48 Gran Turismo!
42 Gran Turismo!
36 Gran Turismo!
30 Gran Turismo!
25 Gran Turismo!
20 Gran Turismo!
15 Gran Turismo!
12 Gran Turismo!
08 Gran Turismo!
06 Gran Turismo!
04 Gran Turismo!
02 Gran Turismo!

260 Aá

AG2R Citroën Team, UCI—ACT (FR)
Est. Briançon; 1992
Chazal, equip. BMC (2021–)

20

Bianchi, SRAM, Cube,
Lapierre, Canyon, Colnago, Cervélo,
BMC, Shimano GRX.

20

Àà

260

Paris-Roubaix
Paris-Roubaix
Paris-Roubaix
Paris-Roubaix
Paris-Roubaix
Paris-Roubaix
Paris-Roubaix
Paris-Roubaix
Paris-Roubaix
Paris-Roubaix
Paris-Roubaix
Paris-Roubaix

02
04
06
08
12
15
20
25
30
36
42
48

TYPEFACE	:	VCTR MONO
DESIGNER	:	TRAVIS KOCHEL
LOCATION	:	PORTLAND, US

		PUBLISHED BY	:	VECTRO
		CHRONOLOGY	:	2017 - 2023
		RELEASED IN	:	2018 - 2023

| LINK | : | HTTPS://VECTROTYPE.COM |
| STYLES | : | THIN, THIN ITALIC, LIGHT, LIGHT ITALIC, REGULAR, REGULAR ITALIC, MEDIUM, MEDIUM ITALIC, BOLD, BOLD ITALIC, BLACK, BLACK ITALIC |

VCTR MONO IS A MONOSPACED TYPEFACE WITH A WARM, SLIGHTLY GOOFY, AND TACTILE DESIGN. INSPIRED BY TEXT FOUND ON THE LENSES AND BODIES OF MANUAL CAMERAS, PARTICULARLY LEICAS AND NIKONS, IT WAS ORIGINALLY NAMED ISO FOR THE PROJECT EXIF.CO. OPTIMISED FOR INTERFACE DESIGNS, IT INCLUDES A SUBSTANTIAL SET OF ICONS AND EMOJIS SUITABLE FOR APPS AND INTERFACES.

CAP HEIGHT

REGULAR — 290PT

X-HEIGHT

Vv

BASELINE

VCTR Mono

THE QUICK BROWN FOX
IT WOULD BE THE CHEE
IT'S A LOVELY DAY IN
AND THE PUNGENT AROM
PROMISE OF A SUMPTUO
THINKING ABOUT THE D

The quick brown fox jumps over a lazy dog. He didn
it would be the cheeky thing to do. After all, he
It's a lovely day in the neighbourhood, with the s
and the pungent aroma of fresh rubbish bins wafting
promise of a sumptuous meal. The sprightly fox rub
thinking about the delicious treasures he's about
the lazy dog remains unperturbed. With her long sno
long black fur fluttering in the breeze, she is in
the mountains are made of beefy treats, the valleys
and the puddles are just the right temperature. Why
It's a dog's life, after all.

The quick brown fox jumps over a lazy dog. He didn't have to, but he thought
it would be the cheeky thing to do. After all, he had a reputation to maintain.
It's a lovely day in the neighbourhood, with the sun shining, the birds chirping,
and the pungent aroma of fresh rubbish bins wafting through the air - the
promise of a sumptuous meal. The sprightly fox rubs his paws together in glee,
thinking about the delicious treasures he's about to dig into. Still in her spot,
the lazy dog remains unperturbed. With her long snout, droopy jowls, and
long black fur fluttering in the breeze, she is in a dreamland far away - where
the mountains are made of beefy treats, the valleys are filled with tennis balls,
and the puddles are just the right temperature. Why be in the rat race?
It's a dog's life, after all.

VCTR

VCTR MONO

VCTR MONO

VCTR MONO

VCTR MONO

MONO

VCTR MONO

VCTR MONO

VCTR MONO

VCTR MONO

TYPEFACE	:	ZETKIN
DESIGNER	:	INGA PLÖNNIGS
LOCATION	:	BERLIN, GERMANY

PUBLISHED BY	:	FUTURE FONTS
CHRONOLOGY	:	2020
RELEASED IN	:	2020

LINK	:	HTTPS://WWW.FUTUREFONTS.XYZ/INGA-PLONNIGS/ZETKIN
STYLES	:	LIGHT, LIGHT OBLIQUE, REGULAR, REGULAR OBLIQUE, MEDIUM, MEDIUM OBLIQUE, BOLD, BOLD OBLIQUE, BLACK, BLACK OBLIQUE, WIDE, WIDE OBLIQUE

ZETKIN IS A CONFIDENT DISPLAY TYPEFACE WITH DETERMINED DIAGONALS, A STRONG SLANT, AND EXTENDED PROPORTIONS. ITS CHARACTERISTIC DESIGN FEATURES, SUCH AS ITS HIGH-WAISTED UPPERCASE LETTERS AND FLARING STROKE ENDINGS, PAY HOMAGE TO VENUS, A TYPEFACE FAMILY RELEASED IN 1907 BY BAUERSCHE GIESSEREI. WITH A DIVERSE RANGE OF WEIGHTS AND WIDE DISPLAY STYLES, ZETKIN IS VERSATILE AND SUITABLE FOR VARIOUS TEXT SIZES AND APPLICATIONS.

CAP HEIGHT

X-HEIGHT

REGULAR — 290PT

BASELINE

Zetkin

THE QUICK BROWN FOX JU

IT WOULD BE THE CHEEKY

IT'S A LOVELY DAY IN THE N

AND THE PUNGENT AROMA

PROMISE OF A SUMPTUOU

THINKING ABOUT THE DELI

THE LAZY DOG REMAINS U

The quick brown fox jumps over a lazy dog. He didn't ha
it would be the cheeky thing to do. After all, he had a re
It's a lovely day in the neighbourhood, with the sun shin
and the pungent aroma of fresh rubbish bins wafting th
promise of a sumptuous meal. The sprightly fox rubs his
thinking about the delicious treasures he's about to dig
the lazy dog remains unperturbed. With her long snout,
long black fur fluttering in the breeze, she is in a dreaml

The quick brown fox jumps over a lazy dog. He didn't have to, but he thought
it would be the cheeky thing to do. After all, he had a reputation to maintain.
It's a lovely day in the neighbourhood, with the sun shining, the birds chirping,
and the pungent aroma of fresh rubbish bins wafting through the air - the
promise of a sumptuous meal. The sprightly fox rubs his paws together in glee,
thinking about the delicious treasures he's about to dig into. Still in her spot,
the lazy dog remains unperturbed. With her long snout, droopy jowls, and
long black fur fluttering in the breeze, she is in a dreamland far away - where
the mountains are made of beefy treats, the valleys are filled with tennis balls,
and the puddles are just the right temperature. Why be in the rat race?
It's a dog's life, after all.

My name is
ZETKIN
but friends call me
ZETQUEEN

abcdefghijklmnopqrstuvwxyz

abcdefghijklmnopqrstuvwxyz

abcdefghijklmnopqrstuvwxyz

abcdefghijklmnopqrstuvwxyz

abcdefghijklmnopqrstuvwxyz

abcdefghijklmnopqrstuvwxyz

ABCDEFGHIJKLMNOPQRSTUVWXYZ

ABCDEFGHIJKLMNOPQRSTUVWXYZ

ABCDEFGHIJKLMNOPQRSTUVWXYZ

ABCDEFGHIJKLMNOPQRSTUVWXYZ

ABCDEFGHIJKLMNOPQRSTUVWXYZ

ABCDEFGHIJKLMNOPQRSTUVWXYZ

abcdefghijklmnopqrstuvwxyz

abcdefghijklmnopqrstuvwxyz

abcdefghijklmnopqrstuvwxyz

abcdefghijklmnopqrstuvwxyz

abcdefghijklmnopqrstuvwxyz

abcdefghijklmnopqrstuvwxyz

ABCDEFGHIJKLMNOPQRSTUVWXYZ

ABCDEFGHIJKLMNOPQRSTUVWXYZ

ABCDEFGHIJKLMNOPQRSTUVWXYZ

ABCDEFGHIJKLMNOPQRSTUVWXYZ

ABCDEFGHIJKLMNOPQRSTUVWXYZ

ABCDEFGHIJKLMNOPQRSTUVWXYZ

TYPEFACE	:	ZIN SANS
DESIGNER	:	CARNOKYTYPE
LOCATION	:	KYSAK, SLOVAKIA

		PUBLISHED BY	:	CARNOKYTYPE
		CHRONOLOGY	:	2016 - 2017
		RELEASE	:	2017

LINK	:	HTTPS://CARNOKYTYPE.COM/FONTS/ZIN_SANS
STYLES	:	10 NORMAL, 10 CONDENSED, 10 EXTENDED STYLES WITH 5
		WEIGHTS + ITALICS

ZIN SANS IS A CONTEMPORARY SANS-SERIF TYPEFACE CHARACTERISED BY A LARGE X-HEIGHT AND A BALANCE BETWEEN THE NEUTRAL LETTER CONSTRUCTION AND DYNAMIC OPEN FORMS. IT FEATURES A NARROWER CONNECTION BETWEEN STEMS AND STROKES. THE FONT FAMILY CONSISTS OF THREE WIDTH PROPORTIONS (NORMAL, CONDENSED, AND EXTENDED) IN FIVE WEIGHTS, MAKING IT VERSATILE FOR BOTH TEXT AND DISPLAY TYPESETTING. ZIN SANS IS SUITABLE FOR VARIOUS APPLICATIONS, INCLUDING MAGAZINE LAYOUTS, EDITORIAL DESIGN, ADVERTISING TYPOGRAPHY, SIGNAGE, AND CORPORATE IDENTITIES. IT IS PART OF THE ZIN SUPERFAMILY, WHICH ALSO INCLUDES SLAB, SERIF, AND DISPLAY FONTS.

CAP HEIGHT

REGULAR — 290PT

X-HEIGHT

BASELINE

Zz

Zin Sans

THE QUICK BROWN FOX
IT WOULD BE THE CHEEK
IT'S A LOVELY DAY IN THE
AND THE PUNGENT ARON
PROMISE OF A SUMPTUC
THINKING ABOUT THE DE
THE LAZY DOG REMAINS

The quick brown fox jumps over a lazy dog. He didr
it would be the cheeky thing to do. After all, he had
It's a lovely day in the neighbourhood, with the sun
and the pungent aroma of fresh rubbish bins waftir
promise of a sumptuous meal. The sprightly fox rul
thinking about the delicious treasures he's about tc
the lazy dog remains unperturbed. With her long sr
long black fur fluttering in the breeze, she is in a dr

The quick brown fox jumps over a lazy dog. He didn't have to, but he thought
it would be the cheeky thing to do. After all, he had a reputation to maintain.
It's a lovely day in the neighbourhood, with the sun shining, the birds chirping,
and the pungent aroma of fresh rubbish bins wafting through the air - the
promise of a sumptuous meal. The sprightly fox rubs his paws together in glee,
thinking about the delicious treasures he's about to dig into. Still in her spot,
the lazy dog remains unperturbed. With her long snout, droopy jowls, and
long black fur fluttering in the breeze, she is in a dreamland far away - where
the mountains are made of beefy treats, the valleys are filled with tennis balls,
and the puddles are just the right temperature. Why be in the rat race?
It's a dog's life, after all.

Zin sans

a member of the ZIN superfamily by CARNOKYTYPE

magazine layouts

risograph

Novinové titulky

03. 06. 2017—15. 08. 2049

Poctivá spoločnosť

(**MUSEUM**)

of Contemporary Art

&

HEADLINES

and running text →

— **ZIN SANS** je komplexný písmový systém navrhnutý pre širokú škálu použitia. Charakteristikou je vysoká stredná výška, ktorá písmo robí výborne čitateľným aj v malých veľkostiach. Konštrukčnou charakteristikou je balans medzi statickým princípom (typické mínusky „b, d, p, q") a otvorenou dynamickou kostrou (otvorené výbehy/nábehy v minuskulách „a, c, e, s").
— Písmová rodina *Zins Sans* pozostáva okrem základnej šírkovej proporcie aj zo zúžených (CONDENSED) a rozšírených (EXTENDED), rezov písma. Samozrejmosťou písma sú malé kapitálky, číselné varianty, alternatívne znaky, paleta zliatkov a množstvo typografických vymožeností v rámci OpenType. Plánovaným rozšírením písmového systému *Zin* je doplnenie o komplementárne písmové rodiny — slabserifový *Zin Slab* a pätkovú verziu *Zin Serif*.

Zin Sans

... is a contemporary sans typeface designed for various situations of typographic usage.¶

Each font includes SMALL CAPITALS, old-style & tabular figures (123/123), standard and discretionary ligatures (fi/ffl/ct/st), alternate glyphs (a/g/y/&) and a many of typographic options applied by the OPENTYPE features. ■

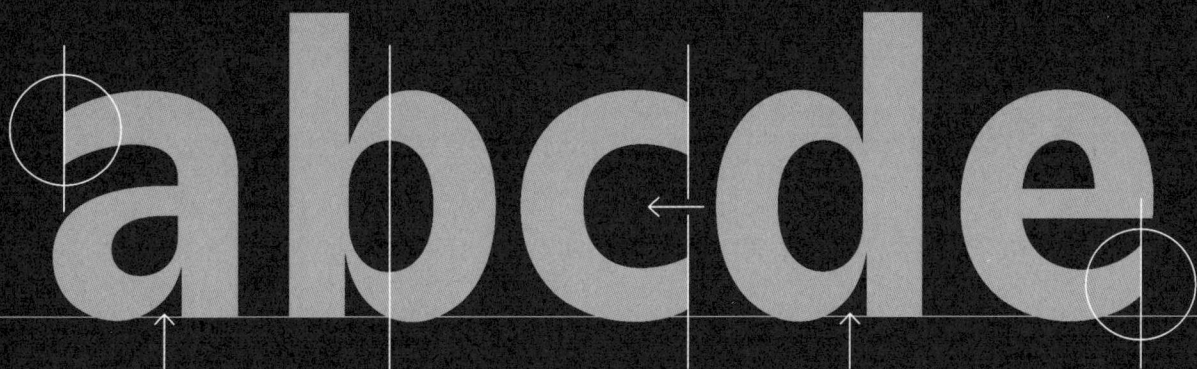

abcde

CONDENSED:	NORMAL:	EXTENDED:
Light	Light	Light
Light Italic	*Light Italic*	*Light Italic*
Regular	Regular	Regular
Regular Italic	*Regular Italic*	*Regular Italic*
Medium	Medium	Medium
Medium Italic	*Medium Italic*	*Medium Italic*
Bold	**Bold**	**Bold**
Bold Italic	***Bold Italic***	***Bold Italic***
Black	**Black**	**Black**
Black Italic	***Black Italic***	***Black Italic***
+	+	+
Demo (Free)	Demo (Free)	Demo (Free)

TYPEFACE	:	ZNVT15
DESIGNER	:	ZIN NAGAO / FOZNT
LOCATION	:	FUKUOKA, JAPAN

		PUBLISHED BY	:	ZIN NAGAO / FOZNT
		CHRONOLOGY	:	2020
		RELEASE	:	2020

| LINK | : | HTTPS://WWW.FOZNT.COM/ZNVT15 |
| STYLES | : | 1 |

THE ZNVIT15 TYPEFACE WAS CONCEIVED SPONTANEOUSLY DURING THE MANUAL CREATION PROCESS, WHICH INVOLVED PLACING SQUARE OBJECTS ON A GRID WHILE SHIFTING AND REASSEMBLING THEM, RESULTING IN AN EXPRESSION DISTINCT FROM CONVENTIONAL PIXEL FONTS. UPON ACTUAL USAGE OF THE FONT, IT PROVES SURPRISINGLY USER-FRIENDLY, LEAVING A UNIQUE APPEARANCE ON PAPER.

CAP HEIGHT

X-HEIGHT

REGULAR – 290PT

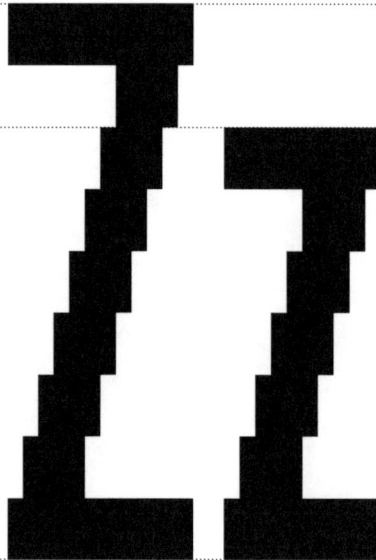

BASELINE

ZNVT15

THE QUICK BROWN FOX JUMPS OVER A

IT WOULD BE THE CHEEKY THING TO DC

IT'S A LOVELY DAY IN THE NEIGHBOURHO

AND THE PUNGENT AROMA OF FRESH R

PROMISE OF A SUMPTUOUS MEAL. THE

THINKING ABOUT THE DELICIOUS TREAS

THE LAZY DOG REMAINS UNPERTURBED.

LONG BLACK FUR FLUTTERING IN THE BR

The quick brown fox jumps over a lazy dog. He didn't have to, but he thought it would be the cheeky thing to do. After all, he had a reputation to maintain. It's a lovely day in the neighbourhood, with the sun shining, the birds chirping, and the pungent aroma of fresh rubbish bins wafting through the air - the promise of a sumptuous meal. The sprightly fox rubs his paws together in glee, thinking about the delicious treasures he's about to dig into. Still in her spot, the lazy dog remains unperturbed. With her long snout, droopy jowls, and long black fur fluttering in the breeze, she is in a dreamland far away - where the mountains are made of beefy treats, the valleys are filled with tennis balls, and the puddles are just the right temperature. Why be in the rat race? It's a dog's life, after all.

AÆBCDEFGHIJKLM
NOŒPQRSTUVWX
YZaæbcdefghijkl
mnoœpqrstuvwx
yzßfifl0123456789※
\:.!#?"'',/_{}[]()——
——"""'$$£¥+=)(~
‰@@&|^'€

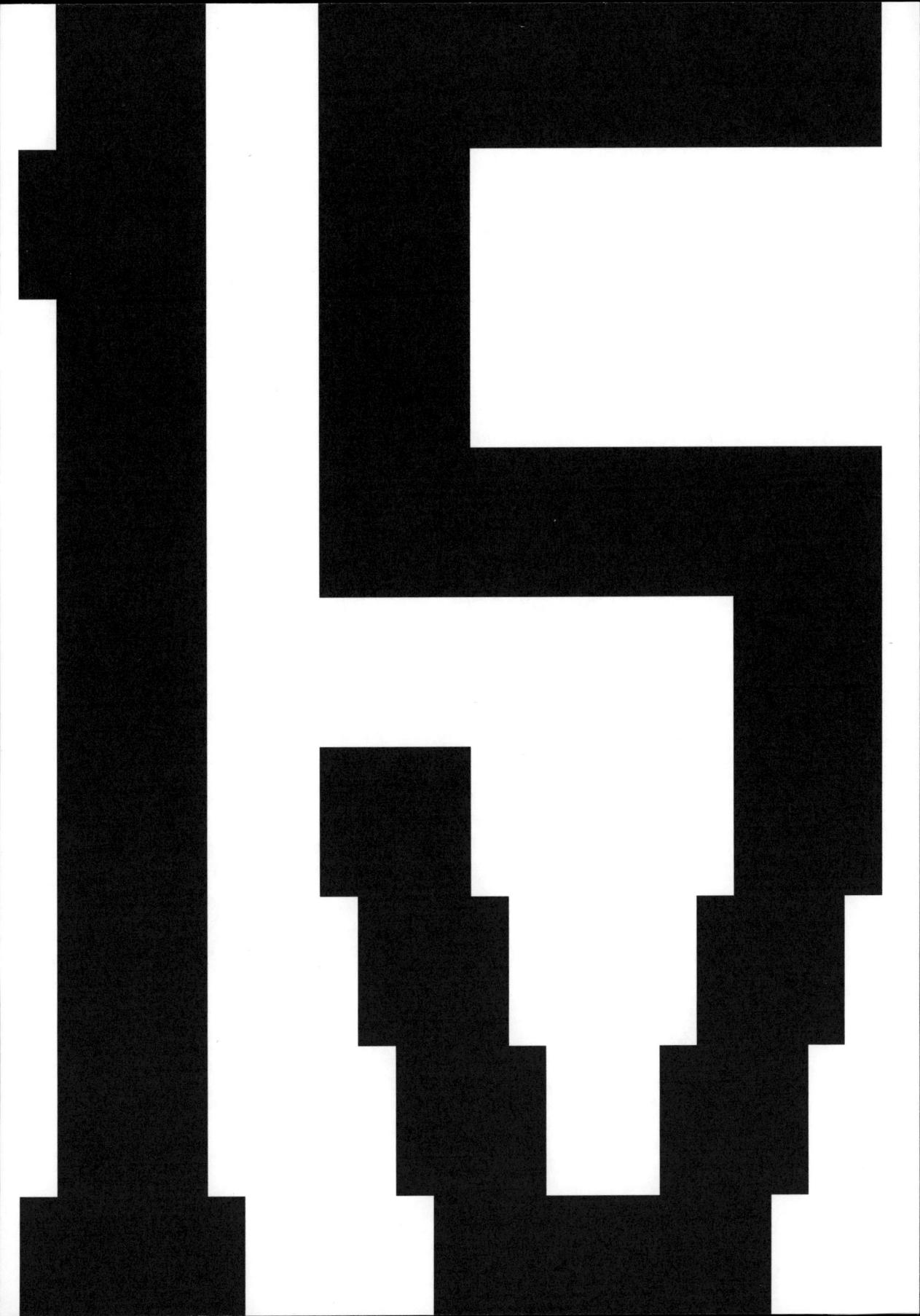

TYPEFACE : ZOOM PRO
DESIGNER : FLORIAN PAIZS
COUNTRY : NEW ZEALAND

PUBLISHED BY : THE DESIGNERS FOUNDRY
CHRONOLOGY : N/A
RELEASE : 2019

LINK : HTTPS://THEDESIGNERSFOUNDRY.COM/ZOOM-PRO
STYLES : 36

ZOOM PRO IS A SANS-SERIF DISPLAY TYPEFACE FAMILY WITH A BRUTALIST YET FRIENDLY AESTHETIC, OFFERING SIX WIDTHS AND SIX WEIGHTS. IT SUPPORTS 219 LATIN-BASED LANGUAGES FROM 212 COUNTRIES AND FEATURES SUBTLE CALLIGRAPHIC CHARACTERISTICS THAT BECOME MORE PRONOUNCED IN LARGER SIZES. THE TYPEFACE IS HIGHLY ADAPTABLE AND ENJOYABLE TO DESIGN WITH, THANKS TO ITS EXTENSIVE RANGE OF ALTERNATES AND OTHER OPENTYPE FEATURES.

CAP HEIGHT

BOOK - 290PT

X-HEIGHT

BASELINE

Zoom Pro

THE QUICK BROWN FOX J
IT WOULD BE THE CHEEKY
IT'S A LOVELY DAY IN THE
AND THE PUNGENT AROM
PROMISE OF A SUMPTUO
THINKING ABOUT THE DEI
THE LAZY DOG REMAINS

The quick brown fox jumps over a lazy dog. He did
it would be the cheeky thing to do. After all, he ha
It's a lovely day in the neighbourhood, with the su
and the pungent aroma of fresh rubbish bins wa
promise of a sumptuous meal. The sprightly fox ru
thinking about the delicious treasures he's about
the lazy dog remains unperturbed. With her long
long black fur fluttering in the breeze, she is in a c

The quick brown fox jumps over a lazy dog. He didn't have to, but he thought
it would be the cheeky thing to do. After all, he had a reputation to maintain.
It's a lovely day in the neighbourhood, with the sun shining, the birds chirping,
and the pungent aroma of fresh rubbish bins wafting through the air - the
promise of a sumptuous meal. The sprightly fox rubs his paws together in glee,
thinking about the delicious treasures he's about to dig into. Still in her spot,
the lazy dog remains unperturbed. With her long snout, droopy jowls, and
long black fur fluttering in the breeze, she is in a dreamland far away - where
the mountains are made of beefy treats, the valleys are filled with tennis balls,
and the puddles are just the right temperature. Why be in the rat race?
It's a dog's life, after all.

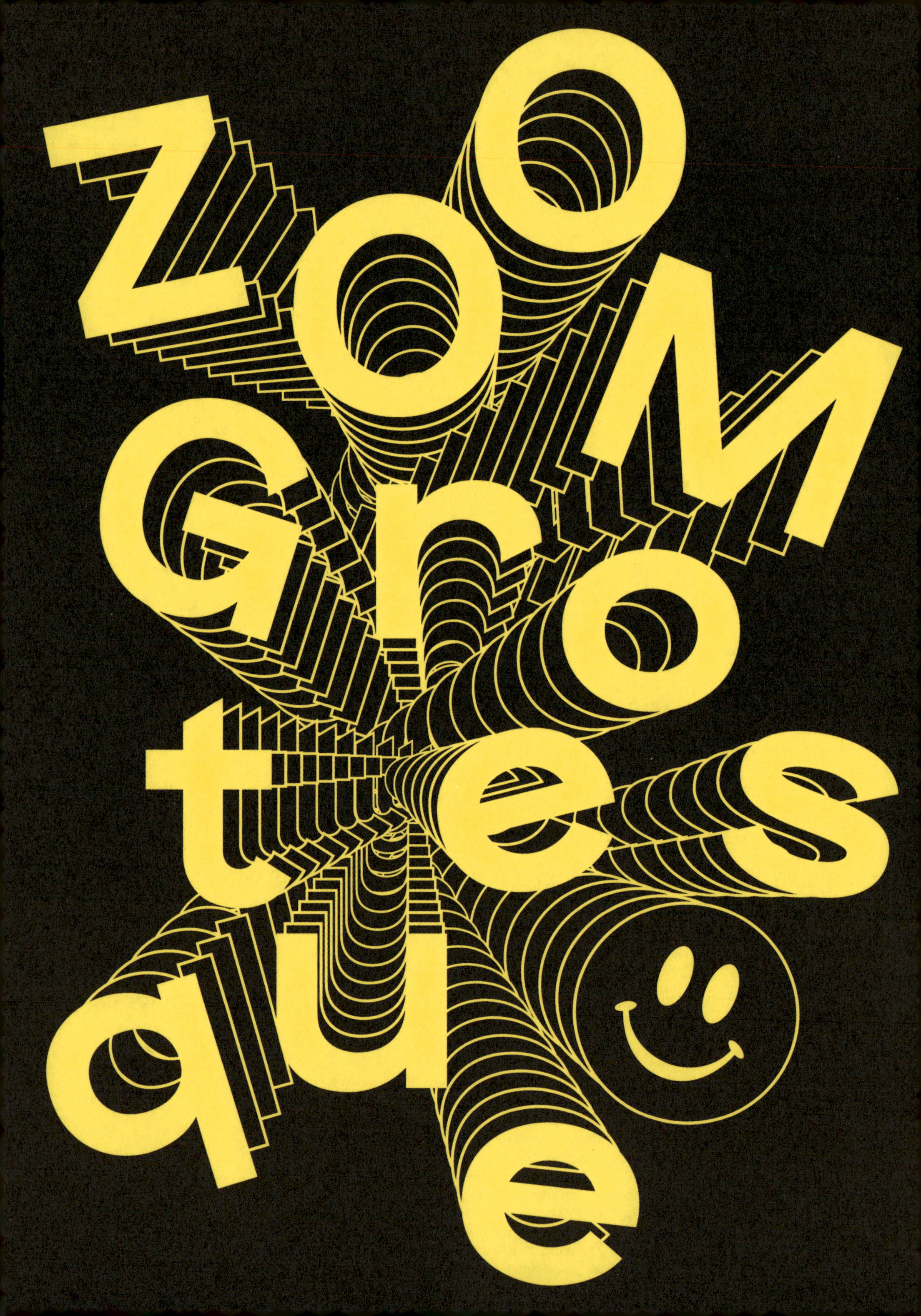
ZOOM
Grotesque

NEW YORK
MOSCOW
TOKYO
BROOKLYN
OSAKA
WELLINGTON
PARIS
LONDON
BERLIN
MILAN
TORONTO

MANEUVER
STREET RACE
ROADSIDES
POWER SLIDE
STRAIGHT
EXHIBITIONS
DRIVE
SNOWFLAKE
RAINBOW
MICRO PLASTIC

NARROW

MEDIUM

HAIR

EXTENDED

LIGHT

COMPACT

BOLD

THIN

NORMAL

REGULAR

WIDE

BRUTAL

known as DJ Bozy. A young father and up-and-coming DJ, Bozy confesses that adding the haka to the track was a spontaneous idea that occurred when collaborating with his friend and fellow producer, Sueno. "The haka is something we all identify with; something Polynesians are very proud of. Mix that with sapa'u and you've got a recipe that's gonna take off," Bozy beams. "We should keep evolving in this way, in collaboration. If we stay united as Polynesians we can go further and keep getting better... [Young people] have so much to offer society but we don't necessarily have

422

the means or the courage to express ourselves, so we do that through our music."

The sound that Bozy and his contemporaries are producing is a radical

islands and relocating to Tah[...] for islanders, particularly you[...] who move for better access t[...] Polynesians live in a rapidly c[...] deck is one way they're explo[...] staying rooted to their Polyn[...]

On the other side of t[...] min and Ennio are two expat T[...] the band QuinzeQuinze. "We a[...] on our side of the planet, tryi[...] culture and electronic music, [...] and modernism," the pair exp[...] dancing to deck because it p[...] synths make us wanna move [...] the sound textures are so sha[...]

We try to use the ima[...] tell our own story."

Made up of fiv[...] and visual artists who[...] QuinzeQuinze aim to r[...] evaluate their expect[...] could be and sound lik[...] that with their latest [...] or spirit in Tahitian. Va[...] intoxicating journey t[...] rules, effortlessly wea[...] from traditional percu[...] futuristic electronic s[...] sung in English, Frencl[...] like something entirely[...]

For Tahitian a[...] music that pays homa[...] up in a strong sense o[...] surrounding this topic[...] Polynesia, an island na[...] colonised by Europear[...] to erase Indigenous cu[...] are French citizens, sp[...] the French school sys[...] and very fabric of soc[...] values and ideals, whi[...] 'modern'. But Polynes[...] are Polynesian. This c[...] between modernity ar[...] Tahitian, is part of the[...] of being an islander to[...]

It's through this lens t[...] scene is evolving. Deck is now[...] subgenres as more artists de[...] music has become the definit[...] life for many Tahitians, as it c[...]

Hair Assistant: **KRESZEND SACKEY**
Makeup Assistant: **ADRIENNE VAN DER MERWE**
Styling: **NICOLE VERNON**
Assistant stylist: **MARIANNE TAOUK**

a Q Leon

e creative **KARLA Q LEON** uses
ing styling skills to tell stories
tory and fine art. When her and
singer Joyce Wrice got together
dio, the results were as powerful
their inspirations.

423

om the
trying
ces] to
Afro-
cky to
ch rich
Since
ced by
ms full
remain
for me

THE COLLECTIONS

hair pieces that clearly showcase
the Asian [references] but also her
African-American roots.

For the looks with
the spikes, I looked to anime
and tried to design a futuristic
piece, adding lots of colour, as
it's something I've noticed in [the
shows] – a love for experimenting
with hair styles by adding vibrant
colours. I really wanted to exhibit
that vibrancy in my work, too.

424

SSSSSSS

425

E.L　　U.L　　L　　R　　M　　E.B

SSSSSSS

F.L.I　　U.L.I　　L.I　　N.I　　R.I　　M.I　　B.I　　E.B.I

MAJO IDEAS
VOL—①①
COLOR

For Ages
4–400

Carmen Herrera
Nubia Navarro

...issue we're taking kids thr... ...that'll t... ...them abou... ...er.
...colour. Our pack is inspired by Nubia Na...rro and ill...ated by Carmen ...rra.

WHAT ARE THE COLORS MOM, Space
THAT SURROUND YOU? ...ring for launch.
Clear skies? Check. Test the engine.
Use the front of this pack to explore
inside your home and create a color... te
palette from what you see. Then go... sta
outside and see what colours are the
in the world. How are they different? ...ers
How are they the same?

TURN
OVER
TO

426

IDEAS is designed with love in
...A. Manufactured in China. All of
...er & Packaging is FSC Certified.
...recycle.

RECYCLE PLEASE RECYCLE
PLEASE PLEASE
FSC

V O L — ①
✱✱✱✱✱✱✱✱✱✱✱✱✱✱✱✱✱✱✱✱✱✱✱✱✱✱✱✱✱✱✱✱
P A C K   C O N T E N T S
✱✱✱✱✱✱✱✱✱✱✱✱✱✱✱✱✱✱✱✱✱✱✱✱✱✱✱✱✱✱✱✱
×1 Poster
×1 Artist Card...ards
×4 Postcards...graphic sticker sheet...
×4 Large full colour sticker sheets...s
×3 Large transparent sticker sheets...ckers
×2 Small sticker sheets...ble MAJO decal
P L U S
A... collective holographic window vinyl
that will throw rainbows about the room!

WWW . MAJO IDEAS . COM

CREATE   LEARN   COLLECT

0101213744134145

427

Jennif

Scott

22/09/

428

Life Ar

Death

Everyt

I've

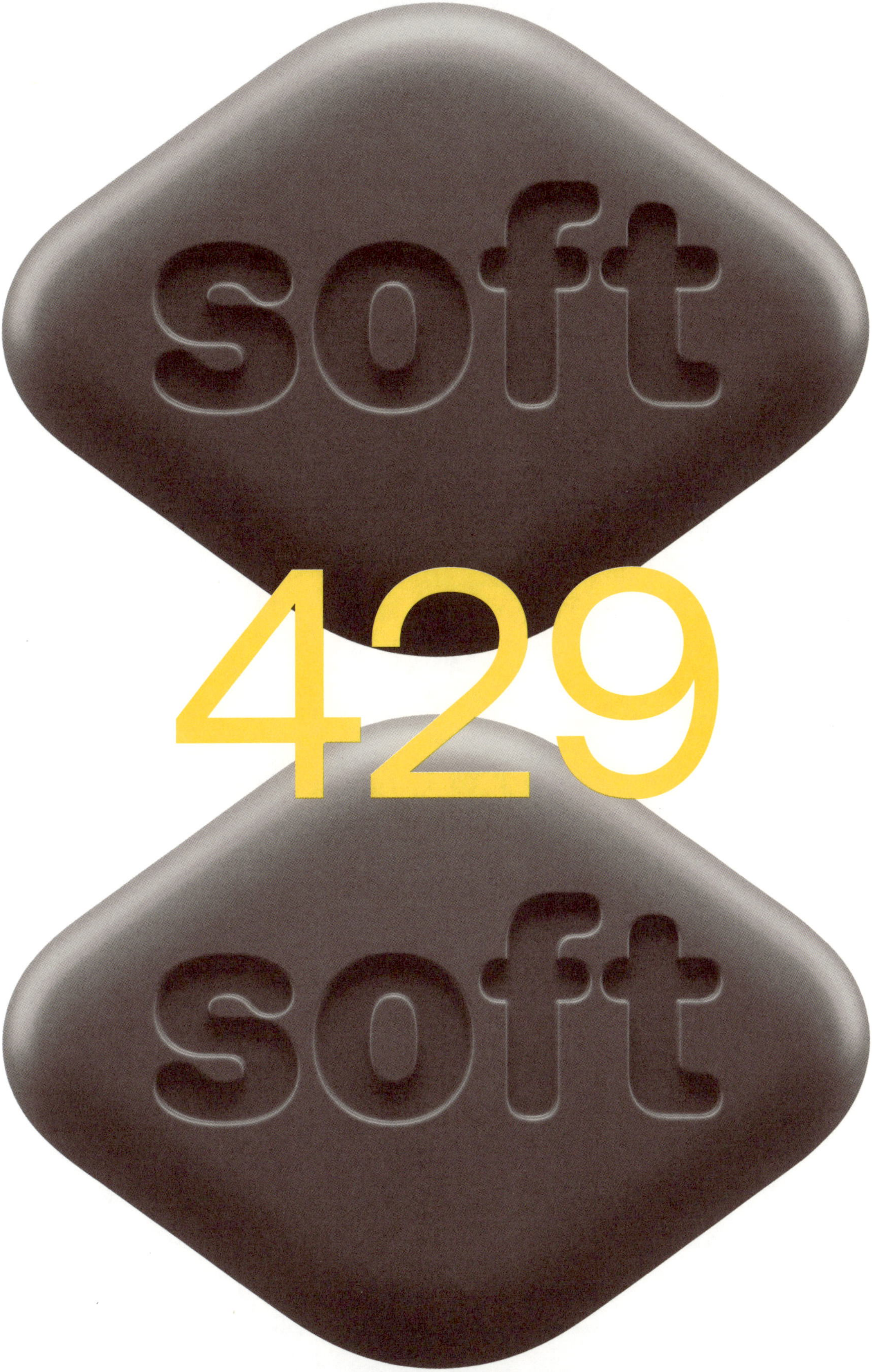
soft
429
soft

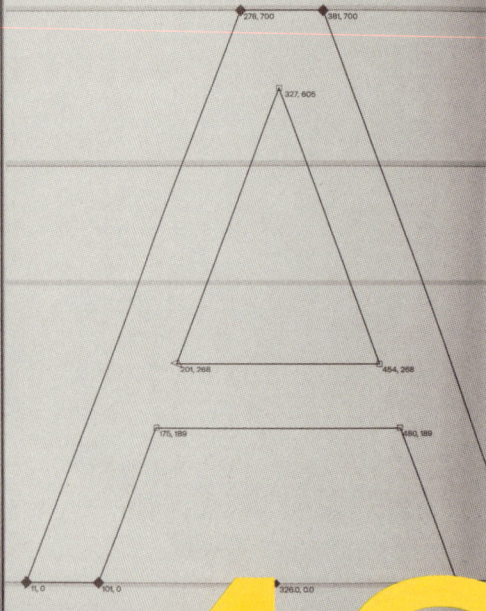

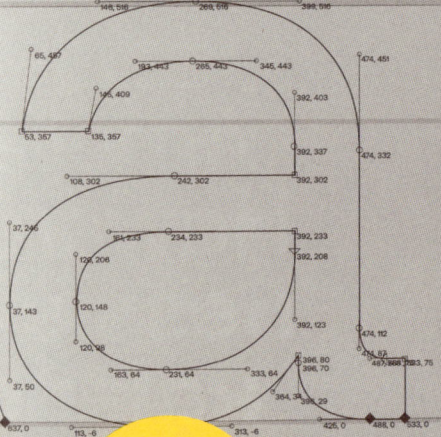

AaBbCc123

430

Aeonik
Boeing 747-400
Livery

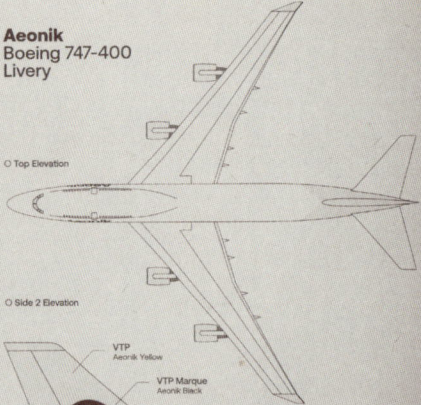

○ Top Elevation

○ Side 2 Elevation

VTP
Aeonik Yellow

VTP Marque
Aeonik Black

Wing Tip
Aeonik Yellow

Registration
Aeonik Bold

Engine
Aeonik Grey

○ Front Elevation

○ Side 1 Elevation

Aeonik

○ Rear Elevation

Engine
Aeonik Yellow

Engine
Aeonik Yellow

Logotype
Aeonik Bold

Ship Name
Aeonik Medium

Landing Gear Flap
Aeonik Yellow

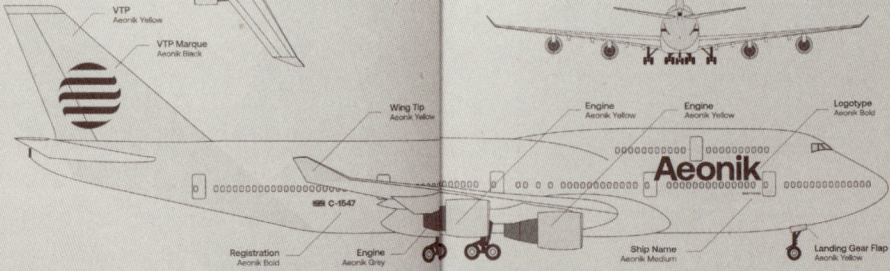

Aeonik

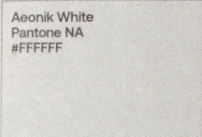

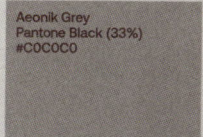

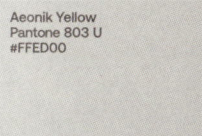

Aeonik

Aeonik White
Pantone NA
#FFFFFF

Aeonik Grey
Pantone Black (33%)
#C0C0C0

Aeonik Yellow
Pantone 803 U
#FFED00

Aeonik Black
Pantone Black U
#1D1D1B

Aeonik

431

747

LHR → ZRH
LHR → ZRH
LHR → ZRH
LHR → ZRH
LHR → ZRH
LHR → ZRH
LHR → ZRH
LHR → ZRH
LHR → ZRH
LHR → ZRH
LHR → ZRH

London → Zurich

Aeonik
Aeonik
Aeonik
Aeonik
Aeonik

C-1578
C-1578
C-1578
C-1578
C-1578
C-1578
C-1578
C-1578

HEATHROW
LHR

ZURICH
ZRH

C-1547
C-1547
C-1547
C-1547
C-1547
C-1547

Oslo
Paris
Berlin
Zürich
London
Hong Kong
Tokyo
New York
Stockholm
Sydney

BCI
BCI
BCI
BCI
BCI
BCI
BCI
BCI
BCI
BCI

BUSINESS CLASS

LHR
ZRH

ZÜRICH
ZRH

HEATHROW
LHR

Aeonik

HEATHROW
LHR

ZURICH
ZRH

LHR → ZRH

432

FO

Mono vs Fono

Aeonik Fono has been designed to live in the space between the classical Aeonik and Aeonik Mono. Its letter shapes are are slightly less exaggerated than a true mono font, making it easier to read. It features proportional spacing and some kerning, all of which make text setting a pleasure.

433

no

DESTINATION

FASCINATING

MASTERFULLY

SUBSEQUENT

434

NEEDLEWORK

ADMIRINGLY

WAVELENGTH

Toothbrushes

Kindergarten

Appointment

Landscaping

435

Gatecrasher

Reinvention

Retractable

AaɑɑBbCcDdEeFff
GgHhIiIiJJjKkLlMm
NnOoPpQQqRrSsTt
UuVvWwXxYyyZz
0123456789

436

Bold - 38pt
OAK
Bold - 30pt
BUZZ
Bold - 23pt
PIZZA
Bold - 19pt
QUARTZ
Bold - 16pt
BILLION
Bold - 14pt
CONCRETE
Bold - 13pt
FABRICATE
Bold - 11pt
STRAWBERRY
Bold - 9pt
OBJECTIFYING

Medium - 30pt
BOOK
Club
Medium - 19pt
SIZZLE
Dazzle
Medium - 12pt
MACAROONS
Dachshund
Radiators

Regular - 11pt
EARTHBOUND
Puzzlement
Chiffchaff
Jazzercise

Regular - 8pt
Apocalypse Now
Special Forces
Walter E.Kurtz
George Cantero

Regular - 6pt
Apple Flagship Shop
@ 235 Regent Street
By appointment only
Saturday 10am - 7pm
Shopping and Pickup

ABCDEFGHIJKLM
NOPQQRSTUVWXYZ
aɑabcdeffghijk
lmnopqrstuvwxy
yz/0123456789
£ß$%&?ℙ±Ä¾©¶

https://CoTypeFoundry.
com © 2022 x 7 weights
AeonikMono-Regular.otf
52 KB WOFF/WOFF2/OTF ¶
LDN,UK aalt/salt/frac/
◊ aɑaffyyJJQQ&&77 ₱£40
CAPS + lwr INT ⑦ **Trial**
#Hashbrown Estd {②①⑨}
¼lb ▶ 100% Beef @ 180°
ZQW / Zweibrücken €uro
Crypto ↔ **₿itcoin** / NFT
Like ✓ Chausseestraße?
Ωmega™ ✳ Play ▶ STOP ■
¥en ₧ ₦aira ₮ ₤ira U$D
Peace ☮ Love & Unity ∞

AEONIK MONO BOLD - 46PT

GLYPHS OpenType

AEONIK MONO MEDIUM - 32PT

TYPOGRAPHY Arrangement

AEONIK MONO REGULAR - 22PT

FIXED-WIDTH Non-Proportional

AEONIK MONO LIGHT - 16PT

AEONIK MONO TYPEFACE
Multiple Font Combinations

437

ss01	a → a	Taramaysalata
ss02	a → a	Taramaysalata
ss03	f → f	Bulletproofed
ss04	y → y	Commutatively
ss05	J → J	Justificators
ss06	Q → Q	Quickstepping
ss07	7 → 7	07747 555 678
ss08	1 → ①	⓪⑦⑦④⑦ ⑤⑤⑤ ⑥⑦⑧
ss09	1 → ①	⓪⑦⑦④⑦ ⑤⑤⑤ ⑥⑦⑧
ss10	1 → 1	07747 555 678
ss11	1 → 1	07747 555 678
ss12	1 → 1	07747 555 678
ss13	& → &	Wayne & Garth

Aeonik Mono/Fono:

- Weights: 7
- Glyphs: 602
- File Size: 54 KB
- Format: OTF
- OT Features: 24
- Languages: 37
- Characters: 467

www.cotypefoundry.com/
our-fonts/aeonik-mono/

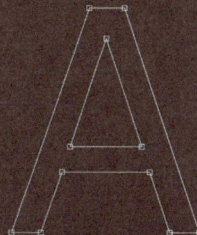

Mono/Fono OpenType Features:

aalt	Access All Alternates
case	Case-Sensitive Forms
dnom	Denominators
frac	Fractions
locl	Localized Forms
numr	Numerators
ordn	Ordinals
salt	Stylistic Alternates
sinf	Scientific Inferiors
ss01	Stylistic Set 01
ss02	Stylistic Set 02
ss03	Stylistic Set 03
ss04	Stylistic Set 04
ss05	Stylistic Set 05
ss06	Stylistic Set 06
ss07	Stylistic Set 07
ss08	Stylistic Set 08
ss09	Stylistic Set 09
ss10	Stylistic Set 10
ss11	Stylistic Set 11
ss12	Stylistic Set 12
ss13	Stylistic Set 13
subs	Subscript
sups	Superscript

This is an OpenType font with 467 characters
Manufactured by CoType® Foundry. Designed by Mark Bloom.
Version 1.000;hotconv 1.0.109;makeotfexe 2.5.65596

CoType™ Foundry

Altform
Specimen
Book V.1

CoType
Foundry.
com

438

Altform m

Rt

439

Default Numerals

0123445 6789

Circled Numerals (White)

⓪ ① ② ③ ④ ④ ⑤ ⑥ ⑦ ⑧ ⑨

Circled Numerals (Black)

0 1 2 3 4 4 5 6 7 8 9

Standard Fractions & Superiors

½ ⅓ ¼ ¾ 0123456789

Tabular Lining Numerals

0123445 6789

Apollo 11

July 20th

July 24th

440

1969

Apollo 11

The primary objective of Apollo 11 was to complete a national goal set by President John F. Kennedy on May 25, 1961: perform a crewed lunar landing and return to Earth.

Crew

Neil Armstrong
Commander

Edwin E. Aldrin Jr.
Lunar Module Pilot

Michael Collins
Command Module Pilot

Backup Crew

James A. Lovell
Commander

Fred W. Haise Jr.
Lunar Module Pilot

William A. Anders
Command Module Pilot

Payload

Columbia (CSM-107)
Eagle (LM-5)

Prelaunch Milestones

11/21/68
LM-5 Integrated systems test

12/06/68
CSM-107 integrated systems test

12/13/68
LM-5 acceptance test

01/08/69
LM-5 ascent stage delivered to Kennedy

01/12/69
LM-5 descent stage delivered to Kennedy

01/18/69
S-IVB ondock at Kennedy

01/23/69
CSM ondock at Kennedy

__/69
command and service module mated

02/__/69
S-__ dock at Kenne

02/__/69
S-__ dock at Kennedy

Combined CSM-107 systems tests

02/27/69
S-IU Ondock at Kennedy

03/24/69
CSM-107 Altitude testing

04/14/69
Rollover of CSM from the operations and checkout building to the vehicle assembly building

04/22/69
Integrated systems test

05/05/69
CSM electrical mate to Saturn V

05/20/69
Rollout to Launch Pad 39A

06/01/69
Flight readiness test

06/26/69
Countdown Demonstration Test

Launch

July 16, 1969;
9:32 a.m. EDT

Launch Pad 39A

Saturn-V AS-506

High Bay 1

Mobile Launcher Platform-1
Firing Room 1

Orbit

Altitude:
118.65 miles

Inclination

32.521 degrees

Du___

Eigh___rs,
Thr___urs,

Dis___ce

953,054 miles

Lunar Location

Sea of Tranquility

Lunar Coordinates

.71 degrees North,
23.63 degrees East

Landing

July 24, 1969;
12:50 p.m. EDT
Pacific Ocean

Recovery Ship

USS Hornet

441

442

7th JA

2 [¤] ≠ Æ
ffi fft (‹›)
¼ { 443
#tt © ;Ä?
᾽95%™

CORNDA

444

CORANDA RACING

Pantone: 811 U
CMYK: 0/68/87/0
RGB: 255/109/32
Hex #: FF6D20

Pantone: Black U
CMYK: 0/0/0/100
RGB: 29/29/20
Hex #: 1D1D1B

Pantone: N/A
CMYK: 0/0/0/0
RGB: 255/255/255
Hex #: FFFFFF

Pantone: Cool Grey
CMYK: 0/0/0/40
RGB: 177/177/177
Hex #: B1B1B1

Pantone: Cool Grey 9U
CMYK: 0/0/0/70
RGB: 110/110/110
Hex #: 6F6F6E

445

COANDA RACING

446

447

448

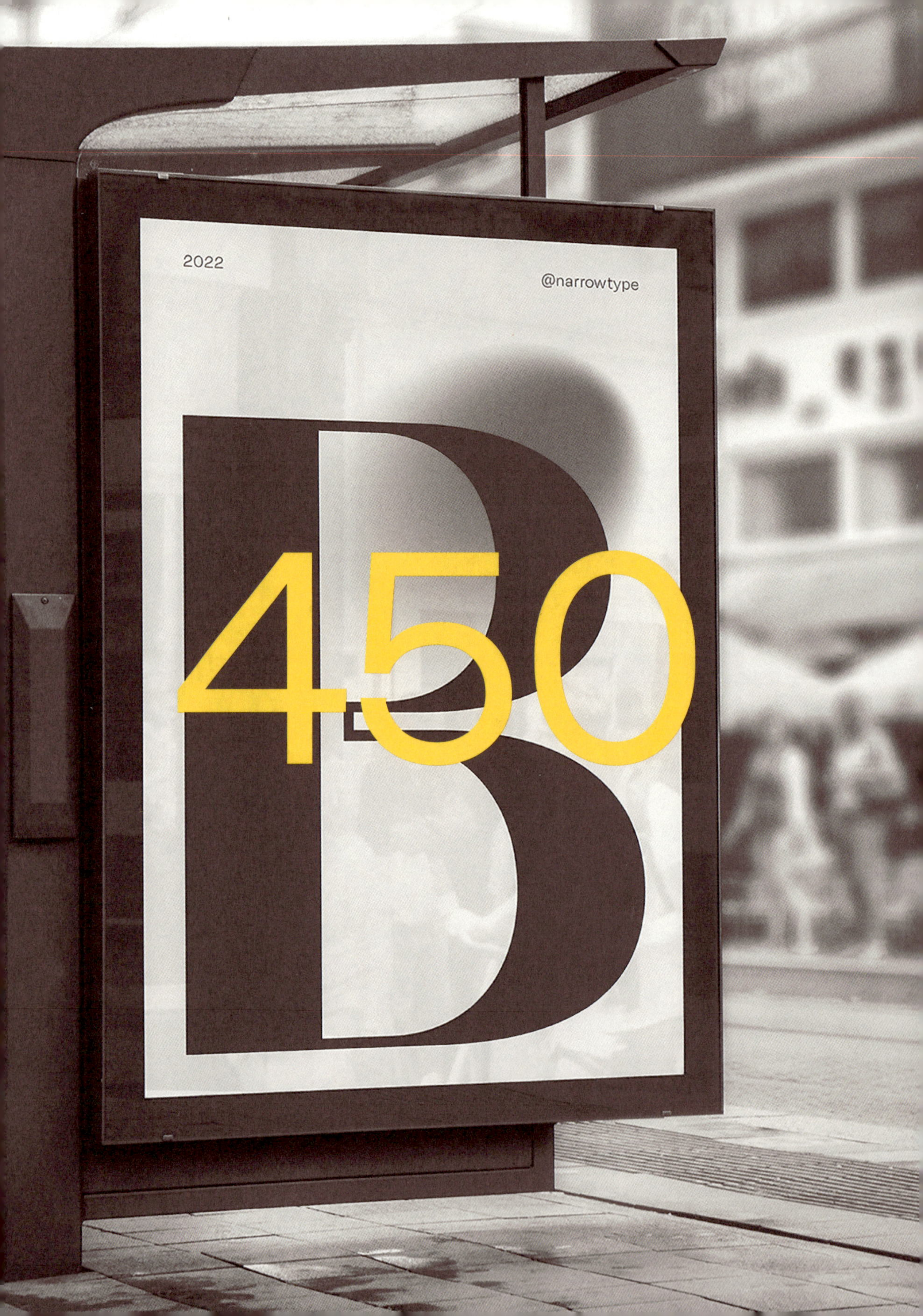
2022
@narrowtype
B
450

1980 × 2035

OUR PORTFOLIO

THANK YOU

FOR CH

J&A

451

J&A

WE ARE ARCHITECTURE
STUDIO LOCATED IN BILBAO

J&A

OUR
JOURNEY 1980

Collection

Aid Kid

452

Aid Kid

Collection

SIDE Ⓐ

1 The Easiest
w/ **NIVVA** 4:34
2 Florence & the Tape Machine 3:55
3   Bux
w/ **Oliver Torr & Terror
Phoenix** 3:01
4 Hyphens in the Flesh
w/ **Isama Zing** 4:28
5 118ms 6:24

Aid Kid Collection

Addict™ sound

All tracks mixed by Aid Kid. Mastered by Gaex at Cargle & Expel Studio (www.gaex.org). Published by Addict Sound. Digitally distributed by Warner Music Group. Art direction by © Anymade Studio 2021.

453

RM MONO
COTYPEFOUNDRY.COM

5   WEIGHTS
494 GLYPHS
17 LAYOUT FEATURES
100 LANGUAGES

RM MONO
COTYPEFOUNDRY.COM

5   WEIGHTS
494 GLYPHS
17 LAYOUT FEATURES
100 LANGUAGES

454

RM MONO
COTYPEFOUNDRY.COM

5   WEIGHTS
494 GLYPHS
17 LAYOUT FEATURES
100 LANGUAGES

RM MONO
COTYPEFOUNDRY.COM

5   WEIGHTS
494 GLYPHS
17 LAYOUT FEATURES
100 LANGUAGES

RM MONO
COTYPEFOUNDRY.COM

5   WEIGHTS
494 GLYPHS
17 LAYOUT FEATURES
100 LANGUAGES

Light	1
Regular	2
SemiBold	3
Bold	4
Black	5

A1	
B2	
C3	
D4	
E5	

RM

ABCDEFGHIJ
KLMNOPQRRS
TUVWXYZ

aabcdeffgh
ijklmnopqr
stuvwxyz
.,;:…!?()

AÄÅÁÀĄÃÅÆĆÇ
ĆÐĐÉÊÈĚËĖĘĜ
ĞĞĦŰÌĨÍÏĮİĬĴ
ĴĶĹĽĿŁÓÔÒÕÖ
ØŒÞŔŘŖŔŖŚŞŜ
ŞßŤŢŢŤŢŰÚŬÙŨ
ŪŴŴŴÝŶŸŹŻ

455

€ 10.00
$ 15.50
£ 18.30
¥ 12.80
$ 15.50

ff

Official
Official
Official
Official
Official
Official
Official
Official

⓪ ② ③
④ ⑤ ⑥ ⑦
⑧ ⑨ ⓪ ①
② ③ ④ ⑤
⑥ ⑦ ⑧ ⑨

1

Aa

AaAaAaAaAa
AaAaAaAaAa
AaAaAaAaAa
AaAaAaAaAa
AaAaAaAaAa
AaAaAaAaAa
AaAaAaAaAa
AaAaAaAaAa

Official
Official
Official
Official
Official
Official
Official
Official

ff

€£Ft&&$

10.00
15.50
18.30
11.80
12.50
15.50

Aa

5 WEIGHTS
494 GLYPHS
17 LAYOUT FEATURES
100 LANGUAGES

RM MONO
COTYPEFOUNDRY.COM

Aa Aa Aa Aa Aa
Aa Aa Aa Aa Aa
Aa Aa Aa Aa Aa
Aa Aa Aa Aa Aa
Aa Aa Aa Aa Aa
Aa Aa Aa Aa Aa
Aa Aa Aa Aa Aa
Aa Aa Aa Aa Aa

TURES

RM MONO
COTYPEFOUNDRY.COM

456

A1
B2
C3
D4
E5
3
4
5

ABCDEF
KLMNOPQRRS
TUVWXYZ
aabcdeffgh
ijklmnopqr
stuvwxyz
.,'':;...!?()

① ② ③
⓪ ① ⑥ ⑦
④ ⑤ ⑨ ⓪ ①
⑧ ⑨ ③ ④ ⑤
② ③ ⑦ ⑧ ⑨
⑥ ⑦ ⑧ ⑨

RM MONO
COTYPEFOUNDRY.COM

1

Official
Official
Official
Official
Official
Official
Official

Aa Aa Aa Aa
Aa Aa Aa Aa
Aa Aa Aa Aa
Aa Aa Aa Aa
Aa Aa Aa Aa

Light
Regular
SemiBold
Bold
Black

RM MONO
COTYPEFOUNDRY .CO

5 WEIGHTS
494 GLYPHS
17 LAYOUT FEATURES
100 LANGUAGES

Official
Official
Official
Official
Official
Official
Official
Offici
Offi.

ff

457

ABCDNOP
KLMNOP
TUVWXYZ
aabcdef
ijklmn
stuw

5 WEIGHTS
494 GLYPHS
17 LAYOUT FEATURES
100 LANGUAGES

RM MONO
COTYPEFOUNDRY.COM

5 WEIGHTS
494 GLYPHS
17 LAYOUT FEATURES
100 LANGUAGES

A1
B2
C3 D4
E5

Light
Regular
SemiBold

5

Weights

Light
+ Italic

aa

Regular
+ Italic

aa

SemiBold
+ Italic

aa

Bold
+ Italic

aa

Black
+ Italic

aa

458

Stonebridge Park
Buckinghamshire
Metropolitan Line
Student Discounts
Regional Transport

Light *Italic*
Regular *Italic*
SemiBold *Italic*
Bold *Italic*
Black *Italic*

459

RM Neue™
— Regular
Size: 170pt
Tracking: -50

Alpha

Scandium
SemiBold 70pt

Bravo

Scandium
Bold 70pt

Charlie

Scandium
Thin 70pt

Delta

Scandium
Light 70pt

Echo

Scandium
Black 70pt

Foxtrot

Scandium
Light Italic 70pt

...foundry.com

Golf

Scandium
Light 70pt

Hotel

Scandium
Bold 70pt

India

Scandium
Regular Italic 70pt

Juliett

Scandium
Light 70pt

Kilo

Scandium
Black 70pt

Lima

Scandium
Light 70pt

460

FM 10 Kreise   AM 6 Kreise

120V
150V/250V 55W

Backup 125V   0.6A
Backup 220V   0.3A

Requires Adapter   USB Adapter

TYPE 97

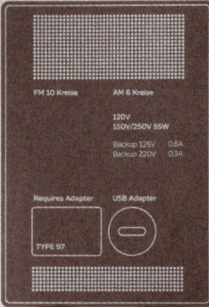

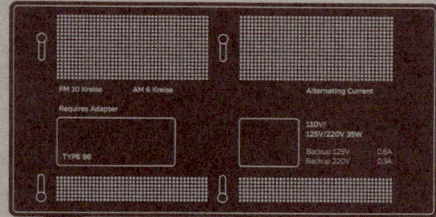

- Extremely low frequency
- Super low frequency
- Ultra low frequency
- Ultra high frequency
- Very low frequency
- Super high frequency
- Low frequency
- Extremely high frequency

FM 10 Kreise   AM 6 Kreise   Alternating Current

Requires Adapter

110V/
125V/220V 35W

Backup 125V   0.6A
Backup 220V   0.3A

TYPE 96

ELF UHF

461

Telemetry
Solar

Automation
Grid

Astronaut
4800km

360
Light

B

g g g g
g g g g

Scandium	Thin
Scandium	ExtraLight
Scandium	Light
Scandium	Regular
Scandium	SemiBold
Scandium	Bold
Scandium	Black
Scandium	Thin Italic
Scandium	ExtraLight Italic
Scandium	Light Italic
Scandium	Regular Italic
Scandium	SemiBold Italic
Scandium	Bold Italic
Scandium	Black Italic

462

463

464

465

THANK
INFAMÜSE
MADE IN USA
HECHO EN USA
FATTO IN USA
FABRIQUÉ EN USA
RN 119376 CA 52192

466

INFAMÜSE

MADE IN U.S.A.
HECHO EN ...
...DE IN U.S.
...QUÉ EN ...
...
CA 52192

468

469

INFAMÜSE

MADE IN USA
HECHO EN USA
FATTO IN USA
FABRIQUE EN USA
メキシコ製

* * *

MEDIUM

INFAMÜSE.COM

INFAMÜSE

HECHO EN USA
FATTO IN USA
FABRIQUÉ EN USA
メキシコ製

* * *

MEDIUM

INFAMÜSE.COM

RN 119376 CA 52192

INFAMÜSE

1-SHIRT

BIANCA SCIUTO

471

Interior & Object Design
+61 411 711 947
hello@biancasciuto.com

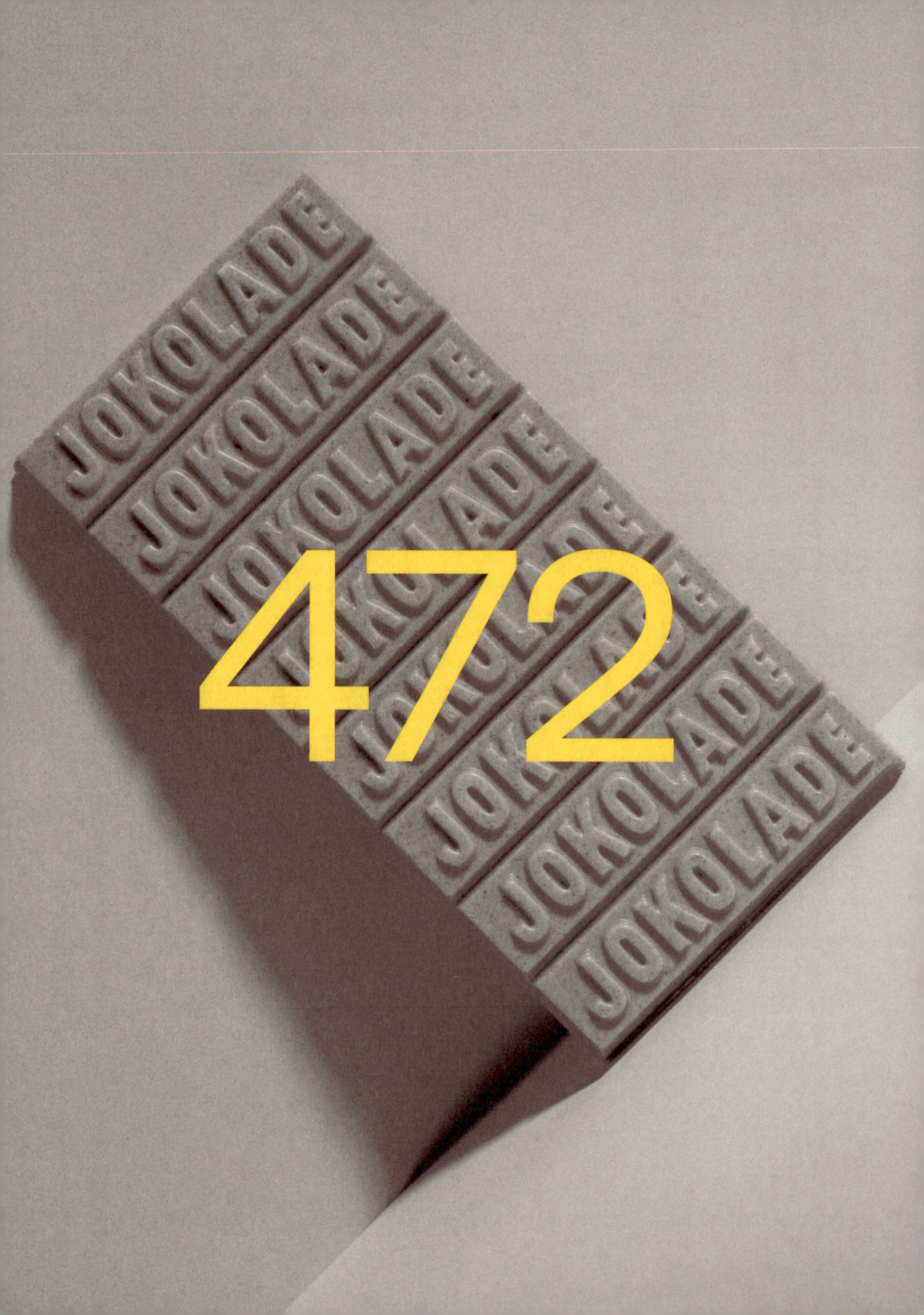
472
JOKOLADE

475

CU MU
LU S

EST.
L 2011

WATTS

LUCY

DESIGNER
B.Env Des, M.Arch

0405 944 412
lucy.watts@oumulus.studio
www.oumulus.studio

Hobart, Launceston,
Melbourne, Adelaide

476

CU
MU US

EST.
2011

BRISBNE

EDWINA

ARCHIT
B.Arch D M.Arch

117 333
ao@oumu studio
oumulus o

our
obart, de,
eston

EST.
2011

CU L US

MU

ANDREW

GRIMSDALE

SENIOR ARCHITECT
Grad.Dip.Arch,
B.Env Des, FRAIA

0438 301 644
andrew.grimsdale@oumulus.studio
www.oumulus.studio

Hobart, Launceston,
Melbourne, Adelaide

478

SLOW
BURNING
SCENTED
SOY
CANDLE

TWELVE
SCENTS

VEGAN-FRIENDLY
INGREDIENTS

TWELVE
SCENTS

BURNS
55—60
HOURS
WEIGHT
NET 250GR

479

BURNS
55—60
HOURS
WEIGHT
NET 250GR

SLOW
BURNING
SCENTED
SOY
CANDLE

TWELVE
SCENTS

VEGAN-FRIENDLY
INGREDIENTS

BLACK VANILLA · BOTANICALS
CITRUS PARADISI · CEDAR BERGAMOT
EARL GREY & BERGAMOT · FIG SAUVAGE

CARE INSTRUCTIONS:
On first use, burn candle until the
surface becomes molten. Also, do not
burn candle for no more than 4 hours of
prolong use. Keep wick trimmed to one-
eue of 5 mm. To prevent smoke and black
soot. If necessary, re-centre wick after or
by guiding the flame, while wax remains molten.

481

roic Actions

RECOGNISE

echnical Education

DEVELOPMENT

Commercial Institutions

LITERARY SUBJECT

Universal Popular Educators

THLY MAGAZINE

482

Grotesque 6

ABCDEFGHIJKLMNOPQ
abcdefghijklmnopqrstuv

ABCDEFGHIJKLMNOPQRSTU
abcdefghijklmnopqrstuvwxyz

ABCDEFGHIJKLMNOPQRSTU
abcdefghijklmnopqrstuvwxyz ,;:-!?'(

ABCDEF
1234567
abcdefghijk

FGHIJKL
bcdefghijklmnop

QRSTUVW
uvwxyzfl

ABCDEFGHIJKLMNOPQRSTUVWXY
Z& 1234567890£$,;:-!?'(
abcdefghijklmnopqrstuvwxyzfiffffifffl

TVERANG

AURLAND, SOGN

Aa Gg

KLm RSu

MNOPQRStuvwxy

ABCDEFGHI
abcdefghijkl

ABCDEFGHI
abcdefghijkl

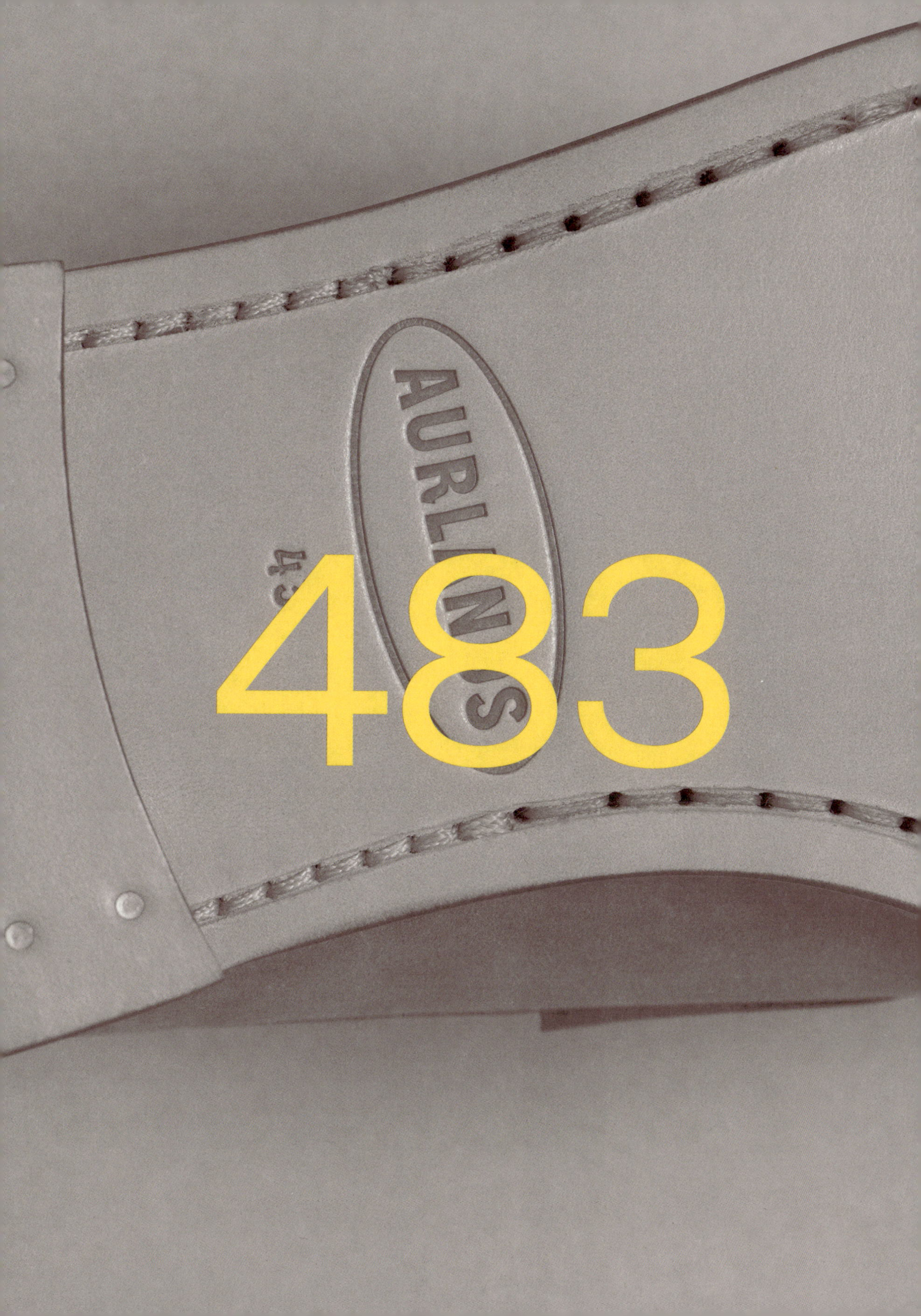

483

CIENNE

484

N Y

485

interactions. We are irreverent intensities. We search for
off-beat movements. We search for happiness and careless
souvenirs of happiness and careless simplicity. We're rooted
in the notion that tomorrow

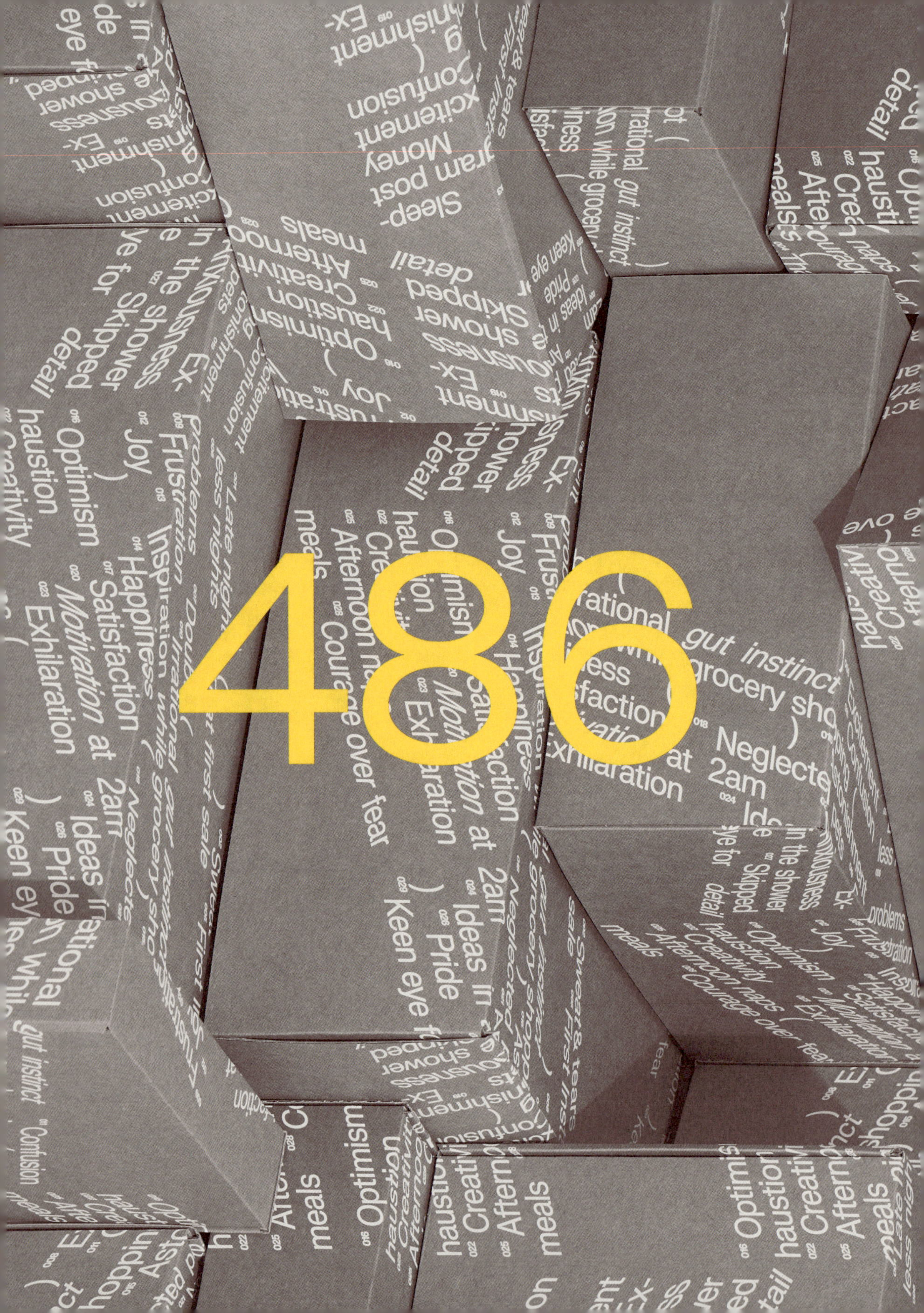
486

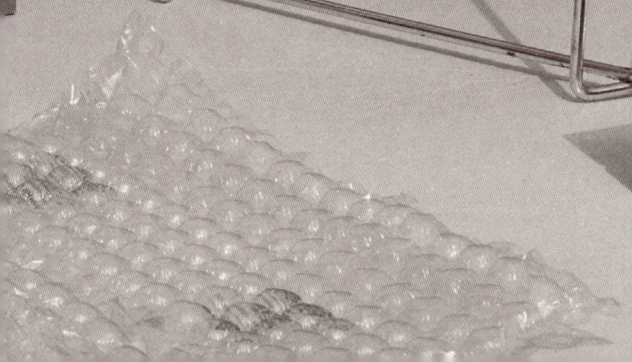

487

Kleman Trevino Studio™

Kleman Trevino Studio™

Kleman Trevino Studio™

Kleman Trevino, Director
hello@klemantrevino.studio
+85 0 4757 9585

klemantrevino.studio

Kleman Trevino
+85 0 4757 9585
Via Atto Vannucci, 15
20135 Milano MI, ITALY

klemantrevino.studio

48

8

MELINA SIMSON VON
+85 0 4757 9585

Via Atto Vannucci, 15
20135 Milano MI, ITALY

hello@klemantrevino.studio
klemantrevino.studio

MELINA SIMSON VON
+85 0 4757 9585

Via Atto Vannucci, 15
20135 Milano MI, ITALY

hello@klemantrevino.studio
klemantrevino.studio

INVOICE

PRODUCT NAME	QUANTITY	RATE	SUM
BROWN CUP LYON SERIES 300 ML	3	$20	$60
WHITE PLATES DIA 25 CM	2	$32	$64
BLACK CUP	1	$25	$25
WHITE VASE HEIGHT 30 CM	2	$40	$80
		TOTAL	$229

PayPal.me/username
002i45653
lpay.me/mubarizyusifzade

Kleman Trevino Studio ™

489

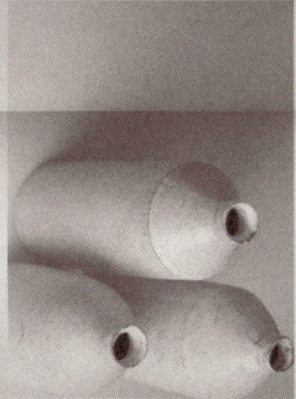

Italy-based artist Kleman Trevino is
known for her distinctive hand-built ce-
ramic objects, characterised by repetitive
patterns and bold colours. We created an
identity system for Kleman that revolves
around consistency, embracing an or-
dered yet unpredictable identity application system to showcase her unique
work.

The identity was combined with a wider
visual strategy, embracing the push and
pull of visual excess and restraint, which
was then applied to various printed deliv-
erables, packaging components and a
website. As a part of the visual strategy,
we created a series of images in collaboration with photographer Shelley Horan
that speak to the contrasting textures
and themes within Kleman's work.

ISBN
9789869758802

img_SP1   img_SP1C img_SP1M img_SP1Y

img_SP1

C→AQUA,
M→FLUOR-
PINK
Y→YELLOW

(GREEN
COVERED)

NO MAGIC
IN RISO
→
a bilingual iso-
graph tool book

4 90

180H*110W*27T
mm, 360-page

img_023

C→AQUA,
M→FLUOR-
PINK
Y→YELLOW

(SCREEN
COVERED)

img_005

C→AQUA,
M→FLUOR-
PINK
Y→YELLOW

(SCREEN
COVERED)

img_005
C

img_005
M

Y

ISBN
9789886

491

NO MAGIC
IN RISO

→

a bilingual riso-
graph tool boo

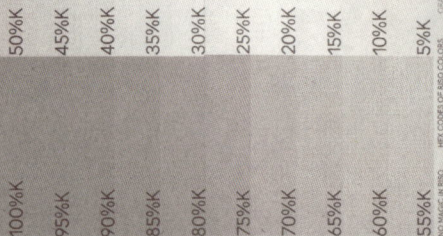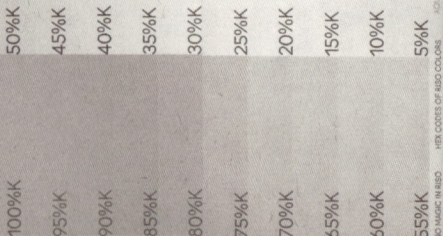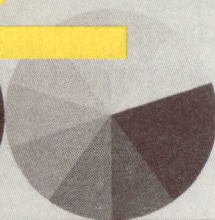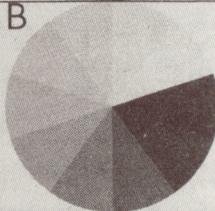
50→45%, 80→90%, 100→95%, 0→95%, 20→50%, 30→25%, 60→50%

NO MAGIC IN RISO

2 COLOR SEPARATION

22° 45°

492

| 50%K | 45%K | 40%K | 35%K | 30%K | 25%K | 20%K | 15%K | 10%K | 5%K |
| 100%K | 95%K | 90%K | 85%K | 80%K | 75%K | 70%K | 65%K | 60%K | 55%K |

ORANGE EFFECT

HEX CODES OF RISO COLORS

NO MAGIC IN RISO

A   B   A+B

C

| 50%K | 45%K | 40%K | 35%K | 30%K | 25%K | 20%K | 15%K | 10%K | 5%K |
| 100%K | 95%K | 90%K | 85%K | 80%K | 75%K | 70%K | 65%K | 60%K | 55%K |

HSV CODES OF RISO COLORS

NO MAGIC IN RISO

100%
0%
100%
0%
100%
0%

50→45%,80→
90%, 100→
100%

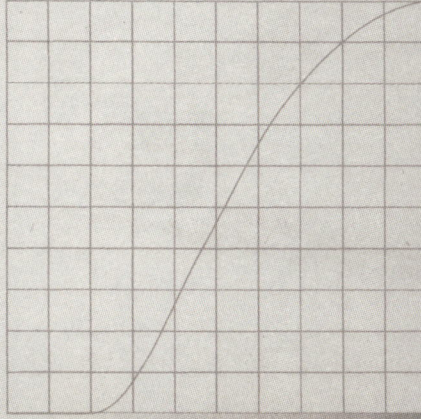

NO MAGIC IN RISO

3 COLOR SEPARATION 0°

231

50%K	45%K	40%K	35%K	30%K	25%K
100%K	95%K	90%K	85%K	80%K	75%K

50%K	45%K	40%K	35%K	30%K	25%K
90%K	95%K	90%K	85%K	80%K	75%K

493

A+C

B+C

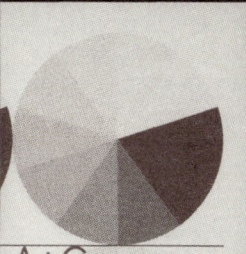

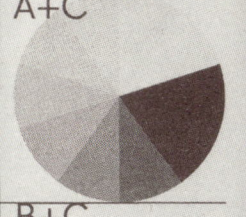

	100%
	0%
	100%
	0%
	100%
	0%

O.OO DESIGN & RISOGRAPH ROOM, TAIPEI TAIWAN/WWW.ODOTOO.COM

NO MAGIC IN RISO IS A BILINGUAL RISOGRAPH TOOL BOOK

0   10   20   30   40   50   60   70   80   90   100

TRITONE COLOR CHART, SCREEN COVERED 60LPI

100 90 80 70 60 50 40 30 20 10

100 90 80 70 60 50 40 30 20 10 0

NO MAGIC IN RISO IS A

PH ROOM, TAIPEI TAIWAN/WWW.ODOTOO.COM

0   10   20   30

100   90   80   70   60   50   40

MIGRANT
1

MIGI

ACROSS
COUNTE

WI
CA

494

MIGRANT
4

MIGI

DARK.
MATTERS

MIG
ODYS

ANT

MIGRANT

2

3

ED

ITAL

FLOWING GROUNDS

495

ANT

MIGRANT

5

6

RO

SEYS

FOREIGN
AGENTS

NO.1-6

MIGRANT

496

497

MIGRANT — EASTERN ASIA • WESTERN EUROPE • NORTHERN AMERICA • WESTERN ASIA • SOUTHERN AFRICA • WORLDWIDE

MIGRANT — NORTHERN EUROPE • AFRICA • OCEANIA • WESTERN EUROPE • SOUTHERN EUROPE • COUNTER SPACE

MIGRANT — WESTERN EUROPE • NORTHERN AMERICA • SOUTHERN AFRICA • WESTERN ASIA • WORLDWIDE

MIGRANT — WESTERN EUROPE • EASTERN EUROPE • SOUTHERN EUROPE • WESTERN ASIA • SOUTH AMERICA • WORLDWIDE

MIGRANT

MIGRANT

1 2 3 4 5 6

498

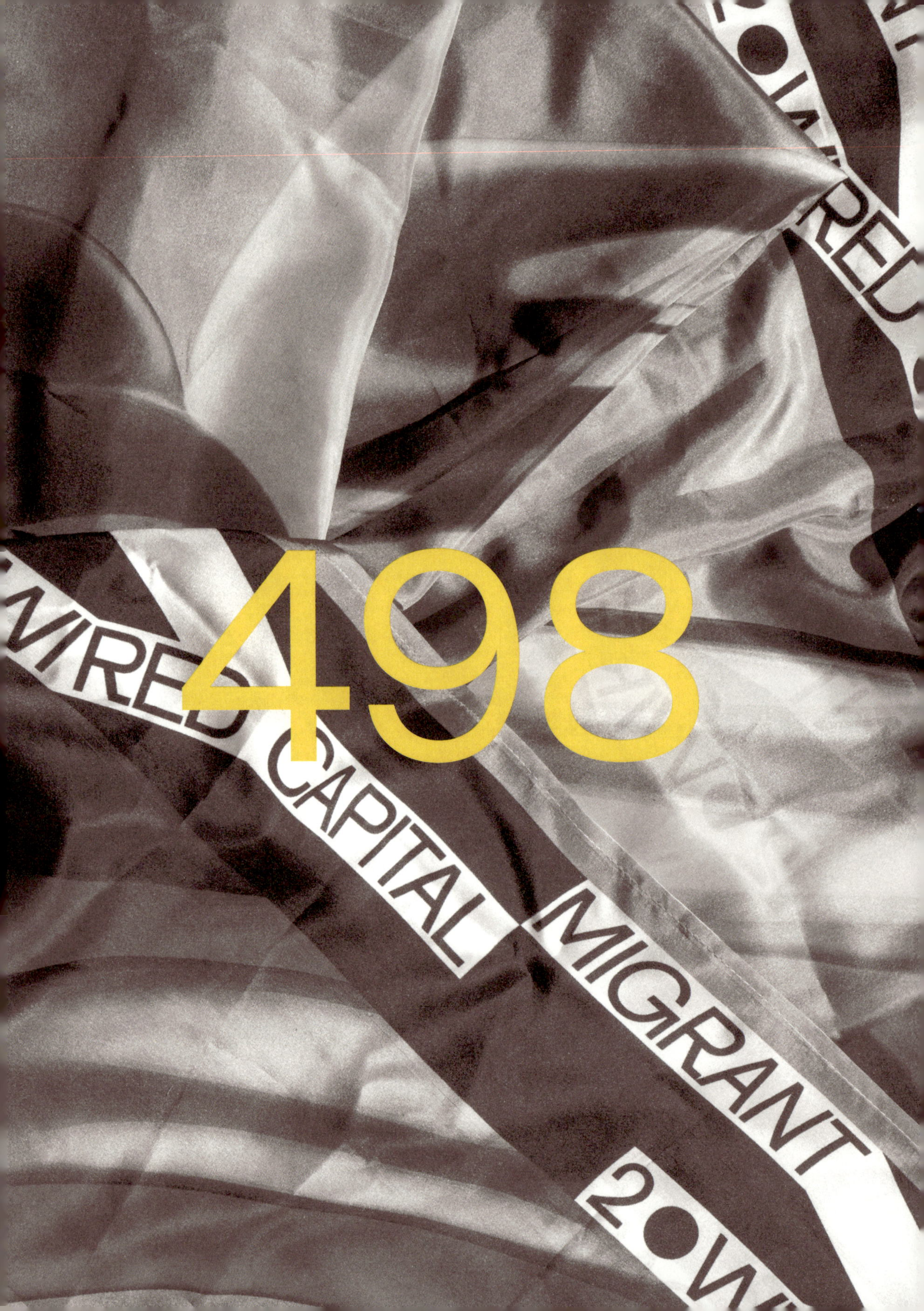

499

MIGRANT ODYSSEUS

5

500

501

502

5

Rucola
Tomato, mozzarella, rocket,
prosciutto crudo, parmesan   10

5
Parmigiana
Tomato, mozzarella, aubergine,
basil, parmesan (v)   10

EXTRA HAPPINESS

Mushroom, olives
mozzarella, salami, sausage
ten free base   1.5
an cheese   2.5
                                   2
                                   2

extra white
Bianco

125/750

4.5/20
6/20
7/30

4.5/20
6/25
7/30

6/25
.5/25
24

3.75
3.75
4.20

503

HAPPY FACE PIZZA

504

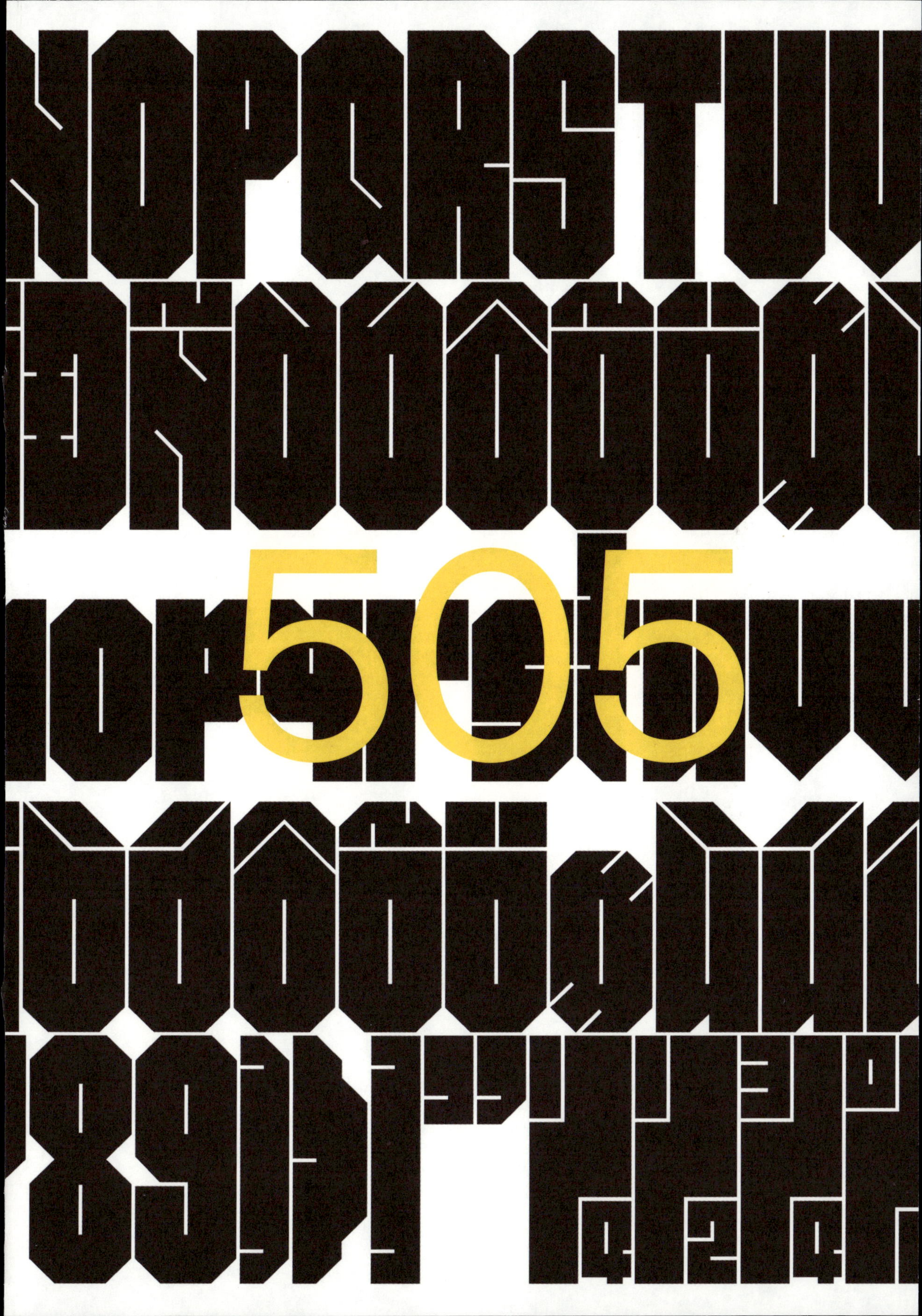
505

clien
l.ent
c ient

p oje
proje

notes

orovioworks.com

n
no
no
not
tébod

506

orov
oro
ovio

Miquel Orovio
Brand Writer

orovioworks.com
m@orovioworks.com
(+34) 629 963 638

Passeig de Sant Gervasi 52,
6è 2a. 08022—Barcelona

Miquel Orovio

Miquel Orovio
Brand Writer

orovioworks.com
m@orovioworks.com
(+34) 629 963 638

Passeig d Miquel Orovio
6è 2a. 08(Brand Writer

DNI : 399131

Think like an agenc
be like a rolling sto

Orovio works with
create and shape b

invo
invo.ce
orov
oro .o
ovio

507

orovioworks.com
m@orovioworks.com

Passeig de Sant Gervasi 6è 2a.
08022 — BARCELONA

Brand Writer

Miquel Orovio

envelo   e
en elope
nvelop

made by Semiotik
semiotikdesign.com
& the team of art
aristotleracing.gr

IANOS E-BOOKS

508

aristotle racing team

20 06
06 —
— 20
20 16

10

IANOS E-ΒΙΒΛΙΟΘΗΚΗ

Ginger Muse is a flagship project of Music Lab in 2020. In line with our spirit to innovate, Ginger Muse connects local musicians from a spectrum of disciplines, records our voices in studio and develops an unprecedented local music label.

Since 2016, Music Lab Festival has been dedicated to promoting and nurturing local music talents. We curate innovative and experimental music programmes, bringing new possibilities to and widening imagination of the public towards music.

Ginger Muse substantiates the vision of Music Lab, from producing and releasing music albums to incubating local talents.

510

GER MU
GER MU
GER MU

GING
GING
GING
GINGER MU
G   R MU
G   R MU
G   R MU

GINGER
MUSE

Ginger Muse substantiates of Music Lab, from produc releasing music albums to local talents.

SET LOOSE

GINGER   MUSE

KAJENG WONG
PIANO

GINGER

GINGER MUSE

Ginger Muse is a flagship project of Music Lab in 2020. In line with our spirit to innovate, Ginger Muse connects local musicians from a spectrum of disciplines, records our voices in studio and develops an unprecedented local music label. Since 2016, Music Lab Festival has been dedicated to promoting and nurturing local music talents. We curate innovative and experimental music programmes, bringing the public towards music. Ginger Muse substantiates the vision of Music Lab, from producing and releasing music albums to incubating local talents. Ginger Muse envisions to identify and develop our city's up and coming musicians and to showcase their programmes to international arenas.

Since 2016, Music Lab Festival has been dedicated to promoting and nurturing local music talents. We curate innovative and experimental music programmes, bringing new possibilities to and widening imaginations of the public towards music.

Ginger Muse substantiates the vision of Music Lab, from producing and releasing music albums to incubating local talents. Ginger Muse endeavors to identify and develop our city's up and coming musicians and to showcase their programmes to international arenas.

Ginger Muse envisions to identify and develop our city's up and coming musicians and to showcase their programmes to international arenas.

GINGER MUSE

511

SMASH: ORIGINALS

ANGEL & DEMON

SET LOOSE

(+850) 2234 5820
KA.ENGWONG@GMAIL.COM
WWW.KA.ENGWONG.COM

TIMOTHY SUN
SAXOPHONE
(+852) 2234 5820
TIMOTHYSUN@GMAIL.COM
WWW.TIMOTHYSUN.COM

GINGER MUSE

GINGER MUSE

GINGER MUSE

512

GINGER MUSE

SMASH: ORIGINALS

ANGEL & DEMON

SET LOOSE

Ginger Muse envisions to identify and develop our city's up and coming musicians and to showcase their programmes to international arenas

Ginger Muse substantiates the vision of Music Lab. from producing and releasing music albums to incubating local talents.

GINGER MUSE

SMASH: ORIGINALS

ANGEL & DEMON

SET LOOSE

513

Ginger Muse envisions to identify and develop our city's up and coming musicians and to showcase their programmes to international arenas

Ginger Muse substantiates the vision of Music Lab. from producing and releasing music albums to incubating local talents.

GINGER MUSE

HALF

HALF

HALF

514

〔序言〕
通過媒體藝術看透
未來，探究共存的意識
意願，並透過照著一面叫
人王智能的鏡子，看清楚
自己的心魔，好好思考舉
步若即的未來跟前該
怎麼走。

願科技有靈，
萬物共生。

[Foreword]
Through media art,
people envisage the future
to explore the apprehensions
and motivations of co-existing
with technology. Like a mirror,
AI lets us scrutinize our inner
demons as we consider
our next steps forward.

May science be kind
and all forms of life
co-exist in peace.

ABCDEFGHI
JKLMNOPQ
RSTUVWXYZ
516

PIXIES
HAIM
FONTAINES D.C.
GANG OF YOUTHS
BECK
PEARL JAM 517
METALLICA
LEWIS CAPALDI
MODERAT

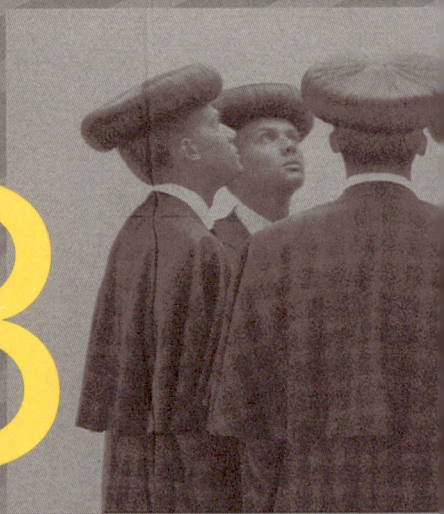

SUNDAY
2 JULY

29 JUNE - 2 JULY

rockwerchter.be ⓇⓌ Werchter Belgium ⓇⓌ rockwerchter.be

STROr

THE 1975
ADEKUNLE GOLD
AMENRA
ANNA CALVI
ARCTIC MONKEYS
AURORA
BABY QUEEN
BEN HOWARD
THE BLACK KEYS
CAVETOWN
CHRISTINE AND THE QUEENS
CITY AND COLOUR

COMPACT DISK DUMMIES
DEAN LEWIS
DOPE LEMON
THE DRIVER ERA
EDITORS
ETHAN BORTNICK
FEVER RAY
FRED AGAIN..
GAYLE
GABRIELS
THE HU
THE HAUNTED YOUTH

HOT MILK
IGGY POP
INTERPOL
THE INTERRUPTERS
J.I.D
JACOB COLLIER
KELSY KARTER &
 THE HEROINES
LIAM GALLAGHER
LIL NAS X
LOVEJOY
THE LUMINEERS

ROCKWERCHTER.BE   ROCKWERCHT   ROCKW

518

MEROL
MACHINE GUN KE
MIMI WEBB
MUSE
NATHANIEL RATE
NIGHT SWEATS
NOVA TWINS
THE OPPOSITES
OSCAR AND THE
PUP
PAOLO NUTINI
PICTURE THIS

PIP MILLETT
PUSCIFER
S OF THE STONE AG
HILI PEPPERS

ROSA
RÜFUS D
RÖYKSOP
SAM FEND
SIGUR RÓ
SLOWTH
SPOO

STORMZ
STROMA
TAMINO
TOUCHÉ A
WARDRUNA
WARHAUS
XAVIER

CHECK
LINE-UP
MORE N
ANNOUNC
FULL
NE &
TO BE

ROCKWERCHTER

THURSDAY
29 JUNE

ⓇⓌ

nae

ROCK WERCHTER

QUEE OF TI STONE

THE 1975
ADEKUNLE GOLD
AMENRA
ANNA CALVI
ARCTIC MONKEYS
AURORA
BABY QUEEN
BEN HOWARD
THE BLACK KEYS
CAVETOWN
CHRISTINE AND THE QUEENS
CITY AND COLOUR

COMPACT DISK DUMMIES
DEAN LEWIS
DOPE LEMON
THE DRIVER ERA
EDITORS
ETHAN BORTNICK
FEVER RAY
FRED AGAIN..
GAYLE
GABRIELS
THE HU
THE HAUNTED YOUTH

HOT MILK
IGGY POP
INTERPOL
THE INTERRUPTERS
J.I.D
JACOB COLLIER
KELSY KARTER &
THE HEROINES
LIAM GALLAGHER
LIL NAS X
LOVEJOY
THE LUMINEERS

ROCKWERCHTER.BE   ROCKWERCHTER.BE

MEROL
MACHINE GUN KELLY
MIMI WEB
MUSE
NATHANIEL FF & THE
NIGHT SW
NOVA TWINS
THE OPPOSITES
OSCAR AN THE WOLF
PUP
PAOLO NU
PICTURE TH

PIP MILL
PUSCIFER
QUEENS OF THE STO GE
RED HOT CHILI PEPP
RELIA
RUFUS DU SOL
ROYAL OPP
SAM FENDER
SIGUR RÓS
SHANGHAI
D

IZY
MAE
NO
THE AMORÉ
UNA
WA
XAVI

CHECK THE FULL
LIN UP ONLINE &
M E NAMES TO BE
AN NED SOON

519

29 JUNE - 2 JULY

2023   rockwerchter.be RW Werchter Belgium RW rockwerchter.be

SUNDAY
2 JULY

TICKETS
ticketmaster.l

Uth KLUB

520

521

522

LIMÓN

524

YERBA

LIMÓN

25 cl

MATÉ

TEA

LA·IÓN

525

526

527

Cuero/Sándalo/Incienso/Humo/Clavo

Fuego

Nuestras velas
son hechas 100%
de cera de soya.

Vertidas a mano
en nuestro taller
de Lima, Perú.

Arde

Recordemos que en algún momento de
la historia aprendimos a controlar
el fuego; gracias a eso hoy somos
lo que somos. El fuego nos da y nos
quita el poder. Nos hace inmensos
e insignificantes a la vez; nos
puede destruir, pero también nos
es prestado para crear. Hoy lo
celebramos en una vela.

528

A B C D E F G H I J K L M
N O P Q R S T U V W X Y Z
a b c d e f g h i j k l m
n o p q r s t u v w x y z

A B C D E F G H I J K L M
N O P Q R S T U V W X Y Z
a b c d e f g h i j k l m
n o p q r s t u v w x y z

A B C D E F G H I J K L M
N O P Q R S T U V W X Y Z
a b c d e f g h i j k l m
n o p q r s t u v w x y z

A	B	C	D	E	F	G	H	I	J	K	L	M
N	O	P	Q	R	S	T	U	V	W	X	Y	Z
a	b	c	d	e	f	g	h	i	j	k	l	m
n	o	p	q	r	s	t	u	v	w	x	y	z

A	B	C	D	E	F	G	H	I	J	K	L	M
N	O	P	Q	R	S	T	U	V	W	X	Y	Z
a	b	c	d	e	f	g	h	i	j	k	l	m
n	o	p	q	r	s	t	u	v	w	x	y	z

A	B	C	D	E	F	G	H	I	J	K	L	M
N	O	P	Q	R	S	T	U	V	W	X	Y	Z
a	b	c	d	e	f	g	h	i	j	k	l	m
n	o	p	q	r	s	t	u	v	w	x	y	z

A	B	C	D	E	F	G	H	I	J	K	L	M
N	O	P	Q	R	S	T	U	V	W	X	Y	Z
a	b	c	d	e	f	g	h	i	j	k	l	m
n	o	p	q	r	s	t	u	v	w	x	y	z

A	B	C	D	E	F	G	H	I	J	K	L	M
N	O	P	Q	R	S	T	U	V	W	X	Y	Z
a	b	c	d	e	f	g	h	i	j	k	l	m
n	o	p	q	r	s	t	u	v	w	x	y	z

A	B	C	D	E	F	G	H	I	J	K	L	M
N	O	P	Q	R	S	T	U	V	W	X	Y	Z
a	b	c	d	e	f	g	h	i	j	k	l	m
n	o	p	q	r	s	t	u	v	w	x	y	z

A B C D E F G H I J K L M
N O P Q R S T U V W X Y Z
a b c d e f g h i j k l m
n o p q r s t u v w x y z

A B C D E F G H I J K L M
N O P Q R S T U V W X Y Z
a b c d e f g h i j k l m
n o p q r s t u v w x y z

A B C D E F G H I J K L M
N O P Q R S T U V W X Y Z
a b c d e f g h i j k l m
n o p q r s t u v w x y z

A	B	C	D	E	F	G	H	I	J	K	L	M
N	O	P	Q	R	S	T	U	V	W	X	Y	Z
a	b	c	d	e	f	g	h	i	j	k	l	m
n	o	p	q	r	s	t	u	v	w	x	y	z

A	B	C	D	E	F	G	H	I	J	K	L	M
N	O	P	Q	R	S	T	U	V	W	X	Y	Z
a	b	c	d	e	f	g	h	i	j	k	l	m
n	o	p	q	r	s	t	u	v	w	x	y	z

A	B	C	D	E	F	G	H	I	J	K	L	M
N	O	P	Q	R	S	T	U	V	W	X	Y	Z
a	b	c	d	e	f	g	h	i	j	k	l	m
n	o	p	q	r	s	t	u	v	w	x	y	z

A	B	C	D	E	F	G	H	I	J	K	L	M
N	O	P	Q	R	S	T	U	V	W	X	Y	Z
a	b	c	d	e	f	g	h	i	j	k	l	m
n	o	p	q	r	s	t	u	v	w	x	y	z

A	B	C	D	E	F	G	H	I	J	K	L	M
N	O	P	Q	R	S	T	U	V	W	X	Y	Z
a	b	c	d	e	f	g	h	i	j	k	l	m
n	o	p	q	r	s	t	u	v	w	x	y	z

A	B	C	D	E	F	G	H	I	J	K	L	M
N	O	P	Q	R	S	T	U	V	W	X	Y	Z
a	b	c	d	e	f	g	h	i	j	k	l	m
n	o	p	q	r	s	t	u	v	w	x	y	z

A	B	C	D	E	F	G	H	I	J	K	L	M
N	O	P	Q	R	S	T	U	V	W	X	Y	Z
a	b	c	d	e	f	g	h	i	j	k	l	m
n	o	p	q	r	s	t	u	v	w	x	y	z

A	B	C	D	E	F	G	H	I	J	K	L	M
N	O	P	Q	R	S	T	U	V	W	X	Y	Z
a	b	c	d	e	f	g	h	i	j	k	l	m
n	o	p	q	r	s	t	u	v	w	x	y	z

A	B	C	D	E	F	G	H	I	J	K	L	M
N	O	P	Q	R	S	T	U	V	W	X	Y	Z
a	b	c	d	e	f	g	h	i	j	k	l	m
n	o	p	q	r	s	t	u	v	w	x	y	z

A	B	C	D	E	F	G	H	I	J	K	L	M
N	O	P	Q	R	S	T	U	V	W	X	Y	Z
a	b	c	d	e	f	g	h	i	j	k	l	m
n	o	p	q	r	s	t	u	v	w	x	y	z

A	B	C	D	E	F	G	H	I	J	K	L	M
N	O	P	Q	R	S	T	U	V	W	X	Y	Z
A	B	C	D	E	F	G	H	I	J	K	L	M
N	O	P	Q	R	S	T	U	V	W	X	Y	Z

A	B	C	D	E	F	G	H	I	J	K	L	M
N	O	P	Q	R	S	T	U	V	W	X	Y	Z
a	b	c	d	e	f	g	h	i	j	k	l	m
n	o	p	q	r	s	t	u	v	w	x	y	z

A	B	C	D	E	F	G	H	I	J	K	L	M
N	O	P	Q	R	S	T	U	V	W	X	Y	Z
a	b	c	d	e	f	g	h	i	j	k	l	m
n	o	p	q	r	s	t	u	v	w	x	y	z

A	B	C	D	E	F	G	H	I	J	K	L	M
N	O	P	Q	R	S	T	U	V	W	X	Y	Z
a	b	c	d	e	f	g	h	i	j	k	l	m
n	o	p	q	r	s	t	u	v	w	x	y	z

A	B	C	D	E	F	G	H	I	J	K	L	M
N	O	P	Q	R	S	T	U	V	W	X	Y	Z
a	b	c	d	e	f	g	h	i	j	k	l	m
n	o	p	q	r	s	t	u	v	w	x	y	z

A B C D E F G H I J K L M
N O P Q R S T U V W X Y Z
a b c d e f g h i j k l m
n o p q r s t u v w x y z

A B C D E F G H I J K L M
N O P Q R S T U V W X Y Z
a b c d e f g h i j k l m
n o p q r s t u v w x y z

A B C D E F G H I J K L M
N O P Q R S T U V W X Y Z
a b c d e f g h i j k l m
n o p q r s t u v w x y z

A	B	C	D	E	F	G	H	I	J	K	L	M
N	O	P	Q	R	S	T	U	V	W	X	Y	Z
a	b	c	d	e	f	g	h	i	j	k	l	m
n	o	p	q	r	s	t	u	v	w	x	y	z

A	B	C	D	E	F	G	H	I	J	K	L	M
N	O	P	Q	R	S	T	U	V	W	X	Y	Z
a	b	c	d	e	f	g	h	i	j	k	l	m
n	o	p	q	r	s	t	u	v	w	x	y	z

A	B	C	D	E	F	G	H	I	J	K	L	M
N	O	P	Q	R	S	T	U	V	W	X	Y	Z
a	b	c	d	e	f	g	h	i	j	k	l	m
n	o	p	q	r	s	t	u	v	w	x	y	z

A B C D E F G H I J K L M
N O P Q R S T U V W X Y Z
a b c d e f g h i j k l m
n o p q r s t u v w x y z

A B C D E F G H I J K L M
N O P Q R S T U V W X Y Z
a b c d e f g h i j k l m
n o p q r s t u v w x y z

A B C D E F G H I J K L M
N O P Q R S T U V W X Y Z
a b c d e f g h i j k l m
n o p q r s t u v w x y z

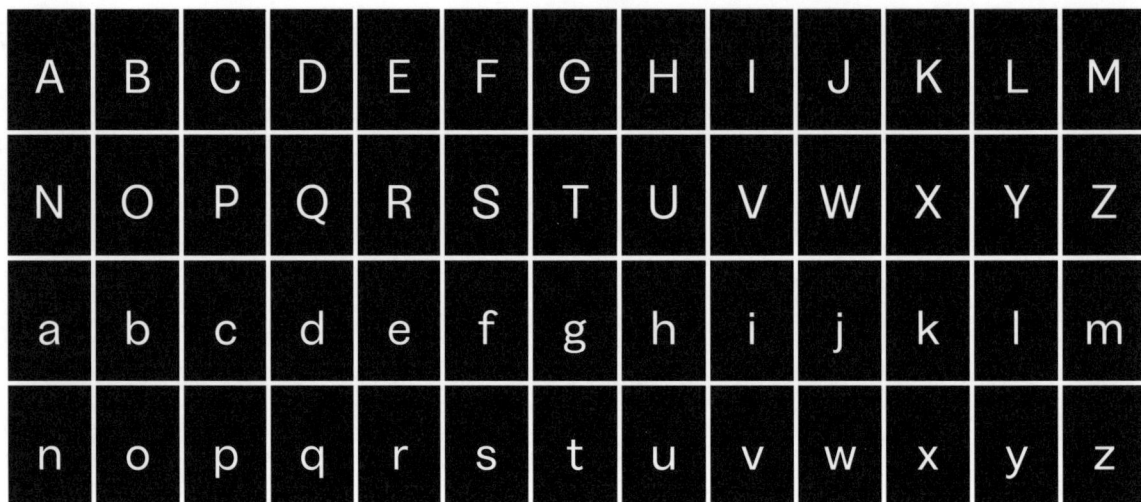

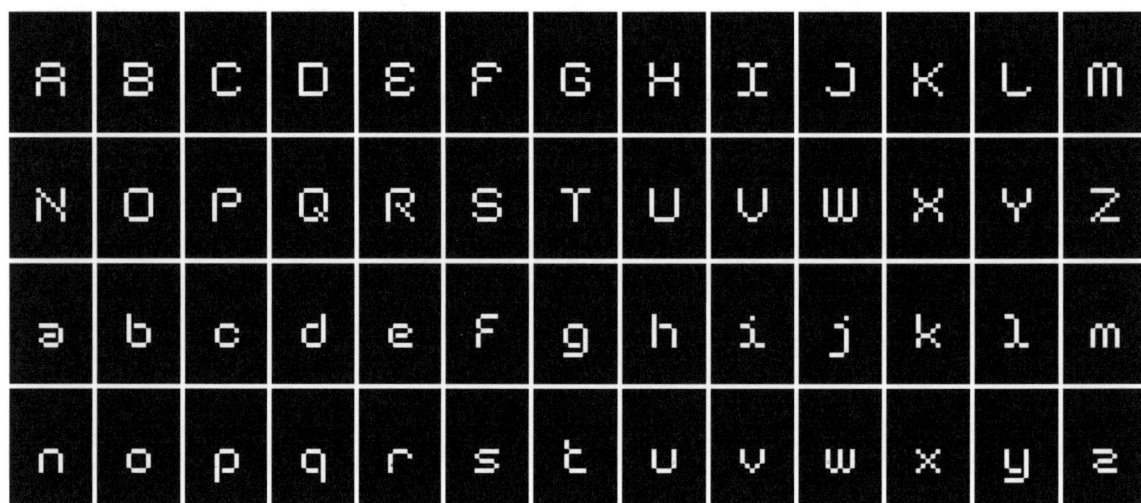

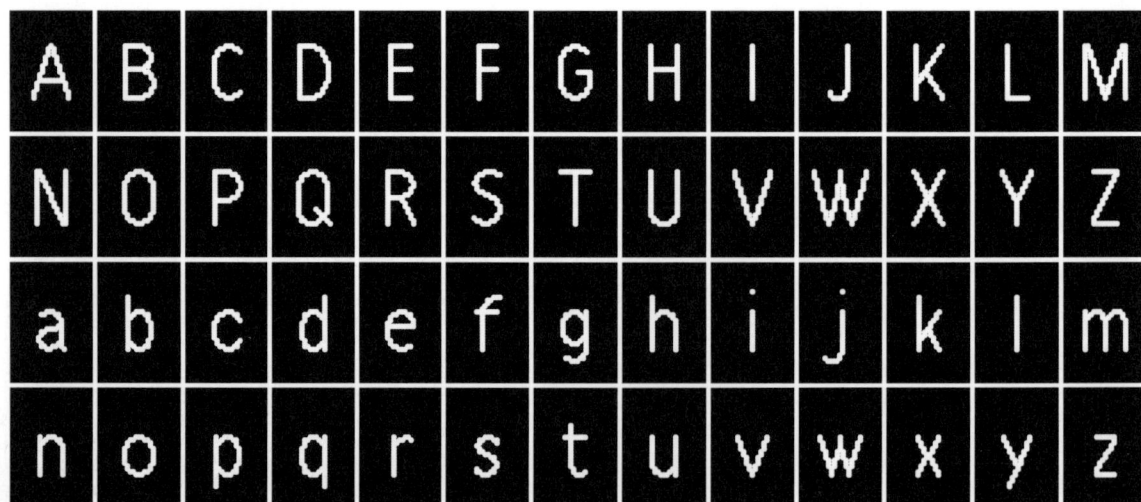

A	B	C	D	E	F	G	H	I	J	K	L	M
N	O	P	Q	R	S	T	U	V	W	X	Y	Z
a	b	c	d	e	f	g	h	i	j	k	l	m
n	o	p	q	r	s	t	u	v	w	x	y	z

A	B	C	D	E	F	G	H	I	J	K	L	M
N	O	P	Q	R	S	T	U	V	W	X	Y	Z
a	b	c	d	e	f	g	h	i	j	k	l	m
n	o	p	q	r	s	t	u	v	w	x	y	z

A	B	C	D	E	F	G	H	I	J	K	L	M
N	O	P	Q	R	S	T	U	V	W	X	Y	Z
a	b	c	d	e	f	g	h	i	j	k	l	m
n	o	p	q	r	s	t	u	v	w	x	y	z

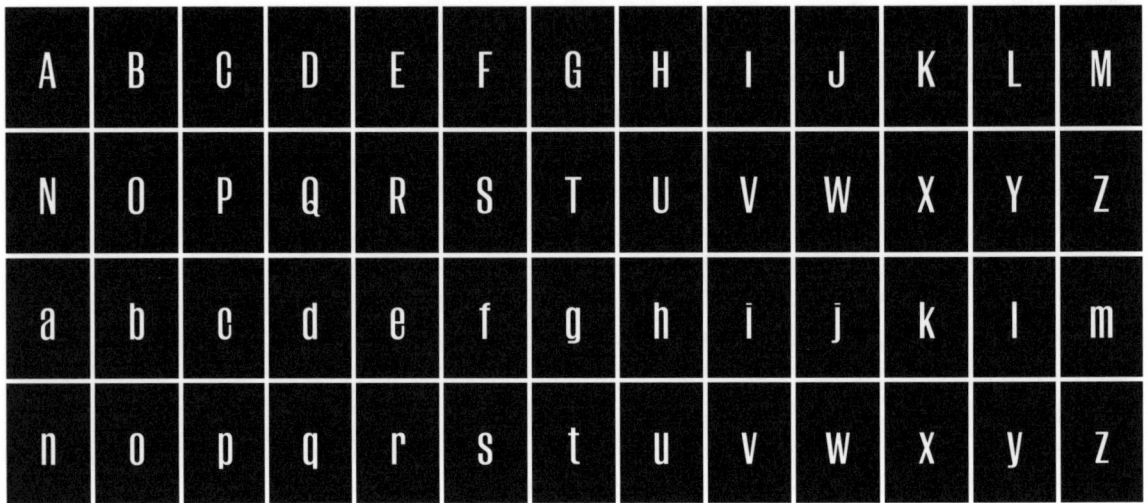

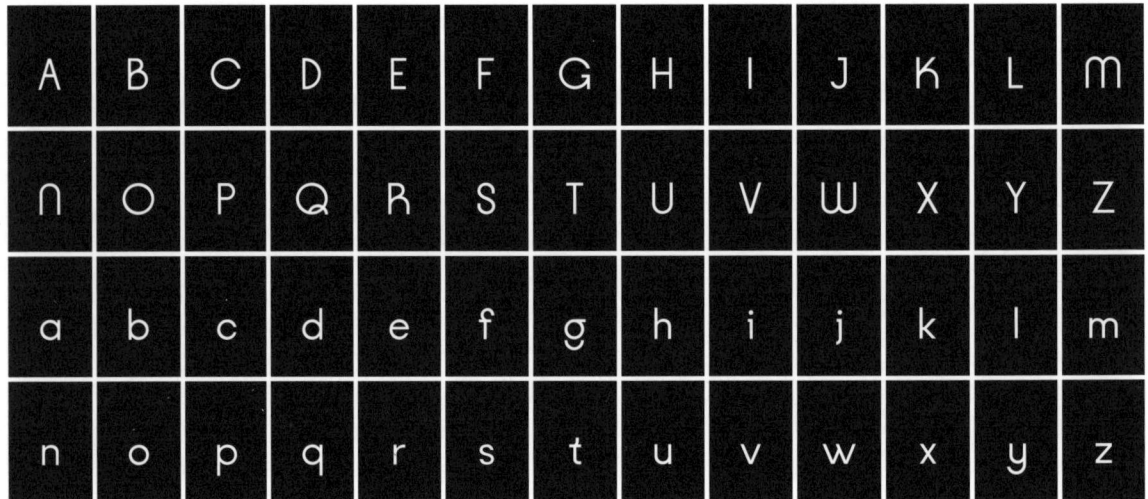

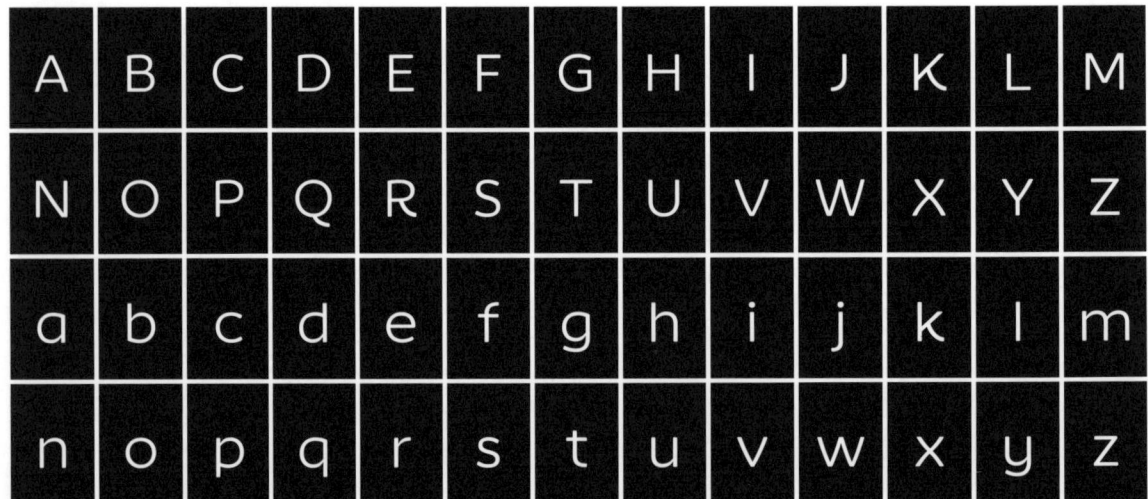

A B C D E F G H I J K L M
N O P Q R S T U V W X Y Z
a b c d e f g h i j k l m
n o p q r s t u v w x y z

A B C D E F G H I J K L M
N O P Q R S T U V W X Y Z
a b c d e f g h i j k l m
n o p q r s t u v w x y z

A B C D E F G H I J K L M
N O P Q R S T U V W X Y Z
a b c d e f g h i j k l m
n o p q r s t u v w x y z

A	B	C	D	E	F	G	H	I	J	K	L	M
N	O	P	Q	R	S	T	U	V	W	X	Y	Z
a	b	c	d	e	f	g	h	i	j	k	l	m
n	o	p	q	r	s	t	u	v	w	x	y	z

A	B	C	D	E	F	G	H	I	J	K	L	M
N	O	P	Q	R	S	T	U	V	W	X	Y	Z
A	B	C	D	E	F	G	H	I	J	K	L	M
N	O	P	Q	R	S	T	U	V	W	X	Y	Z

A	B	C	D	E	F	G	H	I	J	K	L	M
N	O	P	Q	R	S	T	U	V	W	X	Y	Z
a	b	c	d	e	f	g	h	i	j	k	l	m
n	o	p	q	r	s	t	u	v	w	x	y	z

A	B	C	D	E	F	G	H	I	J	K	L	M
N	O	P	Q	R	S	T	U	V	W	X	Y	Z
a	b	c	d	e	f	g	h	i	j	k	l	m
n	o	p	q	r	s	t	u	v	w	x	y	z

A	B	C	D	E	F	G	H	I	J	K	L	M
N	O	P	Q	R	S	T	U	V	W	X	Y	Z
a	b	c	d	e	f	g	h	i	j	k	l	m
n	o	p	q	r	s	t	u	v	w	x	y	z

A	B	C	D	E	F	G	H	I	J	K	L	M
N	O	P	Q	R	S	T	U	V	W	X	Y	Z
a	b	c	d	e	f	g	h	i	j	k	l	m
n	o	p	q	r	s	t	u	v	w	x	y	z

A B C D E F G H I J K L M
N O P Q R S T U V W X Y Z
a b c d e f g h i j k l m
n o p q r s t u v w x y z

A B C D E F G H I J K L M
N O P Q R S T U V W X Y Z
a b c d e f g h i j k l m
n o p q r s t u v w x y z

A B C D E F G H I J K L M
N O P Q R S T U V W X Y Z
a b c d e f g h i j k l m
n o p q r s t u v w x y z

A	B	C	D	E	F	G	H	I	J	K	L	M
N	O	P	Q	R	S	T	U	V	W	X	Y	Z
a	b	c	d	e	f	g	h	i	j	k	l	m
n	o	p	q	r	s	t	u	v	w	x	y	z

A	B	C	D	E	F	G	H	I	J	K	L	M
N	O	P	Q	R	S	T	U	V	W	X	Y	Z
a	b	c	d	e	f	g	h	i	j	k	l	m
n	o	p	q	r	s	t	u	v	w	x	y	z

A	B	C	D	E	F	G	H	I	J	K	L	M
N	O	P	Q	R	S	T	U	V	W	X	Y	Z
a	b	c	d	e	f	g	h	i	j	k	l	m
n	o	p	q	r	s	t	u	v	w	x	y	z

A B C D E F G H I J K L M
N O P Q R S T U V W X Y Z
a b c d e f g h i j k l m
n o p q r s t u v w x y z

A B C D E F G H I J K L M
N O P Q R S T U V W X Y Z
a b c d e f g h i j k l m
n o p q r s t u v w x y z

A B C D E F G H I J K L M
N O P Q R S T U V W X Y Z
a b c d e f g h i j k l m
n o p q r s t u v w x y z

A B C D E F G H I J K L M
N O P Q R S T U V W X Y Z
a b c d e f g h i j k l m
n o p q r s t u v w x y z

A B C D E F G H I J K L M
N O P Q R S T U V W X Y Z
a b c d e f g h i j k l m
n o p q r s t u v w x y z

A B C D E F G H I J K L M
N O P Q R S T U V W X Y Z
a b c d e f g h i j k l m
n o p q r s t u v w x y z

A	B	C	D	E	F	G	H	I	J	K	L	M
N	O	P	Q	R	S	T	U	V	W	X	Y	Z
a	b	c	d	e	f	g	h	i	j	k	l	m
n	o	p	q	r	s	t	u	v	w	x	y	z

A	B	C	D	E	F	G	H	I	J	K	L	M
N	O	P	Q	R	S	T	U	V	W	X	Y	Z
a	b	c	d	e	f	g	h	i	j	k	l	m
n	o	p	q	r	s	t	u	v	w	x	y	z

A	B	C	D	E	F	G	H	I	J	K	L	M
N	O	P	Q	R	S	T	U	V	W	X	Y	Z
a	b	c	d	e	f	g	h	i	j	k	l	m
n	o	p	q	r	s	t	u	v	w	x	y	z

A	B	C	D	E	F	G	H	I	J	K	L	M
N	O	P	Q	R	S	T	U	V	W	X	Y	Z
a	b	c	d	e	f	g	h	i	j	k	l	m
n	o	p	q	r	s	t	u	v	w	x	y	z

A	B	C	D	E	F	G	H	I	J	K	L	M
N	O	P	Q	R	S	T	U	V	W	X	Y	Z
a	b	c	d	e	f	g	h	i	j	k	l	m
n	o	p	q	r	s	t	u	v	w	x	y	z

A	B	C	D	E	F	G	H	I	J	K	L	M
N	O	P	Q	R	S	T	U	V	W	X	Y	Z
a	b	c	d	e	f	g	h	i	j	k	l	m
n	o	p	q	r	s	t	u	v	w	x	y	z

A	B	C	D	E	F	G	H	I	J	K	L	M
N	O	P	Q	R	S	T	U	V	W	X	Y	Z
a	b	c	d	e	f	g	h	i	j	k	l	m
n	o	p	q	r	s	t	u	v	w	x	y	z

A	B	C	D	E	F	G	H	I	J	K	L	M
N	O	P	Q	R	S	T	U	V	W	X	Y	Z
a	b	c	d	e	f	g	h	i	j	k	l	m
n	o	p	q	r	s	t	u	v	w	x	y	z

A	B	C	D	E	F	G	H	I	J	K	L	M
N	O	P	Q	R	S	T	U	V	W	X	Y	Z
a	b	c	d	e	f	g	h	i	j	k	l	m
n	o	p	q	r	s	t	u	v	w	x	y	z

A B C D E F G H I J K L M
N O P Q R S T U V W X Y Z
a b c d e f g h i j k l m
n o p q r s t u v w x y z

A B C D E F G H I J K L M
N O P Q R S T U V W X Y Z
a b c d e f g h i j k l m
n o p q r s t u v w x y z

A B C D E F G H I J K L M
N O P Q R S T U V W X Y Z
a b c d e f g h i j k l m
n o p q r s t u v w x y z

A	B	C	D	E	F	G	H	I	J	K	L	M
N	O	P	Q	R	S	T	U	V	W	X	Y	Z
a	b	c	d	e	f	g	h	i	j	k	l	m
n	o	p	q	r	s	t	u	v	w	x	y	z

A	B	C	D	E	F	G	H	I	J	K	L	M
N	O	P	Q	R	S	T	U	V	W	X	Y	Z
a	b	c	d	e	f	g	h	i	j	k	l	m
n	o	p	q	r	s	t	u	v	w	x	y	z

A	B	C	D	E	F	G	H	I	J	K	L	M
N	O	P	Q	R	S	T	U	V	W	X	Y	Z
a	b	c	d	e	f	g	h	i	j	k	l	m
n	o	p	q	r	s	t	u	v	w	x	y	z

TYPEFACE   :FAIRE SPRIG SANS   REGULAR   P370

A	B	C	D	E	F	G	H	I	J	K	L	M
N	O	P	Q	R	S	T	U	V	W	X	Y	Z
a	b	c	d	e	f	g	h	i	j	k	l	m
n	o	p	q	r	s	t	u	v	w	x	y	z

TYPEFACE   :SURT   REGULAR   P376

A	B	C	D	E	F	G	H	I	J	K	L	M
N	O	P	Q	R	S	T	U	V	W	X	Y	Z
a	b	c	d	e	f	g	h	i	j	k	l	m
n	o	p	q	r	s	t	u	v	w	x	y	z

TYPEFACE   :NB TELEVISION™ PRO   REGULAR   P380

A	B	C	D	E	F	G	H	I	J	K	L	M
N	O	P	Q	R	S	T	U	V	W	X	Y	Z
a	b	c	d	e	f	g	h	i	j	k	l	m
n	o	p	q	r	s	t	u	v	w	x	y	z

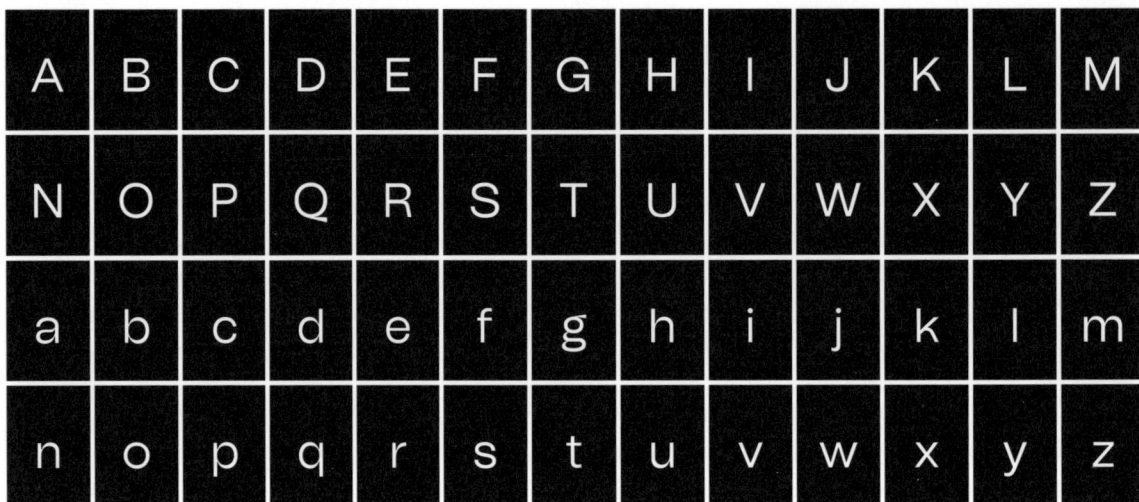

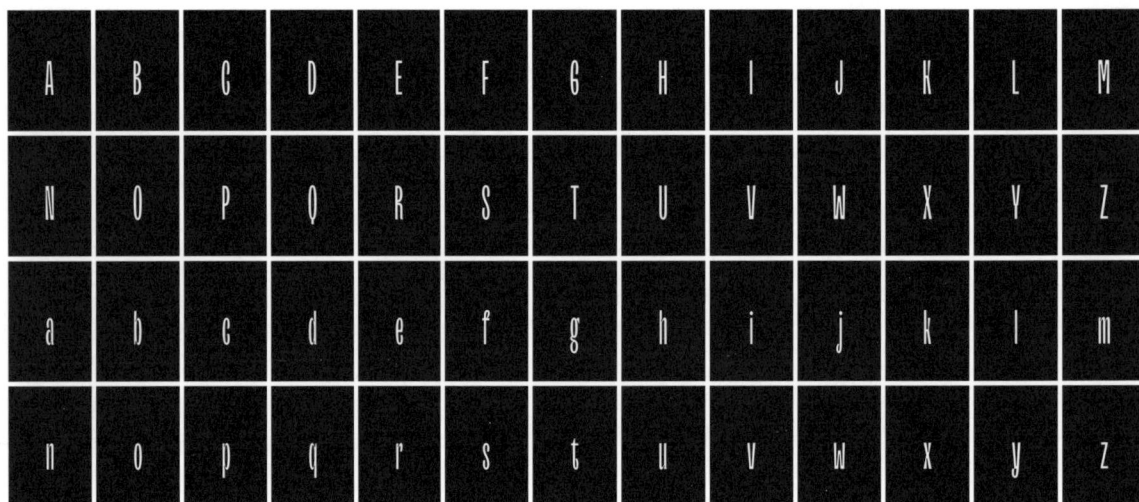

TYPEFACE   :VCTR MONO   REGULAR   P398

A	B	C	D	E	F	G	H	I	J	K	L	M
N	O	P	Q	R	S	T	U	V	W	X	Y	Z
a	b	c	d	e	f	g	h	i	j	k	l	m
n	o	p	q	r	s	t	u	v	w	x	y	z

TYPEFACE   :ZETKIN   REGULAR   P402

A	B	C	D	E	F	G	H	I	J	K	L	M
N	O	P	Q	R	S	T	U	V	W	X	Y	Z
a	b	c	d	e	f	g	h	i	j	k	l	m
n	o	p	q	r	s	t	u	v	w	x	y	z

TYPEFACE   :ZIN SANS   REGULAR   P406

A	B	C	D	E	F	G	H	I	J	K	L	M
N	O	P	Q	R	S	T	U	V	W	X	Y	Z
a	b	c	d	e	f	g	h	i	j	k	l	m
n	o	p	q	r	s	t	u	v	w	x	y	z

A	B	C	D	E	F	G	H	I	J	K	L	M
N	O	P	Q	R	S	T	U	V	W	X	Y	Z
a	b	c	d	e	f	g	h	i	j	k	l	m
n	o	p	q	r	s	t	u	v	w	x	y	z

A	B	C	D	E	F	G	H	I	J	K	L	M
N	O	P	Q	R	S	T	U	V	W	X	Y	Z
a	b	c	d	e	f	g	h	i	j	k	l	m
n	o	p	q	r	s	t	u	v	w	x	y	z

BIOGRAPHY & PROJECT CREDITS

205TF

205TF IS A TYPE FOUNDRY THAT BRINGS TOGETHER THE WORK OF FRENCH INDEPENDENT TYPEFACE DESIGNERS FROM VARYING CAREER BACKGROUNDS. AS A HUMAN-FOCUSED FOUNDRY, IT SUPPORTS TYPEFACE DESIGNERS BY MAKING THEIR CREATIONS AVAILABLE TO A WIDER AUDIENCE, ALLOWING FOR GREATER RECOGNITION OF THEIR WORK.

PP. 86-89

FONT INCLUDED ●
AUGURE

ALONGLONGTIME

HONG KONG-BASED MULTIDISCIPLINARY DESIGN HOUSE ALONGLONGTIME IS DEVOTED TO BRANDING, PRINTED MATTER, AND PACKAGING FOR VARIOUS CLIENTS IN THE CORPORATE, LEISURE, RETAIL, ART, AND CULTURE INDUSTRIES. THE MEANING BEHIND ITS NAME STEMS FROM THE STUDIO'S BELIEF THAT RELATIONSHIPS, TRUST, EXPERIENCE, AND INFLUENCE ARE BEST ESTABLISHED AFTER A LONG, LONG TIME.

PP. 514-515

APPLICATION ●
MICROWAVE INTERNATIONAL NEW MEDIA ARTS FESTIVAL 2022 - HALF HALF

ANAGRAMA

ANAGRAMA IS AN INTERNATIONAL BRANDING FIRM SPECIALISING IN THE DESIGN OF BRANDS, OBJECTS, SPACES, SOFTWARE AND MULTIMEDIA. IT THRIVES ON BREAKING THE TRADITIONAL CREATIVE AGENCY SCHEME, INTEGRATING MULTIDISCIPLINARY TEAMS OF CREATIVE AND BUSINESS EXPERTS.

PP. 466-469

APPLICATION ●
INFAMUSE 2018

BENOÎT BODHUIN

BB-BUREAU IS A GRAPHIC DESIGN STUDIO SPECIALISING IN TYPOGRAPHY. IT WAS FOUNDED BY BENOÎT BODHUIN, WHO WORKS ACROSS THE CULTURAL SECTOR IN VISUAL IDENTITY, SIGNAGE, POSTER, WEB, AND EDITORIAL DESIGN. HE ALSO DESIGNS CUSTOM TYPEFACES.

PP. 182-187

FONT INCLUDED ●
HARBER

BLACKLETRA TYPE FOUNDRY

BLACKLETRA IS A DIGITAL TYPE FOUNDRY RUN BY BRAZILIAN TYPE DESIGNER DANIEL SABINO, WHO IS CURRENTLY BASED IN SÃO PAULO. ESTABLISHED IN 2012, THE FOUNDRY DEVELOPS CUSTOM AND RETAIL TYPEFACES AS WELL AS LETTERING AND LOGOTYPES. ITS TYPEFACES COMBINE HISTORICAL INTEREST WITH CALLIGRAPHIC INFLUENCES AND SOMETIMES UNUSUAL IDEAS.

PP. 278-281

FONT INCLUDED ●
OFELIA

BLAZE TYPE

SINCE 2016, THE INTERNATIONAL TEAM OF EXPERTS AT BLAZE TYPE HAS BEEN WORKING IN CLOSE COLLABORATION TO CREATE STUNNING AND INNOVATIVE FONTS, RESULTING IN A RICH, TIMELESS, AND EVER-EVOLVING CATALOGUE. THE TEAM ALSO PUTS ITS EXPERTISE AT THE SERVICE OF AMBITIOUS BRANDS BY DESIGNING CUSTOM FONTS THAT STAND OUT FROM THE CROWD. COMBINING TYPEFACE DESIGN KNOWLEDGE WITH CONTEMPORARY IDEAS, BLAZE TYPE'S FONTS ARE VALUED FOR THEIR MODERN FEATURES AND AESTHETIC.

PP. 134-139, 376-379

FONTS INCLUDED ●
DIGITAL SANS / SURT

BOTH STUDIO

BOTH IS A BRANDING AND VISUAL COMMUNICATION STUDIO THAT WAS CO-FOUNDED BY SIGIRIYA BROWN AND DAN SMITH IN MELBOURNE. ITS SIMPLE APPROACH IS DRIVEN BY A GENUINE INTEREST IN THE PEOPLE AND COMPANIES WITH WHICH IT CHOOSES TO WORK, LEADING TO THOUGHTFUL AND RELEVANT DESIGN OUTCOMES.

PP. 470-471

APPLICATION ●
BIANCA SCIUTO 2020

CARNOKYTYPE

CARNOKYTYPE IS A SMALL KYSAK-BASED TYPE FOUNDRY RUN BY SAMUEL ČARNOKÝ – A LECTURER, TYPOGRAPHER, AND TYPE AND GRAPHIC DESIGNER. FOUNDED IN 2010, CARNOKYTYPE FOCUSES ON PRODUCING HIGH-QUALITY DISPLAY AND TEXT FONTS FOR VARIOUS KINDS OF TYPOGRAPHIC USE.

PP. 406-409

FONT INCLUDED ●
ZIN SANS

COTYPE FOUNDRY

COTYPE IS THE LONDON-BASED TYPE FOUNDRY OF MARK BLOOM AND CO. ASIDE FROM DESIGNING TYPEFACES FOR DIGITAL AND PRINT, THE TEAM ALSO DESIGNS BESPOKE TYPEFACES AND MODIFICATIONS OF THEIR EXISTING LIBRARY. IT HAS WORKED WITH LEADING DESIGN STUDIOS AND AGENCIES, LICENSING ITS TYPEFACES FOR GLOBAL BRANDS LIKE AMAZON, VIRGIN, AND THE LIKE.

PP. 18-33, 56-63, 106-109, 118-121, 178-181, 326-333, 346-349

FONTS INCLUDED ●
AEONIK / AEONIK FONO / AEONIK MONO / AEONIK PRO / ALTFORM / AMBIT / BETATRON / COANDA / GRIDULAR / RM MONO / RM NEUE / SCANDIUM

PP. 430-447, 454-461

APPLICATIONS ●
AEONIK / AEONIK FONO / AEONIK MONO / ALTFORM / AMBIT / COANDA / RM MONO / RM NEUE / SCANDIUM

DALTON MAAG

DALTON MAAG IS A LONDON-BASED INDEPENDENT TYPEFACE DESIGN STUDIO FOUNDED IN 1991, WITH A PORTFOLIO OF WORK FOR GLOBAL AND LOCAL BRANDS. BEHIND THE WORK AT DALTON MAAG IS AN INTERNATIONAL TEAM OF 50 FONT DEVELOPERS, CREATIVE DIRECTORS, SOFTWARE ENGINEERS, AND SUPPORT STAFF, SPANNING 25 NATIONALITIES AND SPEAKING 14 LANGUAGES.

PP. 48-55

FONTS INCLUDED ●
AKTIV GROTESK / ALDGATE SANS

DDOTT

DDOTT IS A SMALL-SCALE TYPE FOUNDRY AND PUBLISHING PROJECT FOUNDED BY DOMINIK THIEME IN 2017. IT EXPLORES THE HISTORICAL AND TECHNICAL INFLUENCES ON TYPEFACES, STUDIES THE MULTIPLE FEATURES OF ANALOGUE TYPOGRAPHY, AND TRIES TO BRING THAT SINGULAR APPEARANCE BACK ONTO THE SCREEN. THE TEAM BELIEVES THAT THE PERSONALITY OF A TYPEFACE IS HIGHLY INFLUENCED BY THE TRACES AND IRREGULARITIES IT FINDS IN THE LETTERPRESS.

PP. 140-145, 270-273

FONTS INCLUDED ●
DIVERSE / NOUVEAU

DESIGNSTUDIO MATHILDA MUTANT

LAUNCHED IN 2012, DESIGNSTUDIO MATHILDA MUTANT IS AN INTERDISCIPLINARY STUDIO WITH A FOCUS ON CORPORATE, EDITORIAL, AND PACKAGING DESIGN. ESTABLISHED BY MARTINA MIOCEVIC IN MAINZ, IT OFFERS CLEAR CONCEPTS, ATTENTION TO DETAIL, AND BESPOKE SOLUTIONS TAILORED TO EACH CLIENT AND PROJECT. THE TEAM WORKS IN THE FIELDS OF WINE, FOOD, CULTURE, AND FASHION, ON TOP OF OTHER UNIQUE PROJECTS IN BETWEEN.

PP. 472-475

APPLICATION ●
JOKOLADE 2021-2022

DINAMO

DINAMO IS A GERMAN TYPE DESIGN STUDIO THAT PRODUCES RETAIL AND BESPOKE TYPEFACES, DESIGN SOFTWARE, RESEARCH, CONSULTANCY, PHYSICAL OBJECTS, AND EDITIONS. FOUNDED IN BASEL AND BERLIN, IT OPERATES VIA A NETWORK OF SATELLITE MEMBERS ACROSS THE GLOBE, OSCILLATING BETWEEN COMMERCIAL AND CULTURAL PROJECTS OF VARYING SCALES.

PP. 130-133, 150-153, 168-171, 238-241, 334-337

FONTS INCLUDED ●
ABC DIATYPE / ABC FAVORIT / ABC GRAVITY / ABC MONUMENT GROTESK / ABC ROM

DISPLAAY TYPE FOUNDRY

INSPIRED BY SPECIFIC MOMENTS OF IMPERFECTION AND SPONTANEOUS IRREGULARITIES, DISPLAAY IS AN INDEPENDENT TYPE FOUNDRY ESTABLISHED IN 2014 AND BASED IN PRAGUE. WITH A DIVERSE TEAM COMPRISING NUMEROUS COLLABORATORS AROUND THE WORLD, THE FOUNDRY FOCUSES ON RETAIL AND CUSTOM TYPEFACES, AIMING TO DEVELOP DISTINCTIVE TYPEFACES UNSEEN IN THE MARKET.

PP. 90-95, 126-129, 172-177

FONTS INCLUDED ●
BAGOSS / DAZZED / GREED

PP. 452-453

APPLICATION ●
GREED

F37®

F37® FOUNDRY & STUDIO IS AN AWARD-WINNING TYPE FOUNDRY AND DESIGN STUDIO THAT SPECIALISES IN FONTS, BRANDING, CREATIVE CODING, AND PUBLISHING. USING THE LATEST TECHNOLOGY, ITS UNIQUE, STREAMLINED, AND FLEXIBLE TEAM CONVEYS SIMPLE IDEAS IN A BEAUTIFULLY-CRAFTED WAY.

PP. 196-199, 200-203, 210-213, 292-295, 366-369

FONTS INCLUDED ●
F37 JUDGE / F37 K9 / F37 KOOKIE / F37 ORACLE / F37 SONIC

FAIRE TYPE

FAIRE TYPE IS A NEW INDEPENDENT TYPE FOUNDRY BASED IN BROOKLYN. WORKING AT THE INTERSECTION OF GRAPHIC DESIGN AND TYPE DESIGN, IT CRAFTS FONTS, CUSTOM TYPEFACES, AND BESPOKE LOGOS WITH IMPACT. ITS TYPE CATALOGUE IS A DIVERSE MIX OF TEXT AND DISPLAY FONTS, EXECUTED WITH PRECISION AND A RIGOROUS ATTENTION TO DETAIL.

PP. 370-375

FONT INCLUDED ●
FAIRE SPRIG SANS

(FFF) FONTS FROM FOLCH

FFF (FONTS FROM FOLCH) IS A DIGITAL TYPE FOUNDRY THAT WAS FOUNDED BY PABLO FERNÁNDEZ DE LA FUENTE, JOSEP PUY, AND RAFA MARTINEZ IN 2023 IN COLLABORATION WITH ALBERT FILCH FROM THE DESIGN STUDIO FOLCH. WITH AN UNWAVERING COMMITMENT TO EXCELLENCE, FFF DELICATELY CRAFTS TYPEFACES THAT MERGE TIMELESS ELEGANCE WITH CONTEMPORARY SENSIBILITIES.

PP. 12-17

FONT INCLUDED ●
FFF ACID GROTESK

PP. 422-429

APPLICATION ●
FFF ACID GROTESK

FORMAGARI

FORMAGARI IS AN INDEPENDENT TYPE FOUNDRY RUN BY EMMANUEL BESSE IN MARSEILLE, FRANCE. IT AIMS TO PRODUCE QUALITY AND SINGULAR TYPEFACES WHILE HAVING FUN DOING SO.

PP. 188-191

FONT INCLUDED ●
INSITU

FOR THE PEOPLE

FOR THE PEOPLE IS A COLLECTIVE OF DESIGNERS, WRITERS AND STRATEGISTS WITH THE GOAL OF CREATING WORK THAT CREATES SOCIAL AND ECONOMIC IMPACT. THEY SPECIALISE IN BRANDING AND STRATEGY, AND WORK WITH A NUMBER OF IMPRESSIVE AND FASCINATING CLIENTS WHO ARE WILLING TO TAKE BIG SWINGS.

PP. 476-477

APPLICATION ●
CUMULUS 2020

FUERTE TYPE

FUERTE IS AN INDEPENDENT TYPE DESIGN STUDIO WITH A UNIQUE INTERNATIONAL FOOTPRINT, SPLIT BETWEEN THE VIBRANT LANDSCAPES OF DUBAI AND MONTEVIDEO. IT DEVELOPS RIGOROUSLY CRAFTED TYPEFACES WITH A STRONG GRAPHIC APPEAL TO HELP DESIGNERS CREATE MEMORABLE VISUAL EXPERIENCES. ITS PROJECTS COUPLE THE TECHNICAL AND OPTICAL PRECISION OF TYPE DESIGN WITH CONCEPTS ROOTED IN ITS GRAPHIC DESIGN PRACTICE.

PP. 296-299

FONT INCLUDED ●
FT PILAR

GEORGIA HARIZANI

GEORGIA HARIZANI IS AN INDEPENDENT GREEK DESIGNER WORKING WITH BRANDS AND CORPORATIONS WORLDWIDE TO APPLY STRATEGIC DESIGN SOLUTIONS IN THE PHYSICAL AND DIGITAL REALMS. SHE COMBINES HER EXPERIENCE IN THE FIELDS OF ARCHITECTURE, PRODUCT DESIGN, AND VISUAL COMMUNICATION TO OFFER HOLISTIC DESIGN AND COMMUNICATION SERVICES BY EMBRACING THE GENERATIVE POWER OF COLLABORATION.

PP. 478-479

APPLICATION ●
TWELVE SCENTS 2022

GOODS

GOODS BELIEVES THAT A POSITIVE FUTURE REQUIRES COLLECTIVE EFFORT, WHICH IS WHY IT HAS BUILT AN OPEN-SOURCE FRAMEWORK TO SHARE AND DOCUMENT ITS INSIGHTS ON RESPONSIBLE PACKAGING DESIGN WITH DESIGNERS WHO VALUE ETHICS AND AESTHETICS. BY VALUING FACTS AND SCIENCE OVER MYTHS AND SUBJECTIVITY, THE TEAM BELIEVES THAT A MORE SUSTAINABLE CONSUMER GOODS INDUSTRY IS ACHIEVABLE AS A COMMUNITY, AND HOPES TO HELP ELEVATE THE STATUS QUO BY SHARING ITS KNOWLEDGE.

PP. 524-525

APPLICATION ●
LIMÓN

GRILLI TYPE

NOËL LEU AND THIERRY BLANCPAIN FOUNDED GRILLI TYPE IN SWITZERLAND IN LATE-2009 AS A COLLABORATIVE AVENUE FOR WORKING WITH OTHER DESIGNERS. TODAY, ITS TEAM OF EIGHT WORKS ACROSS NEW YORK, COPENHAGEN, AND BEYOND. IT OFFERS ORIGINAL RETAIL AND CUSTOM TYPEFACES WITH A CONTEMPORARY AESTHETIC IN THE SWISS TRADITION. THE RELATIONSHIPS THAT IT FORGES WITH OTHER DESIGNERS ARE ESSENTIAL TO ITS MISSION AND INFORMS ITS DESIRE TO PRODUCE USEFUL TYPE.

PP. 304-307

FONT INCLUDED ●
GT PRESSURA

HAN GAO

HAN GAO SPECIALISES IN CREATIVE DIRECTION, BRANDING, WEB AND GRAPHIC DESIGN. HE WORKS INTERNATIONALLY WITH ARTISTS, MUSICIANS, FASHION DESIGNERS, AND PROGRAMMERS ON A VARIETY OF PROJECTS.

PP. 480-481

APPLICATION ●
NICE CREAM 2019

HEAVYWEIGHT DIGITAL TYPE FOUNDRY

FOUNDED BY FILIP MATEJICEK AND JAN HORCIK IN 2013, HEAVYWEIGHT REFERS TO THE TYPOGRAPHICAL DESCRIPTION OF A VOLUMINOUS FONT STYLE — ITS HEAVY WEIGHT. PRIMARILY, HOWEVER, IT EXPRESSES THE EMPHASIS PUT ON SIMPLICITY, PRECISION OF DETAIL, AND TASTEFUL DESIGN, WHICH CAN BE USED VARIABLY ACROSS GRAPHIC DESIGN APPLICATIONS. BASED ON THIS APPROACH, THE FOUNDRY PRODUCES FONTS THAT ARE USED BY GLOBAL INSTITUTIONS AND SMALL INDEPENDENT START-UPS ALIKE.

PP. 82-85, 274-277

FONTS INCLUDED ●
ATLANTIC / NUCKLE

HEYDAYS

EVERY COMPANY HAS A STORY TO TELL, AND HEYDAYS IN OSLO AIMS TO TELL THEM THROUGH FOCUSED AND FUNCTIONAL IDENTITIES THAT STAND OUT COMMERCIALLY AND CULTURALLY. ESTABLISHED IN 2008 BY MATHIAS HADDAL HOVET, LARS KJELSNES, MARTIN SANNE KRISTIANSEN, TOMAS LEIN, AND STEIN HENRIK HAUGAN, THE STUDIO IS DEDICATED TO BRINGING PROGRESSIVE BRANDS TO LIFE THROUGH PRINT AND DIGITAL MEANS.

PP. 482-483

APPLICATION ●
AURLANDS 2018

INGA PLÖNNIGS

INGA PLÖNNIGS IS AN INDEPENDENT TYPE DESIGNER BASED IN BERLIN WHO DIVIDES HER TIME BETWEEN COMMISSIONED WORK FOR INTERNATIONAL CLIENTS AND SELF-INITIATED PROJECTS. HER WORK IS INSPIRED BY HISTORY, NECESSITY AND THE VERNACULAR. FROM LOGOS AND INDIVIDUAL LETTERS TO CUSTOM TYPEFACE FAMILIES, SHE ENJOYS VECTOR-BASED PROJECTS THAT REQUIRE SKILLED HANDS AND A TRAINED EYE.

PP. 218-223, 402-405

FONTS INCLUDED ●
MAGNET / ZETKIN

KOMETA TYPEFACES

KOMETA TYPEFACES IS A SMALL AND NIMBLE DESIGN STUDIO BASED IN BRNO, PRODUCING HIGH-QUALITY RETAIL AND CUSTOM TYPEFACES THAT MELD TONGUE-IN-CHEEK CONCEPTUALISM WITH A CONTEMPORARY FINISH.

PP. 394-397

FONT INCLUDED ●
KOMETA UNIFORMA

LÉON HUGUES

LÉON IS A FRENCH AND BRITISH, PARIS-BASED TYPE DESIGNER WHO FREELANCES IN VARIOUS FOUNDRIES AROUND THE WORLD, COLLABORATING ON NEW TYPEFACES AND ENGINEERING CUSTOM FONTS. FROM OBSESSING WITH CONNECTED SCRIPT FONTS AND ITALICS TO LEARNING ABOUT SOUTHEAST ASIAN SCRIPTS, HE BELIEVES THAT DIVERSIFYING HIS PRACTICE ALLOWS HIM TO LEARN AND DISCOVER NEW WAYS OF DOING TYPOGRAPHY.

PP. 338-341

FONT INCLUDED ●
RULES

LIFT TYPE

LIFT TYPE IS A MONTPELLIER-BASED DIGITAL TYPE FOUNDRY FOUNDED IN 2014 BY ROMAIN OUDIN. IT OFFERS RETAIL AND CUSTOM FONTS, AS WELL AS LIMITED EDITION TYPEFACES FOR SPECIFIC EVENTS EACH YEAR.

PP. 342-345

FONT INCLUDED ●
SANS PLOMB

LOTTA NIEMINEN

FOUNDED BY LOTTA NIEMINEN, LOTTA NIEMINEN STUDIO CREATES HOLISTIC DESIGN SOLUTIONS ACROSS DISCIPLINES. PASSIONATE ABOUT FINDING THE BEST TOOLS TO EXECUTE CONTENT-DRIVEN VISUALS, THE STUDIO WORKS AS A CREATIVE PARTNER IN ALL ASPECTS BRANDING, BRINGING IDENTITIES TO LIFE THROUGH THOUGHTFULLY CRAFTED PRINT AND DIGITAL IMPLEMENTATIONS.

PP. 484-485

APPLICATION ●
CIENNE 2014-PRESENT

MARINA VEZIKO

MARINA VEZIKO IS AN AWARD-WINNING HELSINKI-BASED DESIGNER SPECIALISING IN BRANDING AND CREATIVE DIRECTION. HER DESIGN PRACTICE IS BASED ON STRATEGIC THINKING AND INTUITION. HER AESTHETIC RANGES FROM SLEEK MINIMALISM TO BRIGHT MAXIMALISM AND LEANS ON NUANCED TYPOGRAPHY AND ARRESTING IMAGERY. IN 2021, SHE WAS SELECTED AS FINNISH GRAPHIC DESIGNER OF THE YEAR.

PP. 486-487

APPLICATION ●
PACKHELP - "WHAT'S IN THE BOX" 2022

MARTIN ESCALANTE

MARTIN ESCALANTE CREATES VISUAL WORK FOR INDEPENDENT CLIENTS, COLLABORATIONS, AND SELF-INITIATED PROJECTS. THROUGH PRINT AND DIGITAL MEDIA, HIS PRACTICE CENTRES ON FINDING VALUE IN THE VISUAL CODES AND THE CONTEXT OF A PLACE. HE WORKS WITH A DEEP INTEREST IN IMAGE-MAKING THROUGH THE EXPLORATION OF SHAPES AND TYPE EXPRESSIONS.

PP. 526-527

APPLICATION ●
ARDE 2021

MASS-DRIVER™

MASS-DRIVER™ IS AN INDEPENDENT STUDIO FOR TYPEFACE DESIGN AND FONT PRODUCTION. FOUNDED IN 2020 AND LED BY RUTHERFORD CRAZE, THE STUDIO AIMS TO DEVELOP ORIGINAL DESIGNS BUILT ON A DEEP UNDERSTANDING OF THE HISTORY AND TECHNOLOGIES BEHIND THEM THROUGH AN INTIMATE KNOWLEDGE OF THE PROCESSES BY WHICH TYPEFACES ARE MADE, AND THE REASONS THEY LOOK THE WAY THEY DO.

PP. 262-265, 308-311

FONTS INCLUDED ●
MD NICHROME / MD PRIMER

MMPX

MMPX IS A MULTIDIMENSIONAL CREATIVE STUDIO SPECIALISING IN THE FIELDS OF DESIGN AND VISUAL ARTS.

PP. 528-529

APPLICATION ●
EDITORI BRANDING 2019

MUBARIZ YUSIFZADE

MUBARIZ YUSIFZADE IS A GRAPHIC DESIGNER AND AN ART DIRECTOR AT AN ADVERTISING AGENCY. SPECIALISING IN GRAPHIC DESIGN, MOTION DESIGN AND 3D DESIGN, MUBARIZ CREATES BOLD AND UNIQUE DESIGNS WITH A MINIMALIST APPROACH.

PP. 488-489

APPLICATION ●
KLEMAN TREVINO STUDIO 2021

NARROW TYPE

FOUNDED BY TYPE AND GRAPHIC DESIGNER ANDREJ SEVCIK, NARROW TYPE IS A TYPE FOUNDRY THAT CREATES CONTEMPORARY, HIGH-QUALITY FONTS WITH PERSONALITY. TO THE STUDIO, AESTHETICS AND UNIQUENESS ARE JUST AS IMPORTANT AS CRAFTSMANSHIP AND FUNCTIONALITY.

PP. 162-167

FONT INCLUDED ●
GIRONA

PP. 450-451

APPLICATION ●
GIRONA

NEUBAU

NEUBAU WAS FOUNDED BY BERLIN-BASED DESIGNER AND AUTHOR STEFAN GANDL IN 2001, BEFORE HE TOOK THE WORLD BY STORM WITH THE RELEASE OF THE BEST-SELLING BOOKS 'NEUBAU WELT' (2005) AND 'NEUBAU MODUL' (2007). DEFINED BY A SYSTEMATIC APPROACH TO TYPE AND DESIGNING FOR SYSTEMS IN PRINT, SCREENS, AND SPACES, THE STUDIO'S WORK WAS EXHIBITED AT MU (THE NETHERLANDS) IN 2008, WITH AN INTRODUCTION BY WIM CROUWEL.

PP. 42-47, 192-195, 380-385

FONTS INCLUDED ●
NB AKADEMIE™ PRO / NB INTERNATIONAL™ PRO / NB TELEVISION™ PRO

NEWGLYPH

NEWGLYPH IS A LAUSANNE-BASED TYPE DESIGN STUDIO SPECIALISING IN THE RESEARCH, DESIGN, AND DEVELOPMENT OF FONTS AND VARIABLE FONT TECHNOLOGY. WITH A MULTICULTURAL TEAM COMPRISING EXPERIENCED PROFESSIONALS IN THE CREATIVE AND TECHNOLOGICALLY-DRIVEN DESIGN FIELD, THE STUDIO STRIVES TO BETTER UNDERSTAND THE VISUAL COMMUNICATION NEEDS OF THE GLOBAL COMMUNITY.

PP. 68-73, 96-99, 246-249

FONTS INCLUDED ●
ANTARCTICA / BAIKAL / NEOGEO

NGUYEN GOBBER

NGUYEN GOBBER IS THE COLLABORATIVE DESIGN PRACTICE OF HOANG NGUYEN AND DAVID GOBBER THAT HELPS CLIENTS FROM CULTURAL AND ACADEMIC FIELDS BY CREATING DISTINCTIVE VISUAL IDENTITIES AND EDITORIAL DESIGNS. THEY ALSO DESIGN EXPRESSIVE DISPLAY TYPEFACES, WHICH ARE USED AND TRUSTED BY GOOGLE, THE METROPOLITAN MUSEUM OF ART, SOUNDCLOUD, WETRANSFER, VICE MEDIA GROUP, AND TOMORROW X TODAY.

PP. 232-237

FONT INCLUDED ●
MONOPOL

0.00 DESIGN & RISOGRAPH ROOM

0.00 IS A TAIPEI-BASED DESIGN STUDIO THAT COMBINES RISOGRAPH PRINTING TECHNOLOGY WITH EXPERIMENTAL DESIGN PATTERNS. THEY SPECIALISE IN FUSING THEIR CREATIVE PRINTING METHODS WITH PRODUCT DEVELOPMENT.

PP. 490-493

APPLICATION ●
NO MAGIC IN RISO 2019

OFFSHORE STUDIO

OFFSHORE STUDIO IS A ZURICH-BASED GRAPHIC DESIGN STUDIO FOUNDED BY ISABEL SEIFFERT AND CHRISTOPH MILER, WITH A FOCUS ON RESEARCH-DRIVEN DESIGN AND VISUAL NARRATIVES. BESIDES COMMISSIONS AND COLLABORATIONS, THE TEAM ALSO ENGAGES IN DESIGN EDUCATION AND INVESTIGATES CRITICAL ISSUES WITHIN THE FIELDS OF DESIGN, MEDIA, AND GLOBALISATION. ITS WORKS HAVE BEEN PUBLISHED, EXHIBITED, AND AWARDED INTERNATIONALLY.

PP. 494-499

APPLICATION ●
MIGRANT JOURNAL NO. 1-6 2016-2019

OR TYPE

OR TYPE IS AN ICELANDIC/DANISH TYPE FOUNDRY FOUNDED IN 2013 TO PUBLISH TYPEFACES DESIGNED BY GUNMAD (GUÐMUNDUR ÚLFARSSON & MADS FREUND BRUNSE). IT AIMS TO CHALLENGE THE CONVENTIONS FOUND IN TYPOGRAPHIC TRADITIONS AND CONTEMPORARY VALUES. WORKING WITH VERNACULAR REFERENCES AND INTRINSIC IDEAS, ITS TYPEFACES ARE DESIGNED TO HAVE THEIR OWN REASON FOR BEING RATHER THAN FILLING A GAP IN THE FONT MARKET. THROUGH ITS GROWING LIBRARY OF ALPHABETS, NEW IDEAS COME, AND ALREADY EXISTING TYPEFACES ARE BROUGHT UP TO CREATE A FRESH TAKE ON PREVIOUS IDEAS.

PP. 354-357

FONT INCLUDED ●
OR SIMILAR

PANGRAM PANGRAM® FOUNDRY

PANGRAM PANGRAM BELIEVES THAT FONTS SHOULD BE SHARED, USED, AND VIEWED BY AS MANY AS POSSIBLE, AND AIMS TO CREATE FONTS THAT AMPLIFY IDEAS AND UNLEASH THE FULL POTENTIAL OF ITS CLIENTS' DESIGNS. ALL FONTS ARE FREE TO TRY ON THE STUDIO'S WEBSITE SO THAT ANYONE CAN FIND THE PERFECT FIT FOR THEIR PROJECT.

PP. 34-41, 154-157, 242-245, 250-255, 312-315

FONTS INCLUDED ●
AGRANDIR / AIR / FORMULA / MORI / NEUE MACHINA / RÄDER

PENTAGRAM - LUKE POWELL

LUKE POWELL JOINED PENTAGRAM AS A PARTNER IN OCTOBER 2015. HE STUDIED GRAPHIC DESIGN AT CENTRAL SAINT MARTINS, GRADUATING WITH HONOURS IN 1996. HE STARTED HIS CAREER AT THE KITCHEN DESIGN STUDIO, AND FOUNDED HUDSON-POWELL WITH HIS BROTHER, JODY HUDSON-POWELL IN 2005. HIS WORK HAS BEEN EXHIBITED INTERNATIONALLY.

PP. 500-503

APPLICATION ●
HAPPY FACE PIZZA 2018

PENTAGRAM - NATASHA JEN

NATASHA JEN WAS BORN IN TAIPEI AND STUDIED GRAPHIC DESIGN AT THE SCHOOL OF VISUAL ARTS IN NEW YORK CITY, WHERE SHE RECEIVED HER BFA WITH HONOURS IN 2002. SHE IS CURRENTLY A DESIGNER, A THINKER, A MAKER, AN EDUCATOR, AND A PARTNER AT PENTAGRAM.

PP. 504-505

APPLICATION ●
CLOSED WORLDS

POWER TYPE™ FOUNDRY

RENOWNED FOR ITS EXCEPTIONAL AND INNOVATIVE TYPEFACE CREATIONS, POWER TYPE'S FOCUS LIES IN CRAFTING TOP-QUALITY FONTS THAT NOT ONLY POSSESS VISUAL APPEAL BUT ALSO OFFER VERSATILITY AND FUNCTIONALITY, WITH A FONT COLLECTION THAT ENCOMPASSES EVERYTHING FROM ELEGANT AND TIMELESS STYLES TO MODERN AND DARING DESIGNS. THE STUDIO OFFERS A DIVERSE SELECTION OF TYPEFACES SUITABLE FOR PRINT, WEB, BRANDING, PACKAGING, AND MORE.

PP. 100-105, 256-261, 282-287

FONTS INCLUDED ●
BASE NEUE / NEUE POWER / OFFBIT

PRODUCTION TYPE

BASED IN PARIS AND SHANGHAI, PRODUCTION TYPE IS A DIGITAL TYPE DESIGN AGENCY THAT CREATES UNIQUE AND INNOVATIVE TYPEFACES BY BLENDING TRADITIONAL AND CONTEMPORARY DESIGN ELEMENTS. ITS FONTS ARE CHARACTERISED BY ELEGANCE, PRECISION, AND ADAPTABILITY, CATERING TO A WIDE RANGE OF DESIGN NEEDS WHILE MAINTAINING A COHESIVE STYLE.

PP. 158-161

FONT INCLUDED ●
GAMUTH SANS

QUATRIÈME ÉTAGE

QUATRIÈME ÉTAGE IS THE COLLABORATIVE DESIGN PRACTICE OF TOULOUSE-BASED OPHÉLIE RAYNAUD AND PARIS-BASED VALENTIN PORTE. TOGETHER THEY OFFER CREATIVE AND ART DIRECTION, VISUAL IDENTITY, GRAPHIC DESIGN, AND WEBSITE DESIGN SERVICES. QUATRIÈME ÉTAGE IS ALSO KNOWN TO EXPERIMENT AND INSPIRE THROUGH SELF-INITIATED VISUAL DESIGN PROJECTS.

PP. 506-507

APPLICATION ●
MIQUEL OROVIO 2019

SEMIOTIK DESIGN AGENCY

SEMIOTIK DESIGN AGENCY WAS ESTABLISHED IN 2014 BY FOUNDER AND DESIGN DIRECTOR DIMITRIS KOLIADIMAS. IT FOCUSES ON BRAND IDENTITY SYSTEMS, TYPOGRAPHY, AS WELL AS PRODUCT AND PACKAGING DESIGN. BESIDES COLLABORATING WITH ESTABLISHED CLIENTS AND ORGANISATIONS, ITS WORK HAS ALSO BEEN AWARDED AND EXHIBITED INTERNATIONALLY.

PP. 508-509

APPLICATION ●
ARISTOTLE RACING TEAM X10 2017

SETUP TYPE

SETUP TYPE IS A SLOVAKIAN TYPE FOUNDRY AND DESIGN STUDIO FOUNDED IN 2009 BY ONDREJ JÓB, A TYPE DESIGNER BASED IN BRATISLAVA. THE STUDIO'S ACTIVITIES INCLUDE DESIGNING RETAIL AND CUSTOM TYPEFACES, DIGITISING HISTORICAL TYPEFACES, BRANDING, AND LETTERING, AS WELL AS RESEARCH AND SOFTWARE DEVELOPMENT IN THE FIELDS OF TYPE DESIGN AND TYPOGRAPHY.

PP. 224-227

FONT INCLUDED ●
MANUAL GROTESK A

SM FOUNDRY

INITIATED BY OPEN STUDIO, SM IS AN APELDOORN-BASED DIGITAL TYPE FOUNDRY THAT DESIGNS AND DISTRIBUTES MODERN RETAIL AND CUSTOM FONTS THAT FACILITATE CLEAR AND DISTINCTIVE COMMUNICATION. AT SM FOUNDRY, FONTS ARE PRODUCED WITH FUNCTIONAL AND AESTHETIC CONSIDERATION, RESULTING IN A LIBRARY OF VERSATILE TYPEFACES. IT ALSO OFFERS BESPOKE DESIGN SOLUTIONS INCLUDING LOGOTYPES, CUSTOM FONTS, CUSTOM CHARACTERS, FONT FAMILY EXPANSIONS, AND COMPLETE CUSTOM TYPEFACES.

PP. 228-231, 362-365

FONTS INCLUDED ●
MAXEVILLE / SOLARIS

SOCIOTYPE

JOE LEADBEATER IS A LONDON-BASED TYPE DESIGNER WHO HAS BEEN HONING HIS CRAFT FOR CLOSE TO A DECADE. HIS TYPEFACES HAVE BEEN USED BY THE LIKES OF VIRGIN, EXPEDIA, AND STOCKX. HE IS ALSO A CO-FOUNDER OF SOCIOTYPE: A PART INDEPENDENT TYPE FOUNDRY AND PART SELF-PUBLISHER OF THE SOCIOTYPE JOURNAL.

PP. 288-291, 320-325

FONTS INCLUDED ●
ONSITE / REWORK

STUDIOWMW

BASED IN HONG KONG BUT WORKING IN THE GLOBAL MARKETPLACE, STUDIOWMW IS A NEW KIND OF DESIGN AGENCY THAT SPECIALISES IN BRAND-BUILDING THROUGH EFFECTIVE, CAPTIVATING, AND CONCEPTUAL DESIGN SOLUTIONS. THE AGENCY DEVELOPS TRUSTED RELATIONSHIPS WITH CLIENTS TO DELIVER VALUE THROUGH VISUAL IDENTITIES, PACKAGING PRODUCTS, INTERIOR, AND WEB DESIGN.

PP. 510-513

APPLICATION ●
GINGER MUSE ALBUM DESIGN 2020

THE DESIGNERS FOUNDRY

THE DESIGNERS FOUNDRY WAS ESTABLISHED IN 2012 AND HOSTS A CURATED RANGE OF TYPEFACES FROM DESIGNERS ALL OVER THE GLOBE. IT ALSO DESIGNS CUSTOM TYPEFACES.

PP. 110-113, 350-353, 386-389, 414-419

FONTS INCLUDED ●
BRIK / SHAPE / TOMATO GROTESK / ZOOM PRO

THE FOUNDRY TYPES

COVERING ALL ASPECTS OF TYPOGRAPHY AND ITS IMPLEMENTATION FROM FONT DESIGN, LANGUAGE EXPANSIONS, WORDMARKS AND LOGOS TO LICENSING, THE FOUNDRY TYPES HAS AN EXTENSIVE KNOWLEDGE OF TYPE DEVELOPMENT. IT SPECIALISES IN THE CREATION, PRODUCTION, AND LICENSING OF NEW RETAIL AND BESPOKE TYPEFACES, AS WELL AS TYPOGRAPHIC BRAND ASSETS FOR CORPORATE USE.

PP. 78-81, 300-303

FONTS INCLUDED ●
FOUNDRY ARKIAS / FOUNDRY PLEK

THINGSIDID

THINGSIDID IS A HONG KONG-BASED CREATIVE STUDIO THAT IS COMMITTED TO BRANDING, PRINT, GRAPHICS, AND PACKAGING WORK FOR CLIENTS IN THE CORPORATE, RETAIL, ARTS AND CULTURAL SECTORS. IT SEEKS TO CREATE WORK THAT LEAVES LASTING IMPRESSIONS AND BRINGS PEOPLE TOGETHER.

PP. 514-515

APPLICATION ●
MICROWAVE INTERNATIONAL NEW MEDIA ARTS FESTIVAL 2022 - HALF HALF

TIGHTYPE

TIGHTYPE IS AN INDEPENDENT TYPE FOUNDRY AND STUDIO ESTABLISHED IN 2015, OFFERING RETAIL TYPEFACES AND CUSTOM TYPE SOLUTIONS FOR DESIGN-ENTHUSIASTIC INDIVIDUALS AND CONTEMPORARY BRANDS. OVER THE YEARS, TIGHTYPE HAS PROVIDED TYPEFACES FOR AND COLLABORATED WITH DESIGN STUDIOS AND COMPANIES RANGING FROM FORTUNE 500S TO YOUR LOCAL COFFEE SHOP.

PP. 214-217, 358-361

FONTS INCLUDED ●
MACAN & MACAN STENCIL / SNEAK

TIN

TIN IS A GLOBALLY OPERATING BRANDING AND DIGITAL DESIGN STUDIO BASED IN AMSTERDAM, SPECIALISING IN CREATING UNIQUE BRANDING, DESIGN, AND ONLINE EXPERIENCES. WITH A TEAM OF PASSIONATE DESIGNERS, SKILLED STRATEGISTS, AND DIGITAL EXPERTS, TIN IS COMMITTED TO BRINGING BRANDS TO NEW HEIGHTS, DRIVEN BY THEIR ENTHUSIASM FOR INNOVATION AND AN INSATIABLE CURIOSITY FOR THE UNKNOWN.

PP. 516-519

APPLICATION ●
ROCK WERCHTER 2022-2023

TOBY NG DESIGN

TOBY NG GRADUATED FROM CENTRAL SAINT MARTINS IN GRAPHIC DESIGN AND FOUNDED TOBY NG DESIGN IN 2014. SPECIALISING IN GRAPHIC DESIGN AND BRAND IDENTITIES, NG RIGOROUSLY TACKLES DESIGN CHALLENGES WITH WIT AND AESTHETICALLY MEANINGFUL COMMUNICATIONS. HIS STUDIO WAS NAMED ONE OF THE TOP HONG KONG AGENCIES IN 2016.

PP. 520-521

APPLICATION ●
UTH KLUB 2020

TYPETYPE.ORG

TYPETYPE IS A TYPE FOUNDRY THAT HAS SPENT THE LAST DECADE MASTERING ITS CRAFT OF CREATING TYPEFACES. ITS CORE VALUES LIE IN STRIVING FOR EXCELLENCE AND CONSTANT SELF-IMPROVEMENT, AS WELL AS BEING DEDICATED TO THE CRAFT. THE STUDIO'S MISSION IS TO CREATE AND SHARE WELL-DESIGNED, HIGHLY FUNCTIONAL, VERSATILE TYPEFACES WHILE REMAINING VISIONARIES AND PASSIONATE ARTISTS.

PP. 122-125, 266-269, 390-393

FONTS INCLUDED ●
TT COMMONS™ PRO / TT NORMS PRO / TT TRAILERS

VECTRO

VECTRO IS A TYPE DESIGN STUDIO THAT OFFERS RETAIL FONTS, CUSTOM TYPEFACE DESIGN, AND FONT PRODUCTION SERVICES. ITS WORK PUSHES WHAT'S POSSIBLE AT THE INTERSECTIONS OF TYPE, TECHNOLOGY, AND BUSINESS. BASED IN PORTLAND, OREGON, VECTRO WAS FOUNDED IN 2021 BY TRAVIS KOCHEL AND LIZY GERSHENZON. THE TWO HAVE BEEN DESIGN PARTNERS FOR ALMOST 20 YEARS, FOUNDING COMPANIES SUCH AS FUTURE FONTS AND THE DESIGN STUDIO SCRIBBLE TONE.

PP. 64-67, 316-319, 398-401

FONTS INCLUDED ●
ANALOG / RAINER / VCTR MONO

VIOLAINE & JÉRÉMY

VJ-TYPE IS AN INDEPENDENT TYPE FOUNDRY BASED IN PARIS, BORN FROM VIOLAINE & JÉRÉMY'S CREATIVE STUDIO WHERE DRAWING CUSTOM FONTS FOR PROJECTS BECAME A HABIT. THE TEAM DESIGNS FONTS LIKE IT WOULD DESIGN EVERYTHING ELSE: WITH ITS OWN ARTISTIC GESTURES AND SENSIBILITIES. ITS FOCUS LIES IN CREATING STRONG, PECULIAR, AND APPEALING FONTS.

PP. 114-117, 204-209

FONTS INCLUDED ●
CATEGORY / KOBE